D1249651

Touch/ Telephone/ Voice Response Registration

A Guide for Successful Implementation

Melanie Moore Bell
Editor

Technology in Higher Education Series

American Association of
Collegiate Registrars and Admissions Officers
Washington, DC

1993

Contents

Figures

Tables

Foreword

It has been said that the ideal instructional setting occured when a student sat at one end of a log and the teacher sat at the other. The moment this mythical instructor jumped off the end of the log and invited another faculty member to share the teaching load, registration and class scheduling presented a challenge to even the most exotic instructional enterprise. Long lines seemed an unavoidable consequence of registration.

Eavesdrop on nearly any alumni gathering and you may likely hear at least one story about how college sweethearts met while waiting in a registration line. Some registrars even claim that registration and course add/drop lines are central to the social life of the institution; campus life would be dreary without them. Most registrars, however, continue to look for ways to eliminate the inconveniences associated with registration.

Finally, technology has presented an alternative that seems to offer the ideal solution to course registration—touchtone telephone registration with voice response. This book describes the historical development of touchtone telephone registration and introduces the reader to the many factors that must be considered when designing and implementing a comprehensive telephone registration system. It also introduces the reader to other administrative applications supported by voice response technology.

Registration is a complex undertaking that involves nearly every segment of the college or university community. Planning for a replacement system necessarily involves faculty, students, advisors, curriculum specialists, classroom assignment personnel, computer analysts, and, in this case, data communications or telephone service representatives. Whether designing a custom touchtone telephone registration system or adapting one designed by a software vendor, the registrar will ultimately be held responsible for the success of the system. With the help of this guide, registrars can benefit from the lessons learned by others who have worked on the leading edge of this technology. Each institutional setting is unique, but the information shared by Melanie Moore Bell and her associates in this book will facilitate the successful installation of the most elaborate telephone registration system.

W. W. (Tim) Washburn
Executive Director
Admissions and Records
University of Washington
February 6, 1993

Acknowledgements

The authors, whose biographical sketches and institution profiles appear in the back of this publication, represent expertise in the field of touchtone telephone/voice response registration. I am indebted to the writers collectively and individually for the quality of their submissions and their suggestions guiding the general development of this book, and to their colleges and universities for providing support for this project.

My thanks go to Wayne Becraft, AACRAO Executive Director, who had the vision for this project, and to Henny Wakefield, AACRAO Director of Communications, who played a major role in the preparation of this publication. Ms. Wakefield's professional expertise and close scrutiny improved all our work markedly. Thanks also to Kathy Plante, AACRAO Vice president for Professional Development, Research, and Publications, and to Louise Lonabocker, Chair of the AACRAO Publications Policy Committee for their support. Many thanks, too, to Eileen Kennedy, Senior Editor; Laurie Mathews, AACRAO Editorial Secretary, and to George Spack, AACRAO Director of Computer Services, for their computer skills, and to other AACRAO staff who so diligently assisted with this project.

A special debt of gratitude is given to the vendors who endorsed this publication, provided funding for this AACRAO project, and lent their expertise in the field of voice response technology.

There are other groups of individuals whose support made it possible for me to complete this work. Staff in the Registrar's Office at Gonzaga University (Shari Cameron, Karen Carlson, Esther Evans, Cheryl Luchini, Jean Martin, Sharon Sewell, Carolyn Tucker), at Whitworth College (Roberta Garner, Ramona Kinniman, Mardelle Shagool, and Gail Wolf), and at the University of Washington (especially Verla Boss, Frank Byrdwell, Earl Hawkey [now at the University of Nebraska], Van Johnson, Amy McKenzie and Bill Shirey) offered me support during the development and completion of this project while they handled their regular duties with their usual attention and devotion. Elizabeth Carras and Ken Pecka at Whitworth College and Joan Allbery, John Bujosa, Cole Hanford, Peter Hanlon and Kai Uahinui at Gonzaga University, contributed their computer expertise extensively. Thanks to W. W. (Tim) Washburn at the University of Washington, Tammy Reid at Whitworth College, and Harry Sladich at Gonzaga University for being great bosses whose spirited support and continuing encouragement contributed greatly to this professional endeavor.

My thanks to the reviewers who have experience in touchtone telephone/voice response registration—John Bujosa and Fr. J. Alfred Carroll, S.J. (Gonzaga University) and David Stones (University of Texas at Austin)—and those who are considering moving to this technology—Carol Foster (Concordia University in Montreal), Steve Nieheisel and Michael Schmitt (Eastern Washington University), and Faith Weese (Grand Canyon University in Arizona)—for their insights and suggestions for improving this publication.

To my husband, Dr. David S. Bell, who has been a vital helpmate and constructive critic and who knows more about touchtone telephone/voice response registration than he ever wanted to, I give my loving appreciation for his patience, cooperation, guidance, and moral support during the many long evenings, weekends, and holidays taken up by this assignment.

Melanie Moore Bell
University Registrar
Gonzaga University
June 15, 1993

MATHEMATICS

ARCHAEOLOGY

FINE ARTS

FRENCH

CHEMISTRY

LITERATURE

PHILOSOPHY

URBAN STUDIES

LINGUISTICS

Melanie Moore Bell
Gonzaga University

The telephone came first, and then the computer. Now, the linking of these two powerful technologies, computer power and telephone simplicity, is creating vast new opportunities for colleges and universities. What once could only be accomplished with computer keyboards can now be performed with touchtone telephones.

By pressing a telephone number on a touchtone telephone, a student directly keys registration data through a telephone keypad by generating corresponding tones that communicate with the touchtone telephone/voice response registration system. The voice response system on the other end of the telephone line converts the tones back into their numeric equivalents and sends this information to the computer in a form that a registration program understands. The registration program, in turn, processes the information and passes the results back to the voice response system. The system interprets the codes and starts a corresponding prerecorded spoken response on the appropriate telephone line.

Colleges and universities are using this new application with an old technology, the computer, to collect analog or digital signals and manage and distribute voice response information. Before they can tap this automation of voice and computer information to achieve successful touchtone telephone registration, however, they need to carefully design and test the system, and understand the human factors involved.

Implementing a touchtone telephone/voice response (TT/VR) registration system is both one of the most exciting and one of the most frightening experiences a college or university can experience. Registrars and computer personnel had to overcome a lot of anxiety to allow themselves to daydream about students registering on touchtone telephones. In 1980 it seemed like a space age dream. Many colleges and universities were still using arena registration. Some had experienced computerization in some mode of computer batch processing, several had optical scanning registration, others had moved to on-line terminal registration.

Some efforts were successful, others were not. Those registrars' offices that had adopted a nice comfortable on-line system discovered the registration process was manageable—mostly, except when the computer went down, or when large numbers of students came to register on the last day or in the last hour. Often these institutions were able to eliminate the overnight lines that found students camping out in sleeping bags to be first in line for the best choice of courses.

As we enter the last decade of the twentieth century, those colleges and universities with TT/VR technology are finding registration is no longer the negative activity it once was. TT/VR registration offers pluses for students, faculty, and almost every administrative office on campus.

Touchtone Telephone/Voice Response Registration: A Guide for Successful Implementation reviews the development and application of this high technology know-how to college/university activities. It chronicles the way voice response technology improves an institution's communication processing, increases productivity and enhances student services all at the same time. Finally, it guides the prospective user through the stages that take an idea through design, development, and implementation. Figure 1.1 graphically presents the elements in any touchtone telephone/voice response registration project.

Figure 1.1. Elements in a TT/VR Registration Project

Identify Need
Use Team Approach
Ask a Lot of Questions
Develop a Reasonable Plan
Prepare Cost/Benefit Analysis
Develop Feature Requirements
Understand Application Developments
Identify Desired Min/Max Requirements
Develop Scenarios, Flow Charts, Script
Select Voice, Record Script, Install Script
Find Ways to Present Project Favorably
Prepare and Send Request for Proposal
Wait...Wait...Wait for Vendor Response
Receive Bids from Multiple Vendors
Evaluate Bids and Select Vendor
Implement...Train...Train...Train
Test...Test...Test...Test...Test
Pursue New Enhancements
Increase Effectiveness
Write NewsReleases
Avoid Negatives
Apply New Ideas
Surprise Folks
Do Not Panic
Pay Vendor
Have Fun
E n j o y !

Source: Prepared by Melanie Moore Bell

PSYCHOLOGY

MARKETING

ART HISTORY

BIOLOGY

GERMANIC LANGUAGES

PAINTING

ASTROPHYSICS

COMPUTER SCIENCE

CIVIL ENGINEERING

Melanie Moore Bell
Gonzaga University

The touchtone telephone/voice response industry is growing and changing rapidly, and so is the language used to describe it. Below are definitions recognized in the industry and in colleges and universities using voice response technology.

ACD. See Automatic Call Distributor

Analog Transmission. Analog signals are continuous; they are like waves. An analog signal may move from 1 to 2 volts. In the process of changing, it will take on every intermediate value (i.e., 1.375972 volts is one of the infinite signposts that will be passed on the way from 1 to 2 volts). Natural phenomena (at least above the quantum physics level) tend to be analog. The method of transmitting analog signals is fairly straightforward but does have some disadvantages. The chief disadvantage of analog transmission is the ability of the signal to take on any given value. Electrical noise (which is everywhere in varying degrees) and the inherent resistance of electrical cabling will distort an electrical signal as it is transmitted. Although predictions and adjustments for many types of distortion can be made, the exact amount of distortion can never be known. And since an analog signal can take on any value it can never be perfectly regenerated.

ANI. See Automatic Number Identification

Application Generator. These are menu-driven software tools that help users develop voice processing application programs. They are usually written in an industry standard, fourth-generation language (i.e., 4GL) or a proprietary language developed by the vendor.

Application Processor Unit. This is the part of a voice processing system that provides, minimally, call flow logic, data manipulation verification, and host computer interface. It may include local database functions, system management, and application development tools. It can be a physically separate unit or built into a unit that also embodies the voice processing system.

Application Program. This is the software residing on an application processor or host computer that controls a voice processor through caller transac-

tions; it may also be referred to as a voice application, scenario application, or channel application. It may also be a program residing on a host computer that is accessed by an application processor to retrieve or enter caller data and may be referred to as a host application, or host process.

APU. See Application Processor Unit

ASCII. American Standard Character for Information Interchange, a standardized code used by many computers to store characters, digits, and other symbols.

Asynchronous Transmission. Transmission protocol in which each information character (or sometimes each word or small block) is individually synchronized, usually by using start and stop elements. The gap between characters (or words) is not necessarily a fixed length. Asynchronous transmission is also called "start-stop transmission." Although, there will be a maximum transmission speed that can be supported in any given situation, within this maximum the speed used is not critical and may vary.

Attenuation. A decrease in signal strength when transmitting from one point to another. This decrease is usually expressed as a ratio in decibels.

Audiotext. The use of voice communication to retrieve information that is stored digitally via telephone, e.g., the Internal Revenue Service (IRS) uses audiotext for taxpayer assistance.

Automatic Call Distributor. A switching device attached to a telephone system to route calls to a number of different answering points. Advanced features may include an automated attendant feature to answer the telephone, and stack the calls, sometimes with cueing messages and a dynamic display of how many calls are waiting.

Automatic Number Identification. Used in telephony signalling systems.

Binary Synchronous Communication. Also called BISYNC, this is the most common character-oriented communications protocol. BSC is a synchronous form of transmission which uses special characters (SYN) to maintain consistent clocking between the sending and receiving device.

IBM's BSC (which has become a default standard) is one of the most widely used protocols.

Call Bridging. The ability to ask the switch(es) to "add" another line to the pair.

Call Classification. The ability to recognize the "special" sounds heard when a called number is busy, not in service, unassigned, etc.

Call Service Levels. A "grade of service" is defined as the probability of a call receiving a busy signal. Consider a one-line system receiving two one-minute calls per hour. When caller A places a call, there is only one chance in 60 that the line is being used by caller B. The "grade of service" is 59/60 or 98.3%. The grade of service is a function of 1) the distribution of calls, 2) the number of lines, 3) the length of calls, and 4) the number of calls. Calls may not be received evenly throughout the day. To achieve a desired minimal level of service, the base used must be the most demanding time of day, day of week or time of year.

The more lines available, the better the service. If the one-line, two-caller-per-hour system, referenced above, added an additional line, the service level would increase to 100%. This is true since the second caller is assured a line would be available. Note, however, that it may not make sense to double the line cost in order to increase service 1.7%.

The shorter the length of an average call, the better the service. If the one-line, two-caller-per-hour system, referenced earlier, had a typical call increase from one minute to ten minutes, the level of service would drop to 83% (50/60).

The fewer calls received, the better the service. If a third caller was added to the one-line, two-caller-per-hour system, the level of service would drop from 98.3% to 96.6% since two minutes out of each hour would be consumed by other callers. In systems with more than one line, the principles are the same but the computations become more complex. For example, with two lines and four callers the level of service is NOT identical to that offered by the one-line two-caller situation since there are more ways for the four callers to interact. The study of this type of problem, called "queuing theory," has been going on for years and the results of this effort are available in graphic form on PC programs. As a point of reference, the telephone company has a PO1 (i.e., level of busy signals for a given call volume) level of service. Typically, voice response vendors have graphs showing the number of lines required to provide a given level of service for a given load.

Central Office. The central office is that section of the American telephone system that contains the power supplies and equipment for transmission, signaling, and primary switching equipment for all interconnecting functions. Each central office has a theoretical capacity of 10,000 numbers, based on the last four digits of the telephone number; the first three numbers identify the central office.

Centrex. Central office switching system leased by telephone companies and residing on the telephone company's rather than the customer's property.

Data Transactions Format. The technical definition of a data element specifying alpha, numeric, or a combination of characters appropriate to the data field to be processed.

Dialed Number Information System. Used in telephony signalling systems.

Digital Transmission. Digital signals take on only specified signal levels. A digital signal may jump from 1 volt to 2 volts. A digital signal of 1.93334572 volts transmits 2 volts. Since any signal received must be 1 or 2 volts, a signal which is almost 2 volts can be regenerated to take on its "exact" original value.

Digitized Speech. Speech stored by means of digital representation of its analog form. See Vector Quantization

DNIS. See Dialed Number Information System

Driver. A software module that "drives" the data out of a specific hardware port. See Protocol

DTMF. See Dual-Tone Multi-Frequency

Dual-Tone Multi-Frequency. Push button or touchtone data entry dialing entered by the caller.

E&M Connections. Ear and mouth leads (2 and 4 wire) which carry signals between trunk equipment and a separate signaling equipment unit.

Flow Charting. A graphical representation of system relationships.

Gateway. A data communication connection between two systems. Generally the connection is an wide-area network of some kind between two or more dispersed local networks.

Grade of Service. See Call Service Levels

Ground Start. Ground start lines are sometimes used on loops connecting PBXs to the central office. Ground start is a method of signalling between two machines where one machine grounds one side of the line and the other machine detects the presence of the ground. The alternative signaling method is "loop start."

Handler. Software which interfaces directly with hardware. See Protocol

HDLC. See High Level Data Link Control

High Level Data Link Control. HDLC is a protocol that addresses the physical connection standards for layer two of the International Standard Organization's OSI (Open Systems Interconnection). HDLC provides synchronous, bit-oriented data transmission for simplex, half-duplex, or full-duplex communication. Network configurations may be point-to-point or multipoint over switched or nonswitched facilities.

Host Application. An application program that is accessed by an application processor to retrieve/enter caller data. See Application Program

Host or Host Computer. External computer connected to a voice processing system usually in one of two ways: 1) it may be accessed via a standard communication protocol by an application processor as a database resource to retrieve and update records, or 2) it may directly drive a voice processor, controlling the caller transactions.

Host Screen Format. Typically refers to voice response emulation of a host mainframe screen that may already be utilized in the registration process.

Hunt Group. A collection of telephone lines supporting a single telephone number that allows one telephone number to receive multiple calls at once. The telephone switch is constructed to use any one of a number of telephone lines for calls. Named for the "hunting" for an unused line feature. Inbound calls receive a busy signal if all lines in the hunt group are busy.

Interactive Voice Response. A voice response application considered "interactive" when the caller can both receive and enter data.

IVR. See Interactive Voice Response

LAN. See Local Area Network

Line Conditioning. Two types of line conditioning are provided: C Conditioning and D Conditioning. C Conditioning controls attenuation, distortion and relay so they stay within specific limits. D Conditioning controls harmonic distortion and signal-to-noise ratios so they lie within specific limits. Even if random events such as physical destruction and electrical interference (electrical storms) are disregarded, telephone lines are not perfect paths for electrical signals. A given circuit will have a level of resistance or impedance which is a function of the physical properties of the line. This means there will be some level of corruption of both the amplitude and phase of signals transmitted over the line.

Given that perfect transmission is not possible, the telephone company simply insures lines meet a standard acceptable for voice transmission. The line quality acceptable for voice transmission, however, may not be acceptable for data transmissions at high data rates. One way to minimize problems with a leased line is to pay a premium for a line that is "conditioned." The telephone company then either selects a path that meets the more stringent requirements of conditioning or upgrades the performance of an existing circuit by placing amplifiers and/or delay equalizers on the line.

Local Area Network. A datacomm system that allows a number of independent devices to communicate directly with each other, within a moderately sized geographic area, over a physical communications channel of moderate data rates. According to

Byte magazine (July 1987), "To be a LAN, a network must have full connectivity between the stations, be fully administered by the owner (not the Federal Communications Commission), and run on a single set of cables."

Logical Unit. Supports sessions with a host-based system.

Loop Start. The majority of telephone lines are "loop start." This means they signal off-hook by completing a circuit at the telephone. The alternative signaling method is ground start. Loop start is a method of signaling where one machine completes a circuit causing current to flow and the other machine detects the signal by the presence of current.

Loop start operates as follows. While the telephone is "on-hook," both the line relay and the cut-off relay are inactive; that is, they allow the battery to supply current to the line. No current flows because the receiver holds the switch down and the circuit is open at the telephone. When the receiver is lifted, the switchhook closes and completes the circuit. This causes current to flow. The current flow signals the switch that subscriber service is desired.

LU. See Logical Unit

Millisecond. Disk access time is measured in milliseconds, i.e., one-thousandth (1/1000) of a second. The term millisecond is used frequently in some vendor's training for the setting of trimmers, i.e., a circuit element (as a condenser) used to tune a circuit to a desired frequency. A disk access time below 20 milliseconds is relatively fast; an access time above 50 milliseconds is relatively slow.

MODEM. Acronym for MOdulate and DEModulate. A modem is a device used to convert digital signals to analog signals for transmission across an analog telephone link. Modems operate in pairs with the modem on the receiving end converting the analog signal back into a digital signal. Modems modulate digital signals used by computers or other digital equipment into audio tones that can be carried by a public telephone network.

Modulation. The process of converting digital signals to analog signals. A modem's modulation technique is key to its compatibility with other modems. Most modems transmit a continuous sinewave, i.e., a waveform that represents periodic oscillations and that is visualized as a sine curve. This sinewave is defined by its amplitude, frequency, and phase. Modems use circuits designed for voice. It is not only convenient, therefore, but realistic to think of modems as generating songs. The amplitude of the signal is the volume of the song, the frequencies of the signal are the tones being played (they are all within audio range), and the phase is the rhythm of the song.

Some modems sing simple songs. They simply vary the volume (amplitude) of the signal. Most modems vary the tone frequencies of the signal to create a song. The highest data rates (most complex songs) are generated by modems capable of varying volume, tone, and rhythm. The modem on the other end of the line must understand the rules used to generate the song in order to convert the song received back into the notes (digital input) which created them.

On-Line System. A computer application that is interactive and operating in real time.

Optical Mark Read. A process used in registration that requires a student to pencil in bubbles on an optical mark sense readable form that is passed through a scanning device which reads the marks and sends the data to the host computer.

Outsourcing. The process by which a company arranges for a third party to implement and manage a specific function of a department of an organization.

PCM. See Pulse Code Modulation

PBX. A private branch exchange system allowing communication between a business and between the business and the outside world. A switching device is placed on the premises so calls can be routed using fewer "lines." The lines become trunks at that point. These are used to allow entities with many telephones the alternative of connecting them to the telephone network as "extensions." Recently, these switching devices have been used to provide additional features to the telephones they serve.

Phonemes. The set of sounds which make up a language. See Text-to-Speech

Project Team. Representatives from the registrar's office, computing center, telecommunications department, academic deans and/or advising, and the purchasing department who plan and implement touchtone telephone/voice response registration. Ad hoc work groups may be formed to assist in their areas of expertise throughout a project.

Protocol. A formal set of rules governing the exchange of information between two or more devices. For example, in a classroom, the "protocol" may be; 1) the teacher may speak (lecture), request a student to speak (call on a student who has not raised a hand), or permit a student to speak (call on a student who has raised his hand); 2) a student may speak only if given permission to speak (called on); or 3) a student may raise his or her hand to request permission to speak. These rules can be considered the classroom protocol. Since the teacher may speak at any time and the student must wait for permission to speak, a master/servant relationship has been established.

Since part of a protocol may be implemented in hardware, the distinction between driver or handler software (software which interfaces directly with hardware) and protocol software is often fuzzy. In general, communications software has drivers at the bottom layer, protocols in the middle layers, and application software in the higher layers.

The trend is towards layered protocols where each layer on one machine interfaces only to the corresponding layer on another machine and the layers directly above and below it on the base machine. This means modifications or enhancements do not affect the entire protocol but are limited to these well defined interfaces. Examples of protocols are Asynchronous Communication (ASC), Binary Synchronous Communication (BSC), High Level Data Link Control (HDLC), and Synchronous Data Link Control (SDLC).

PTSN. See Public Switched Telephone Network

Public Switched Telephone Network. Refers to the worldwide voice telephone network accessible to all those with telephone and access privileges.

Pulse Code Modulation. This is a method of digitizing speech. An analog signal can be faithfully reconstructed from digital data if the voice is "sampled" a given number of times per second. This is the same manner in which music is recorded on digital compact disks. In the case of the voice grade telephone lines, the sample rate is 6,600 samples per second. Using PCM, 8-bit samples are taken 8,000 times per second (i.e., a value from 0 to 256 is assigned to the height of the waveform). PCM recording at this sample rate insures the quality of the recorded voice is better than the voice an analog telephone is able to transfer.

Most of the information in a voice response system is carried at frequencies around 1,000 Hz (a hertz is a measurement of frequency in cycles per second; a hertz is one cycle per second). The very low frequencies are important in male voices. The highest frequencies (around 3,000 Hz) add individuality and aid in recognition but do not contain as much critical information. By sending a complete description (1 byte of information) of the voice wave in each sample, PCM is able to handle analog waves that jump from one extreme to the other. But this ability is required only during the loudest phrases with the highest frequencies.

Pulse Telephones/Pulse Dialing. These are the older telephones which do not use touchtone. Instead a number of pulses (clicks) are used to signal the number dialed. For example, dialing a 5 creates five quick clicks. When these telephones are connected directly to a central office, the "clicks," really a series of shorts and opens that can be easily detected, are not passed beyond the central office.

Queuing Theory. See Call Service Levels

Request for Proposal. A set of requirements for a voice response system or other procurement used to solicit information about hardware, software, system specification and pricing. Typically, the RFP has less detail than the RFQ.

Request for Quotation. A document prepared by colleges or universities that requests specific information on a vendor's product, service, support, implementation, etc. Vendors may use the RFQ to prepare responses and bids.

RFQ. See Request for Quotation

RFP. See Request for Proposal

Scenarios. Narratives made up of TT/VR to script prompts and default paths occurring when students access the TT/VR system.

Screen Emulation. A hardware device or a combination of hardware and software that permits programs written for one computer to be run on another.

Script. The dialog of all the voice responses used in a TT/VR registration system.

SDLC. See Synchronous Data Link Control

SNA. See Systems Network Architecture

Specifications. Functional requirements of a voice response system.

Start-Stop Transmission. See Asynchronous Transmission

Synchronous Data Link Control. A bit oriented synchronous communications protocol developed by IBM.

Synchronous Transmission. A transmission process that insures a fixed number of bits (characters or words) is transmitted during a given unit of time. Since both sender and receiver are clocking the data, it is important to insure the send and receive clocks are in sync. This is done by sending some sort of sync character or flag, or by including timing information within the data itself.

Systems Network Architecture. A product of IBM.

T-1 Links. Digital transmission links.

Telephony. The use or operation of an apparatus for transmission of sounds between widely removed points with or without connecting wires.

Text-to-Speech. Text-to-speech typically uses nine layers of software to convert text to speech in the following manner:

1. An ASCII text string is received.

2. The text is "normalized." Numbers are converted to text (e.g., 24 becomes twenty-four) and abbreviations are spelled out (e.g., Dr. becomes doctor in the default case or drive if context switches dictate).

3. Words whose spelling does not follow standard phonetic rules are converted to a phonetic form. This step converts the word "of" (the only case of the letter "f" being pronounced as a "v") to a phonetic spelling ("ov"). A dictionary of these nonphonetic words and their desired conversions is maintained. Users can add words to this dictionary.

4. The (now phonetic) words are converted to phonemes, the set of sounds which make up a language. English uses about 5,000 sounds or phonemes.

5. The phonemes created in step 4 are modified according to rules of prosody, i.e., the systematic study of metrical structure. There is an innate timing or cadence to speech. This step modifies the phonemes to put the rhyme back in the speech. Note that there is a trade off between the insertion of a very human-like cadence to speech and intelligibility. Some vendors have opted to sacrifice cadence for clarity.

6. Phonetic rules are applied. These rules make the fine distinction between the "t" in Tom and the "t" in cat.

7. The phonemes are broken into utterances, the shortest sounds humans make. Possible utterances are a function of the size and shape of the vocal passages. Since each person is different, the utterances of each person are also different. Nevertheless each person creates unique utterances from the same set of utterance types. This step identifies the types of utterances required to build the required phonemes.

8. The utterances are digitized. By using different sets of rules to create the finite set of utterances, different sounding voices can be created. After this step, text-to-speech and voice response create the same form of voice data.

9. The digitized speech is sent to a digital-to-analogue converter and sound (speech) is created. This step uses the same hardware used for voice response.

Throughput. The time it takes for the telephone to be answered, a message to be spoken, input received, and a response completed in voice response technology.

Touchtone Telephone. A telephone which creates tones as signals rather than clicks as in rotary telephones. These tones are easy to decode to generate the codes used in TT/VR registration systems.

Touchtone Telephone Registration. Registration achieved through telephone and computer technology. A student keys data through a telephone keypad that serve as a minicomputer keyboard/terminal, generating corresponding tones that communicate with the on-line telephone registration system on a mainframe computer. Telephone voice response equipment on the other end of the telephone line converts the tones back into their numeric equivalents and passes this information to the host computer in a form that the registration program can understand and utilize. The registration program, in turn, processes the information and passes the results back to the voice response equipment. The system interprets the codes which prompt corresponding prerecorded spoken responses to be played over the appropriate telephone line for each student transaction entry.

Each student is provided with instructions and a worksheet for accessing the touchtone telephone registration system. After the worksheet is completed, the student keys in a personal access number (institutional-assigned student number or social security number) and date of birth or personal access code (PAC) for verification of eligibility by the system. When the system has verified eligibility (admitted, in good academic standing, no holds on registration, is appropriate day to register, etc.), the student enters his or her course request. The registration system responds that the student is registered in each course, or informs the student why registration has not occurred.

Vector Quantization. A method of digitizing voice. Vector quantization is considered the "state-of-the-art" voice compression technology. It is based on the concept that, although voices are quite variable, a number of recurring patterns (this is similar to the

text-to-speech concept of a finite number of utterances) exist. Instead of storing an image of the voice patterns, only a code identifying a base pattern, such as an utterance, is stored along with a limited amount of information that defines how that utterance differs from the stored template of that utterance. This approach requires quite a bit of processing in order to digitize the voice since the first step is to identify the best pattern match. Less memory, however, is required to store the voice. Converting digitized voice to analog is not processor intensive since no pattern matching is required for this step.

Vocabulary. Sentences, words, phrases, letters and numbers scripted to affect the direction of the voice response application.

Voice Mail. People-to-people communication via computer. Interactive (but nonsimultaneous) voice communication. Voice mail system features typically include one-to-one communication, message answering and forwarding, and distribution lists.

Voice Messaging. Ability to store and retrieve voice messages from telephone callers.

Voice Processing. Capturing, storing, manipulating, and retrieving voice information via telephone. Includes voice mail, voice response, audiotext, call routing, speech recognition, text-to-speech, etc.

Voice Processing System. Computer which interfaces to telephone network and potentially other computer(s) to perform any or all types of voice processing. Typically, a voice processing system consists of a voice processor and application processor, and/or other auxiliary processors.

Voice Processing Unit. A tool for providing access to database information. Voice response units interface with a human via telephone, using voice out (generally prerecorded digitized voice) and touchtone in. Voice processing units are distinguished from other voice technologies (voice mail, etc.) primarily by their ability to interface to a host computer. May also be referred to as Voice Response Units (VRU).

Voice Processor. The part of a voice processing system which provides, minimally, voice storage and retrieval, and a telephone network interface. Operates under direct control of another computer.

Voice Recognition. The ability to recognize human utterances as specific words and to recognize a person's identity by his or her voice.

Voice Response Technology. The category of speech technology relating to the recording of human voice, the reduction of that voice to a digital signal, and the storage of that signal in small units of words and phrases that can then be randomly combined on command from the host computer to form specific word sequences and sentences. Because voice response is digitized human voice, it provides high quality speech which retains pitch and tone variations that artificial speech synthesis cannot create. Simply stated, voice response technology is people-to-computer communication sent remotely via touchtone telephones. It uses a touchtone telephone as a computer terminal to enter and retrieve computer data.

Waveform. The characteristic shape of a period signal usually shown as a plot of amplitude over a period of time.

Will Call. The activity of a student requesting service documents with the intention of "picking up" the documents in person after preparation by an office.

Landmark

Developments

BUSINESS

ASTRONOMY

SCULPTURE

NURSING

ARABIC

LAW

URBAN PLANNING

INDUSTRIAL DESIGN

ELECTRICAL ENGINEERING

Erlend D. Peterson,
Brigham Young University

Significant achievements in voice computer technology during the 1980s made possible the application of touchtone telephone data entry with digitized human voice response computer systems. These developments literally transformed a touchtone telephone into a computer keyboard/terminal capable of interacting with a mainframe computer. The application of this technology to university registration meant students could use a touchtone telephone to gain access to the university registration system, enter the registration data by pressing touchtone telephone keys, and listen to a "human" voice verify each transaction. The procedure potentially offered convenience, ease, and an uncomplicated method for untrained computer users to personally interact with a computer system.

Independent of each other, the admissions and records personnel at Brigham Young University (BYU) and Georgia State University (GSU) pioneered the development of a paradigm for integrating touchtone telephone/voice response technology with a registration system. However, it was not until the 1984 American Association of Collegiate Registrars and Admissions Officers (AACRAO) conference when BYU personnel presented a session on touchtone telephone/voice response (TT/VR) registration that the two universities became aware of each other's developments and began to collaborate.

Early Years of Development

The banking industry, led by Seattle First National Bank, first used touchtone technology to offer bill payment by touchtone telephone in 1971. However, problems put a stop to the service shortly after it was introduced. Telephone bill payment services began again in 1974 with Farmers and Mechanics Savings of Minneapolis. The idea soon caught on, and by 1982 approximately 450 financial institutions offered touchtone banking services.

In a conference on Home (Banking) Delivery Services, Koenig (1982) stressed telephone banking as a service that would be convenient for customers,

would wean them from paper transactions, and would free the bank from labor-intensive and expensive services. The banking industry pursued touchtone telephone/voice response banking to offset labor costs, which were increasing at about 10% a year during the 1980s, even as computer costs were decreasing significantly. Banking officials could charge customers ten or fifteen cents for a touchtone telephone bill payment transaction and still save customers five to ten cents in postage. One study concluded both the bank and customer could come out ahead financially by using touchtone telephone technology (Ryan 1982). Telephone banking cost the bank an average of 6.27 cents a transaction. In contrast, paying a bill over the counter cost the bank 42.96 cents per transaction.

In the early years of development, the banking industry believed home banking and the use of high technology by the customer were inevitable. However, the banking industry still had concerns about technology, security, privacy, and its general strategy.

IBM introduced touchtone telephone/voice response technology to university computer personnel in 1969 at the College and University Machine Records Conference (CUMREC) in Ann Arbor, Michigan. Presentation of a model touchtone banking system included a live demonstration of an electronic payment transfer from a customer's bank account to a store's bank account. The demonstration began with a telephone call made to the host computer. The host computer voice asked the customer to identify the type of transaction. The customer inserted a transaction number by pressing the touchtone keys on the telephone. After verifying the user's identification (ID) number, the computer "talked" the user through a series of directions; the user responded by keying in appropriate data through the touchtone process. The directions asked for the customer's account number, the store's account number, and the amount of the purchase. The computer then confirmed there was sufficient money in the customer's account to pay for the purchase and asked if the transfer of funds should be made. After confirmation, a computer voice verified the transaction.

The touchtone telephone demonstration impressed university computer personnel. They were intrigued with the possibilities of applying the concept to a registration system. Unfortunately at that time, the technology was well ahead of computer developments on campuses and implementation would not be feasible until university student information computer systems were on-line.

The Brigham Young University Model

BYU'S GOALS

Brigham Young University developed its TT/VR system primarily as an efficient and inexpensive way for students to register. It sought a registration system that would be convenient and simple, would give students immediate feedback, and would provide up-to-the-minute information for departmental chairpersons and registration administrators.

In the past, most registration systems required students to enroll in a university arena at a scheduled time when faculty would be present. Waiting, long lines, and rushed academic advisement characterized the process. Other systems required students to submit course request forms and wait for an extended period to get the registration results by mail. The new touchtone telephone system would allow students to register from home at their convenience.

The ready availability of current course information and student eligibility for particular courses often posed problems. The computer design in the new touchtone telephone system would provide alternative information for students when problems arose at any stage of registration. The immediate feedback would give students complete control over the course selection process and enable them to select the teacher, time, and place for each course. The system would operate within the university's

on-line system and would allow academic managers to maximize the use of the university's two most expensive resources, its faculty and facilities.

BYU'S EIGHT-STEP PLAN

The development of the TT/VR registration system at BYU actually began with a model voice recognition/voice response system. Although the voice recognition model became functional, it was only reliable approximately 95% of the time. Five percent unreliability inhibited implementation. However, altering the system to accommodate touchtone input created a more reliable system. The changes took a few weeks to complete.

The modifications resulted in a working TT/VR model that allowed students to register for classes and make schedule changes by interacting directly with the microprocessor. The telephone, with its key pad, functioned like a computer keyboard/terminal. Registration could be initialized or changed for any student record in the test file.

Students accessed the system by entering the telephone number given in the registration materials. After gaining access to the system, they used the numeric action code plus the five-digit class index code for each course. The system confirmed the action and stated the department name and course number.

Several groups of students tested the touchtone telephone model. In addition, after a formal presentation on the program the university administration gave its enthusiastic support.

In the summer of 1983, a development team of four administrative users, two systems analysts, and a systems programmer organized the design and implementation of the system. The team focused on eight steps in developing the TT/VR registration system:

1. Examined hardware and software sufficient to accommodate large numbers of students. A search of current providers of touchtone telephone/voice response equipment serving the banking industry located a system from Perception

Technology that used a PDP 1124 minicomputer to answer the telephone and speak to students; 32 telephone lines could be used simultaneously. The system would interface with an IBM 4341 host computer.

2. Flow charted all student interactions with the computer and the computer replies. All options the students would need to register and possible errors the student might make were included in a flow chart. The flow chart also included all computer verbal promptings and replies and was eventually used as the source document for programming the system and as the basis for identifying vocabulary phrases, department names, and numbers to be recorded in the script.

3. Selected the voice for the computer replies. Based on the recommendation of a panel of students, the development committee chose a male voice for the voice responses; the banking industry had typically used female voices.

4. Installed and linked the minicomputer (Perception Technology's VOCOM) to a host computer (IBM 4341). The VOCOM unit answered the telephone, interpreted the tones, and sent messages to the host computer. The host completed all processing and returned messages that triggered voice responses from the VOCOM to the student. In essence, the VOCOM made it possible to give voice responses for an existing on-line system that previously had given only visual responses. The linking of the systems and programming took approximately 90 working days for one programmer.

5. Drafted instructions for the students. The committee reviewed the touchtone instructions of various banks and drafted and tested instructions for students. Student employees tested the instructions and suggested refinements.

6. Piloted the program. Another group of students participated in a pilot program to test the system. After programming was complete, computer science classes provided a test file and helped debug the system. Students were very satisfied and eager for the project to proceed. In December 1983, 400 newly admitted students registered with the system. As a final pilot in January 1984 the math department used the system for its high demand courses during the add and drop period. Primary problems were experienced in the linkage between the mini-and host computers. Otherwise, the system functioned well and the students were exuberant.

7. Tested the system capacity. In an analysis of the system's capacity, the committee discovered it took approximately four minutes and ten seconds for a student to register for six courses on the new system. If three of the six courses were full, it took a typical student five minutes and five seconds to complete registration.

Three different approaches used to project the length of time needed to register 27,500 students indicated it would take between 85 and 90 hours of computer time to register the students. The committee implemented staggered starting times to prevent overloading the 32 telephone lines.

8. Developed management controls. Management controls regulated student entry into the system. The Registration Office scheduled student entry into the system by characteristics such as honors program, class standing, number of credit hours, and alphabetical letters of the last name (Spencer, Peterson and Bell 1986).

BYU implemented its TT/VR registration system in April 1984. Initially, approximately 16,000 students used the touchtone telephone registration system. Another 4,000 students used the new telephone registration system to add or drop classes. During this first year, students could also use the mail registration system.

In October 1984 the touchtone system became the primary system used for winter semester registration. That month the system received over 28,000 calls; by the end of December almost 54,000 calls had been made by over 26,000 students. Of the 32 telephone lines dedicated to the system, only 13 lines received constant use during the highest volume month of October.

While there was an initial cost of $110,000 for the TT/VR system, other registration cost savings paid for the system within a year. TT/VR has been very reliable at BYU. Very little has been done to improve the system except to purchase hardware upgrades and additional telephone lines for new applications.

The Georgia State University Registration System

In 1982 Georgia State University (GSU) began looking for a way to improve the on-line, optical scanning registration system it had implemented in 1972. It wanted to provide better service to its students. Because of the popularity of touchtone telephone banking in the literature, GSU's admissions and records personnel began researching the technology and considering the application to the registration system.

One of the system developers obtained a copy of the book *Teaching Your Computer to Talk* (Teja, Tab Books, Inc., 1981). GSU personnel sent letters to over 25 companies listed in the book to request further information on speech technology and equipment. The response was dismal with only two or three responding.

In 1983 GSU received a mass-mailing letter from Periphonics Corporation which began, "Dear College Administrator: How would you like to handle Student Registration more easily and more accurately . . . A Periphonics Voice Response System will enable your students to call from any standard push-button telephone and register in a matter of minutes." In response, Georgia State University began its pursuit, in earnest, of touchtone telephone/voice response technology for registration. It was not until February 1985 that GSU actually piloted the system. In August of that year the system became operational.

The variables related to implementing a new system had to be worked out from scratch and were largely based on educated guesses and intuition.

There were no widely distributed examples of registration scripts. The script had to be painstakingly developed. Also, voice response systems had limited capabilities and costly voice memories. The script developer had to be extremely frugal with every word and phrase. Every phrase had to be designed for reusability.

Sizing a system was largely guesswork. There was no history on how long an average transaction might last. Nor were there data to predict with any certainty the average number of return calls per student. Because of the dramatic convenience of the touchtone telephone medium, previous data from walk-in registration models were not good predictors. The vendors insisted that their experience in the banking industry was relevant. However, the development personnel soon found the registration requirements quite different from those of the banking industry.

Showcasing the TT/VR Registration Model

With the preliminary success of the touchtone telephone registration system, the Brigham Young University admissions and records personnel began a series of professional presentations at several conferences, including the 1984 American Association of Collegiate Registrars and Admissions Officers (AACRAO) Annual Meeting, the College and University Machine Records (CUMREC) Annual Conference, and several regional conferences.

A positive response to their new registration approach prompted Georgia State University personnel to sponsor the first Touchtone Telephone Registration seminar on their campus in December 1985. Over 250 admissions and records personnel nationwide attended.

Brigham Young University hosted a similar conference in June 1986. The program at the seminar showcased the agenda of the day and the early pioneers.

"Data Collection for Batch Registration Systems" by Ralph Boren, University of Utah

"Fee Payment by Telephone" by Mark Elliott, Georgia State University

"Flowcharting and Script Developments for a Touchtone Telephone Registration System" by John T. Reed, Metropolitan State College

"Implementing a Turnkey Solution" by Jim DeVere, Maricopa Community Colleges

"Learning from Others to Bring Touchtone Telephone Technology to Your Campus" by Hugh King, University of Alberta

"Methods for Matching Student Demand to Limited Telephone Resources" by Douglas J. Bell, Brigham Young University

"Teaching Registration to Talk: Touchtone Telephone Registration Issues and Answers" by James E. Green, Jr. and Mark Elliott, Georgia State University

"Technical Considerations for Adapting Touchtone Telephone to Your Environment" by Walter Nicholes, Brigham Young University

"Touchtone Telephone Registration at Brigham Young University: Its Development and Capabilities" by Robert W. Spencer and Erlend D. Peterson, Brigham Young University

"Touchtone Telephone Registration: Establishing a Timetable and Management Checklist" by Ruth Jass, Bradley University

"Vendor Selection: Technical Specifications and Other Issues" by H. Garth Rasband, Brigham Young University

Campus Implementation Grows

Most college and university administrators recognized the potential benefits of a touchtone telephone registration system. A TT/VR system is only the front end of the system, however, and requires an existing on-line registration interface. Although this caused a delay for some, by 1988 the following colleges and universities reported having implemented a touchtone telephone/voice response registration system:

Bowling Green State University (Ohio)
Bradley University (Illinois)
Brigham Young University (Utah)
Colorado State University
Ferris State College (Michigan)
Florida International University
Florida State University
Georgia State University
Iowa State University
Lane Community College (Oregon)
Miami-Dade Community College (Florida)
North Carolina State University
Northeast Louisiana University
The Ohio State University
Pennsylvania State University
Ricks College (Idaho)
Rochester Institute of Technology (New York)
San Jose State University (California)
Texas A&M University
University of Akron, The (Ohio)
University of Alaska
University of Alberta (Canada)
University of Arizona
University of British Columbia (Canada)
University of Central Florida
University of Colorado at Boulder
University of North Texas
University of Southern California
University of Southern Mississippi
University of Utah
University of Washington
University of Wisconsin-Madison
Weber State College (Utah)

Vendor Hardware/Software Improvements

Although institutions, particularly admissions and records offices, gained sophistication from each other via collaborative efforts, improvements in vendors' hardware made enhancements to the registration systems possible.

In 1988 there were advances in processor speeds, progressions to 16 and 32 bit data paths, and increased data storage capacities at dramatically reduced prices. Products of the microcomputer (r)evolution made voice memory capacity a non-issue. The evolution made many PC-based solutions viable and brought reliable technology within the financial reach of the higher education market.

In 1989-90 advances in voice response scripting tools and host communication software eliminated most of the development bottlenecks associated with the customization of voice response scripts to host applications for both vendors and customers. This evolution brought the technology within the reach of institutions that previously did not have the technical wherewithal to implement it.

In 1990-91 improved hardware and software paved the way for the convergence of voice mail, automated attendant, and voice response (host computer dependent) applications. The result has been the opportunity to integrate voice response applications for a variety of enrollment service functions with call management for those same functional areas and a blurring of the lines between voice response, bulletin board, and automated attendant applications.

Summary

During the 1970s, touchtone telephone data entry and computer voice response technology introduced in the banking industry found its way into higher education. As with the banking industry, client service and economic pressures prompted colleges and universities to pursue tech-nological applications. During the 1980s, college and university admissions and records personnel adopted touchtone technology in the registration process to provide:

1. an efficient and inexpensive means for registration;

2. students with course selection and immediate feed-back in the registration process;

3. students with a registration system designed to meet their needs and natural responses, and

4. up-to-the-minute management information for department chairpersons and registration administrators.

As recently as the 1980s, college and university students dreaded the registration process. It generally took place in an enormous, confusing arena or through a mail-in computer algorithm course scheduling system. Now touchtone telephone adopted by colleges and universities in the 1980s transforms registration into a convenient and easy process. The TT/VR registration system has given department chairpersons and registration administrators up-to-the-minute management information. Students can telephone from the comfort of their home, resident hall or apartment. Touchtone telephone/voice response registration provides alternatives when courses close. Best of all, ongoing registration changes are easily accommodated, eliminating unnecessary delays and waste in student time.

Chapter

4

Selling the Idea

HISTORY

EDUCATION

ACCOUNTING

ITALIAN

TOPOLOGY

LATIN

STATISTICS

ALGEBRA

METEOROLOGY

Donald J. Wermers
University of Wisconsin-Madison

First, Sell the Larger Concept

The first step in selling touchtone telephone/voice response (TT/VR) registration is to develop the general concept of applying the many existing and emerging electronic technologies to all student and academic support services on a campus. Once the concept that multiple, more efficient, and more humane technically based methods exist to serve students, faculty, and staff is recognized and accepted, selling any one specific application of electronic technology to improve a service becomes less difficult.

Recent professional publications call for institutions to apply electronic technology vigorously and creatively to the many processes that serve students and staff in the academic environment (Evert 1990; Jones 1990; Lonabocker 1990). The significant use of automated technology in higher education that began during the 1960s with keypunch cards and sorters evolved into real progress in the 1970s when data were entered and accessed directly on-line with staffed terminals. Key breakthroughs occurred in the 1980s with TT/VR registration, distributed processing, FAX, etc. Higher education is now poised to take advantage of the opportunities and challenges of the 1990s to catch up with available and emerging technologies by increasing its applications of these tools to the many daily processes serving students and staff.

A partial listing of these processes performed routinely in student academic support service areas of most colleges and universities is shown in the right column of Figure 4.1 below. The left column lists the powerful electronic tools available for use by higher education. The processes in the right column remain relatively constant. Recent history suggests, however, that the number and types of electronic tools in the left column will grow rapidly in the immediate and continuing future.

Although certain institutions can be cited as rare exceptions, higher education in general is not keeping pace with technical developments. For example, out of the thousands of postsecondary institutions in this country, only a few hundred have TT/VR registration applications or other student direct access capabilities. Even fewer use laser image or electronic data interchange (EDI) technologies. The difference between the technologies available and the way business is conducted in higher education may be referred to as the "electronic technology utilization gap." Figure 4.2 illustrates this concept.

Electronic technology tools available in the 1990s are represented at level X. The use of these tools in higher education is represented at level Y. The difference between X and Y represents the level of underutilization of available technologies in supporting the academic mission of colleges and universities. Since the X and Y levels cannot be quantified, these values are placed arbitrarily on the table for illustrative purposes only. In reality, the difference between X and Y varies among individual institutions.

The challenge for education in the 1990s is to close this gap or, at the very least, keep the gap from widening as new technologies emerge. This challenge can only be met with more creative, imaginative, and increasingly effective strategies to apply these tools to daily processes. With each successful implementation, student service offices will be able to provide more timely and accurate services to its many constituents (students, faculty, staff, and administration) in more effective, efficient, and increasingly humane and user-friendly ways.

Out of this larger picture emerge some relatively simple applications that have been around for decades and call for minor adaptations from users: touchtone telephone/voice response registration, and other daily processes in registrar, admissions, financial aid, bursar, and residential life offices that may include providing students with access to . . .

➤ advisement/degree summaries
➤ the status of their admissions, financial aid, or housing applications
➤ grades
➤ fee assessments and payment activity
➤ sign up for new student orientation

➤ their biographical and educational data
➤ information on course/section availability and
➤ requests for transcripts and verification-of-enrollment

Obviously, this technology has many applications in college and university environments but the most popular (and generally the first) application of TT/VR is registration. However, several colleges and universities have implemented grade inquiry (students hear their grades and GPA spoken) first as a means of familiarizing students and personnel in registrar, computer, and telecommunication offices with TT/VR technology prior to implementing registration.

Moving Ideas to Implementation

Even proponents of other registration systems agree that the application of TT/VR technology to registration is an excellent idea. However, having a good idea is not enough. Careful maneuvering of a TT/VR registration project will increase the possibility of its successful implementation and acceptance by those who are affected by its installation.

There are two basic assumptions to consider at the outset. First, every college and university has its own set of characteristics, its own formal and informal political and communications channels. Thus, there is no single right answer or formula to ensure that any given good idea will be accepted on campus, or, indeed, be successfully implemented. The second assumption seems to oppose the first. That is, even though each campus is unique and no one right approach exists, most campuses share certain similarities that make it possible to develop a process that moves an idea to successful implementation. Four general principles and three strategies appear, at least on the surface, to be common threads throughout the entire process.

Confidence, risk-taking, patience, and openness — four elements of common sense — can guide the entire process as the project moves from the embryonic stage through final delivery.

1. Confidence in the idea. Someone once said that the art of successful politics is doing the doable — the key word being "doable." Confidence, not only that the idea is an excellent one, but is possible within the unique environment in which it is to be developed, is vital. Skeptical administrators, faculty, and students only need to talk informally to their counterparts on other campuses with touchtone technology to develop confidence that TT/VR technology should be explored for registration and other applications on campus.

In the past five to ten years the large number of registrars and data processing administrators ready to share technical and procedural information, as well as data about TT/VR experience, include the following:

➤ Large public universities such as Arizona State University, University of Arizona, Florida State University, Georgia State University, Michigan State University, The Ohio State University, University of California-Los Angeles, University of Washington, and the University of Wisconsin-Madison;
➤ Private universities such as Bradley University, Brigham Young University, Gonzaga University, University of Notre Dame, and the University of Southern California;
➤ Community colleges such as Cerritos College, Daytona Beach Community College, Florida Community College at Jacksonville, Miami-Dade Community College, and Riverside Community College;
➤ Canadian universities such as the University of Alberta, University of British Columbia, and University of Calgary; and
➤ Smaller colleges such as Dixie College, North Florida Junior College, and Rancho Santiago College.

Skeptics raising questions related to security, control, accuracy, etc. can be reminded that the technology is used in banking, finance, and investment industries to permit customers to access

Figure 4.1. Applications of Electronic Technologies to Processes in Higher Education

ELECTRONIC TECHNOLOGY TOOLS		HIGHER EDUCATION PROCESSES

- ATMs
- automated multi-function IDs
- computer terminals:
    - ✓ "dumb"
    - ✓ laptops
    - ✓ notebooks
    - ✓ PCs (smart)
    - ✓ palmtops
    - ✓ touchscreen
- electronic data interchange (EDI)
- facsimile (FAX)
- local area networks (LAN)
- laser image
- mainframes
- **touchtone telephone/ voice response (TT/VR)**

APPLIED TO:

- applications for and **status of:**
    - ✓ **admissions**
    - ✓ **financial aid**
    - ✓ housing
- **advisement/degree summaries**
- course equivalency evaluations
- **grade** transmission/entry/**reporting**
- **fee assessment/payment**
- financial aid distribution
- ID cards
- **new student orientation:**
    - ✓ information about
    - ✓ **registering for**
- record archiving/foldering
- **registration**
- **student access to own data**
- student financial accounts
- **student access to course/section availability**
- transcript/**certification requests**
- transcripts (send and receive)

Figure 4.2. Electronic Tools Used in Higher Education

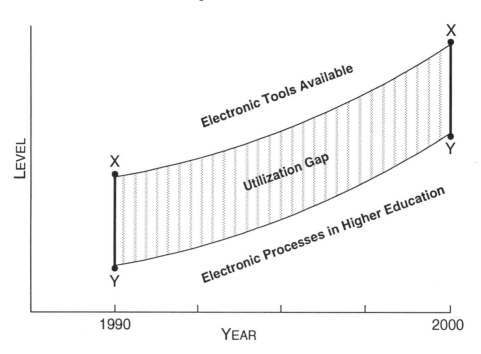

Reprinted with permission from Donald Wermers, University of Wisconsin-Madison

their accounts for inquiry and bill payment, and to transfer investment funds. The amounts of money handled by TT/VR technology in these environments should relieve doubts about its use in academic environments.

2. Willingness to take risks. Even the greatest idea may meet up with opposition, as reflected in the following "Seven Steps to Stagnation."

> "We are not ready for that."
> "We are doing all right without it."
> "We have never done it that way before."
> "We tried that once before."
> "It costs too much."
> "That is not our responsibility."
> "It just will not work." (author unknown)

Since those who oppose new ideas and resist change are always around, colleges and universities must be prepared to take risks—not precautions—that will enable them to use current and emerging technologies to enhance services to students and faculty. If a campus waits until there is a 100% chance of success, or until every question has been answered and every issue resolved, progress will be extremely slow and painful.

3. Patience. Risk-taking must be tempered with a prudent dash of patience. The project should neither be forced nor rushed. Pushing the project forward when the campus is not ready to accept it strengthens opposition and slows progress even more. Rallying support for TT/VR in the campus community is essential to acceptance of the technology.

4. Open to input. As the idea of TT/VR registration develops from the germinal stage to a well formulated plan, keeping an open ear to what others are saying is crucial. A college or university environment is highly complex; it is comprised of people with different perceptions, ideas, and opinions. Registration is the most visible administrative process on a campus and the one activity each term that directly involves every student, school or college office, academic department, most advisors and faculty members, and a number of administrative offices.

No one professional nor officer can possibly identify all the concerns and needs related to registration campus wide. Both the supporters of a new registration system, and their learned opposition may suggest excellent new applications that can be incorporated into the development. Being receptive to the comments of others also supports continuing dialogue.

Having confidence in an idea encourages the visionary to take necessary risks. Exercising patience and inviting active participation moves an idea forward at an acceptable pace. The objective is to push the walls of opposition back and gradually erode them, not knock them down.

Three Strategies for Obtaining Approval

Major activities associated with implementing a TT/VR registration system on a college or university campus include 1) obtaining formal administrative approval, 2) gaining broad campus support, and 3) initiating a comprehensive informational campaign. Certain phases of these activities usually occur simultaneously although the emphasis may be on one or the other activity. The sequential order of these activities may differ depending on the project and the campus political environment at the time of the project's conception. For example, on one campus where formal administrative approval for the TT/VR registration system is necessary, the task of gaining broad campus support may be the focus. On another campus a registrar may use the broad endorsement and recommendations for change in the registration process advocated by students, faculty, advisors, and departments to support a proposal advocating TT/VR registration to top administration. The order in which these activities occur is interchangeable as needs dictate, as the politically savvy registrar will recognize.

1. Obtain formal administrative approval.
First, know the objective. Understand precisely what it is that requires approval. For example, one campus administration that had recognized the need to replace the in-person, paper, batch, arena-type registration system in place for 20 years wanted to know what type of automated system was needed, not that automation was needed. The administration was ready to commit funds to this, even though it had previously rejected a staffed-terminal system primarily because of the costs of development, hardware, and on-going staffing. Armed with this knowledge, the development team narrowed its focus to identifying the most cost-efficient automated system. The TT/VR registration system proposed fitted the administration's criteria. Formal administrative approval was obtained within months after the decision was made to move in that direction, within a time-frame most colleges or universities would regard as just slightly less than miraculous. Knowing the objective precisely saved valuable time in developing the proposal.

Second, understand the specific channel of formal approval for each new project. The waters can be muddied easily if more than the minimum number of governing bodies, committees, or administrators are involved in the decision-making process. For example, it was during the first meeting of two ad hoc committees on automated registration that the least complex formal approval channel jumped out like a flashing neon sign. Simply stated, the chairpersons of the two ad hoc committees were charged with proposing the new registration system to the chancellor. No more, no less. Thus, the idea for a TT/VR registration system was not subjected to endless "sifting and winnowing" by a number of committees, student and faculty senates, or the dean's council. The interests of these groups were not ignored, but they were not formally involved in the approval process. Recognizing and following the most direct route to formal approval contributed significantly to the short period of time from idea to approval.

Third, remain sensitive to the informal sources of influence throughout this and all other phases of the project. Who are the opinion makers? Who will be consulted? Who is likely to support the idea? Oppose it? Why? Although there is a formal channel of approval in most if not all political environments, an endless variety of informal sources of influence—some real, some imagined—exists. The importance of knowing and using the real campus "influencers" cannot be overstated. Chances of approval are substantially weakened if these sources are not cultivated and convinced of the merits of TT/VR registration.

Describing precisely what requires approval and concentrating on the most direct channel to obtain approval, while consulting those who informally influence the decision-makers, will greatly increase the chances of obtaining formal administrative approval.

2. Gain broad campus support. Mobilizing broad campus support for TT/VR registration before or after formal administrative approval has been obtained is extremely important to its successful implementation. Getting the entire campus on the project's bandwagon, developing a sense of campus ownership, and moving from the "yours/mine" mentality to an "ours" mentality should be a major objective.

How can this needed broad base of support be mobilized? In the retail world, even the best of products must be vigorously marketed before it will be accepted by the buying public. One phase of marketing is simply educating the public about the product — what it is, what its benefits are, and why it is the best available product. So, too, the campus needs to be educated early in the discussion with input solicited from all segments. The lines of communication opened in the beginning need to be used frequently and in every possible form.

Shortly after formal approval of the TT/VR registration proposal on one university campus, for example, a working paper was distributed to deans' offices and departments briefly describing the concept, how it would work on campus, and the issues and problems that would require resolution. Meetings were then scheduled with each of the colleges and departments. Without question, the most effective aspect of these one-to-one, three-hour-long meetings was a simple five-minute, on-line demonstration that used a speaker telephone to show how another university's TT/VR registration system worked. The demonstration occurred after a ten-minute general introduction which informed each small group that the campus was developing a system to permit students to register in an on-line environment from anyplace in the world at any time of the day with a touchtone telephone. The closed, obviously incredulous (not skeptical) expressions on most people's faces turned to open expressions of interest and inquiry during the demonstration. The mind set changed immediately from "no way" to "yes, but . . . ." The demonstration, thus, was a tool that immediately turned the meetings into positive question and answer sessions.

During these meetings, valuable input, from the ultimate users of the system permitted the analysts to address questions raised. These open communications were instrumental in gaining campus-wide acceptance of the idea. Being receptive to the concerns expressed generated the sense of community ownership essential for successful implementation. Once the lines of communication were opened, they remained open throughout the stages of development, installation, and review.

The value of establishing just the right tone, style, and methods of communication, along with the virtues of patience and openness-to-input during this phase, cannot be overstated. What is being proposed will, after all, change the way many people do things. Not understanding exactly how life will be changed generates a natural tendency to resist, to be skeptical, and to want more information than may be readily available. These kinds of emotions must be recognized and handled in ways which will allay the doubts of the skeptics and retain them as positive supporters of the project.

The result of the discussion papers and meetings may be the publication of the Project Definition paper. This "final" description, on which development of the project will be based, emerges as little more than a formality reflecting the agreements reached throughout the mobilization of broad campus support.

3. Initiate a comprehensive information campaign. Formal administrative approval has been obtained. Efforts to develop broad campus support have begun and are continuing. The computer analysts and programmers are engrossed in their developmental activities. A technical committee is creating the touchtone hardware Request for Proposal (RFP). Simultaneously, the registrar's office is working with colleges, departments, and other administrative offices to develop the procedures to implement the new project, which is still several months into the future. Momentum for the project is building. This is the time to initiate a comprehensive information campaign to promote the high visibility of the project and to eliminate any potential elements of surprise when the implementation begins.

This stage can be viewed as a continuation and enhancement of the previous campus mobilization activities. A well orchestrated campaign will a) keep the campus informed of the status of the project, b) educate the campus about its characteristics, c) describe new procedures, and d) ensure that the entire campus is in step throughout the development phase in preparation for a smooth installation.

Several approaches may be initiated to accomplish the above objectives. First, of course, is to continue the in-person discussions and meetings begun during the campus support phase. As the development nears completion and the details of the product become increasingly clear, the registrar's office may conduct detailed orientation workshops for those involved directly with the project. It may also develop and broadly distribute more specific descriptions and instructions to departments, advisors, faculty, administrative offices, and students. One registrar, for example, launched a comprehensive plan for advertising the campus's new registration and advising system. The plan included a farewell-to-the-arena party called "Arenaderci," several news releases in the local and student newspapers, posters, a video, a professionally developed registration guide, and small group training sessions. The training sessions were held to introduce faculty advisors and students to the new registration procedures. (See Exhibit A.1 from the University of Wisconsin-Madison.) Another university developed a skit to show how TT/VR registration worked.

Throughout the development phase, the potentially most effective vehicle for distributing information is a well written, widely disseminated newsletter. One university published 25 issues over a two-year period for faculty and staff. The newsletter contained articles written by staff in college offices and departments, as well as the data processing, instructional space, and registrar offices. It served as the constant link between the "developers" and the "users." It was key in maintaining and enhancing the campus ownership concept. See Exhibit A.2 for a newsletter from The Ohio State University.

The available routes to a campus information campaign are many. Each campus will, of course, develop its own approach. It is most important, however, to acknowledge the need and value of an informational, promotional, and educational campaign before a new idea reaches the operation phase.

Summary

Each campus possesses its own unique characteristics and political climate. There is no single approach to moving a good idea, like TT/VR registration, from acceptance to implementation. There are similarities among campus environments and in processes that can lead to successful implementation based on four common sense principles—confidence in the idea, willingness to take risks, patience, and openness to input. Based on these principles, colleges and universities can incorporate a variety of strategies to obtain formal administrative approval, gain broad

campus support, and initiate a comprehensive informational campaign.

The general principles and strategies may provide guidelines colleges and universities can use to chart a course of action that will move the idea of a TT/VR registration system to reality. Variations on these general guidelines are limitless. Strategies can be modified creatively to address unique campus characteristics.

Acknowledgements:

This section combines ideas and concepts contained in papers presented previously at AACRAO Annual Meetings, Touchtone and Standardization of Postsecondary Education Electronic Data Exchange (SPEEDE) Workshops, and Regional ACRAO Meetings. Some of these were joint presentations that included R. Steve Gawkoski, Registrar, Marquette University; Ronald C. Niendorf, Director of Computing Services for Academic Services and Outreach Administration, University of Wisconsin-Madison; Laura McCain Patterson, Registrar, University of Wisconsin-Eau Claire; and Thomas J. Scott, Special Assistant to the Director, Administrative Data Processing, University of Wisconsin-Madison. Their contributions to this section through co-authoring and co-presenting the original papers are greatly appreciated.

Laying the Foundation

BIOCHEMISTRY

CHICANO STUDIES

SPEECH

KOREAN

ANATOMY

PHYSICS

ORAL MEDICINE

POLITICAL SCIENCE

PRINT MAKING

PRIMARY AUTHOR:

Joneel Harris
University of North Texas

SUPPORTING AUTHORS:

Robert F. Askins
University of South Carolina

Melanie Moore Bell
Gonzaga University

James H. Bundy
North Carolina State University

Donald D. Carter
Texas A&M

T. Luther Gunter
University of South Carolina

Sally Hickok
*University of California,
San Diego*

William L. Salter
University of South Carolina

R. Eugene Schuster
The Ohio State University

Once a college or university decides to implement a touchtone telephone registration system, it must do its homework to ensure the success of the project. Each institution must analyze its own particular situation, plan accordingly, and determine the amount of risk it is willing to take to implement change. This is particularly true for touchtone telephone/voice response (TT/VR) technology which is less familiar than other technologies admissions and records offices have used for the last 30 years.

Who Should Be Involved? The Team Approach

A team approach is critical because of the complexity of the project and the number of departments and other operational areas impacted by the implementation of such a system. Designing and implementing a TT/VR registration system demands expertise in a wide range of disciplines and a broad-based knowledge of the institution itself. Unlike any other system implemented on campus, TT/VR registration draws together more elements in the planning and development stage than any other student-related software application. The team approach, possibly multi-tiered, encourages a broad input of ideas for evaluation and testing and identification of potential problems and solutions. Many campuses already have some sort of committee structure or procedure in place to guide the development of new administrative systems. If so, a TT/VR registration project may be driven by these existing guidelines.

The TT/VR team should include policy and decision makers and detail-oriented implementers. Six to ten participants can provide the appropriate mix. In addition, a steering committee and/or advisory group to oversee the effort, a project team to bring the system to production, and ad hoc work groups that include faculty and students may be formed to work out the exact details of the systems. Existing academic committees on campus may be tapped if policy changes or procedural reviews (e.g.,

those related to academic advising) are necessary. A suggested team structure is represented in Figure 5.1.

Since touchtone registration is basically another type of computerized course scheduling system, the registrar or a designated representative from that office probably will be involved along with one or more computing center systems analysts and/or programmers. Though logically the best chair for the project team, politically the registrar might not be the best leader. If there is resistance to TT/VR registration from the academic community, a faculty member who supports the change may be a better choice.

Telecommunications must be represented in all phases of planning and implementation. Is there a manager of telecommunications? If not, it is critical that someone know and understand the telephony implications, requirements, options, and interfaces necessary for successful and painless implementation of such a system. Some campuses own and operate their own telephone systems. Those totally dependent on a local telephone service provider should have a representative from that company involved in the TT/VR registration project that can generate thousands and, perhaps, hundreds of thousands of telephone calls. Depending on the geographic location and sophistication of telephone equipment in the area of a college or university, its impact on telephone services can be far reaching. Some TT/VR registration projects have caused complete breakdowns in telephone services for campuses, surrounding areas, entire cities, and even counties.

Faculty and students should also be represented on the project team. Key supporters from the faculty as well as skeptics can contribute equally to the successful outcome of the project. The need for student participation is rather obvious since they are the end users of the touchtone registration system.

Ad hoc committee members should represent the areas directly and indirectly affected that may require technical systems interface. These areas might include admissions, bursar or student accounts,

Figure 5.1. Touchtone Registration Organizational Structure

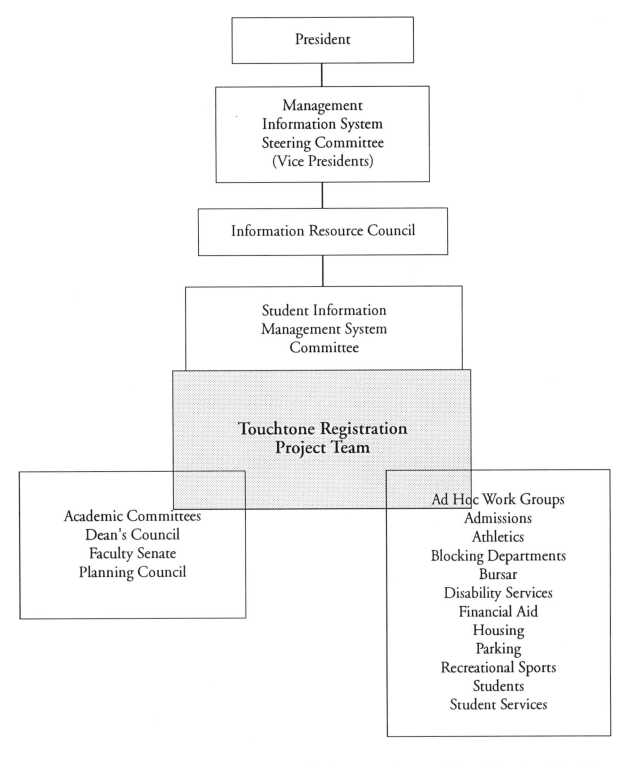

Source: Adapted and reprinted with permission from Joneel Harris, University of North Texas

financial aid, housing or residential life, parking, departments placing bars or holds on registration, athletics, student services, disability services, recreational sports, etc. Membership in work groups will ultimately be driven by the needs that must be met functionally by the system or interfaced programmatically and/or procedurally in another way.

Preparing for the First Meeting

Once the project participants have been identified, the chair should prepare for the first team development meeting by reviewing the team's goal and clearly outline the responsibilities of team members. Successful completion of the charge means that each member actively participates.

The team does not have to re-invent the wheel to prepare for a touchtone registration project but it does need to identify the broad-based institutional needs that the new system must meet. It might start by doing some homework:

➢ Call registrars, data processing and telecommunications managers at the colleges and universities that have implemented TT/VR.

➢ Request samples of their Request for Proposals (RFP), final contracts, scenarios, flow charts, specifications, scripts, work sheets, computer configurations, etc.

➢ Ask those who have implemented a TT/VR registration system to share their experiences and observations.

➢ Ask vendors to forward marketing publications.

➢ Ask colleagues on campus to contact their counterparts at other colleges and universities for information specific to their area.

➢ Contact TT/VR users on other campuses through electronic mail, such as BITNET and INTERNET.

The team's careful review of all information should precede its development of the needs/cost/benefit analysis and other assessments (see below).

Preparing the Needs/Cost/Benefit Analysis

The project team must identify the broad-based institutional needs that the new system must meet. Assuming funding is an issue, it must then prepare a needs/cost/benefit analysis. Contacting similar institutions that have implemented TT/VR can be extremely helpful both in documenting needs and preparing the analysis. If the project team has not already done so, members should attend voice response workshops, visit exhibit shows where vendors are present, and invite vendors to their campus.

THE NEEDS ANALYSIS

The needs analysis begins with an overview of current registration practices and calls upon lengthy interaction between users and potential users of the TT/VR registration system. It does not try to fully document circumstances that may or may not be applicable in the future. Whatever system is put in place must accommodate new requirements as they arise and be flexible and adaptable in its structure and characteristics. Input from users will clarify such processes as information flow across office boundaries, identify the kinds of data processing and analyses that are institution-wide rather than department or school/college-specific, and point out where users see limitations in the way students are currently registering. The participation of the entire college or university community is one critical component sometimes overlooked in the needs analysis. The new TT/VR registration system is not a system solely for administrators; it will be used directly by students and will affect the roles faculty play in the registration process. Participating in the needs analysis helps the team identify the diverse information requirements of these groups, and gets people involved. TT/VR registration is, after all, a major undertaking; the more widespread the support for such an effort, the more likely it is to be successful (EDUTECH International 1990).

The final needs analysis document describes . . .

➤ the assumptions used to define registration needs;

➤ the characteristics of the "ideal" registration system, such as flexibility, integration, and ease of use;

➤ the data and the tools required to store and manipulate the data; and the functional needs in broad rather than detailed terms (pp. 3-4).

Because it helps define institutional and user expectations, the needs analysis is critical to the successful implementation of a new TT/VR registration system.

Setting Goals

What does the college or university hope to accomplish by implementing TT/VR registration? Are there obvious problems that the new system must solve? Can student services be improved, for example? Will TT/VR registration eliminate the need for faculty to perform such clerical tasks, as handing out class cards, and give them more time for academic advising. Administratively, would the TT/VR system ...

➤ save registration space for other purposes?

➤ save money?

➤ improve the efficiencies of the scheduling process by providing instant feedback to students in a dynamic environment?

➤ encourage early/pre-registration? or

➤ replace a batch process of short timeframe, high volume registration?

From a public relations standpoint, how would TT/VR allow the institution to keep pace with area schools or gain an edge on student recruitment and retention?

Defining System Characteristics

Some institutions buy their own hardware and do their own development and programming. Others demand a turnkey system with the vendor providing, for a price, all the resources necessary to implement the system. (A word of caution here. Colleges and universities must be sure vendors under consideration understand their institution's definition of "turnkey" system.) The number of factors to be considered could go on and on but ultimately the project's success depends on an institution's insightful self-analysis of its own circumstances. The outcome of the needs assessment process will become the basis for the bid specification process, usually referred to as the Request for Quotation (RFQ) or the Request for Proposal (RFP). See Exhibit B for a sample RFP from The Ohio State University.

What should a college or university look for in a touchtone telephone registration system? Components of a "good" systems solution, applicable and essential to every TT/VR registration system, should be determined early in the project. Their value can be assessed using the findings of the needs analysis and factoring in those characteristics deemed critical by the college or university. Adopting a scoring system that will allow the project team to weight each element according to its importance to the institution and keep score when the responses to the RFP are multiplied by the weighting factor helps keep the process objective.

EDUTECH International, a private company of higher education computer professionals, observes the following characteristics are usually most important to the college or university considering purchasing an administrative system such as touchtone telephone/voice response registration.

1. The institutional functions supported by the system. These functions usually include processing for registration, closed class authorizations, advisor permission, student accounts, and often some or all of the administrative tasks usually handled in academic departments. Most, if not all, of the requirements identified in the needs analysis should be part of the "basic" system. Those that are not there already should be added in a relatively routine, inexpensive way (p. 5).

2. Quality of technical support. Hardware and software systems go through generations of development. Applications software in general is currently undergoing a major transition in its underlying technology from third to fourth generation. Third-generation products are considered very much at the end of their technical life cycles. Fourth-generation technology is more cost effective, less labor intensive, and will be supported by vendors for a much longer period.

The TT/VR registration system should have technical underpinnings which take advantage of recent developments, and are closer to the beginning of product life cycles than to the end. It is not necessary, nor even desirable, to be right on the cutting edge, but newer technology tools generally provide much better price-to-performance ratios, and tend to be less labor intensive (pp. 5-6).

3. Ease of learning and ease of use. These characteristics balance the issue of familiarity with the current systems environment with the ease of use associated with newer technology, as well as with the training and support available from the vendors of the applications software under consideration. The system should be both easy to learn and easy to use, with a consistent and understandable user interface. Documentation should be well written and extensive. Support staff should be knowledgeable and experienced, and ongoing training should be readily available (p. 6).

4. Availability of system to end users. System procedures should be oriented toward users. The goal is maximum availability of hardware, systems software, and applications software during the users' normal working hours (p. 6).

5. Integration among the system's components. Integration (i.e., changes entered at one point in the system automatically propagate throughout the system) is a design characteristic that takes into account the need to reduce duplication of effort and information and to promote instead a smooth and consistent flow of information.

The system should be integrated across offices, so that different departments can use the same data. The system should follow consistent standards in coding, in documentation, and in procedures, so that data and information can be shared both internally and externally (p. 7).

6. Flexibility for future growth. Flexibility depends on two factors: whether the software readily and easily permits changes, and whether there are sufficient opportunities to make those changes. The first factor is determined by software design and the underlying technology, and the second is determined by control over the computing environment. Flexibility usually suggests a lot of computing power and often leads to a longer learning curve and a more difficult implementation for the computing staff. However, no system is either totally inflexible or completely and easily adaptable. The extremes of this characteristic may represent ideals, not realistic expectations.

Selection of a system, in a sense, should be made with a built-in assumption that it will be maximally flexible and adaptable to growth, enhancement, and modification to accommodate changing needs (p. 7).

7. Quantity of technical support. Technical support is a crucial element in planning and implementing voice response technology. This criterion represents a quantitative measure of the amount of technical support hours that are available and can be devoted to the system's design, installation, and ongoing maintenance (pp. 7-8).

THE COST/BENEFIT ANALYSIS

Costs

Once institutional needs are identified, estimated fixed costs can be determined. Calculating variable costs is slightly more difficult, and projecting "soft dollar" savings is even more subjective.

Fixed expenses, minimally, will usually include hardware and operating system software, an application generator, the application programs, hardware and software maintenance, telephone lines and possibly additional technical staff. At this juncture, some assumptions, based on the needs analysis, may have to be made regarding the size (i.e., processing power and number of telephone lines) of the voice response system needed. The college or university may decide it needs, for example, a 12-, 14-, or 32-line voice system and that the project must be turnkey. Most vendors will provide a quote for their hardware and standard software package system and maintenance over the telephone. Costs for custom application programming may be included in the total price or quoted as a separate charge per hour of application. Telephone interface hardware and line costs will vary depending on whether the institution uses the local telephone service provider or has its own on-campus telephone system.

It is advisable to prepare a best case/worst case analysis and include a contingency for unanticipated costs which may occur later, e.g., more telephone lines, air conditioning the room housing the voice response equipment. Care should be taken not to use the lowest figure for possible cost/benefit and decision analysis purposes. Variable costs may include, but are not limited to, technical support (analyst/programmer time in-house or vendor provided), the effect of the TT/VR technology on batch processing and other computing operations, mass mailings, advertisements, changes to the schedule of classes publication, etc.

The cost analysis should represent the capital outlay for system start-up, any other expenses, and maintenance for the next several years. It may be offset by hard dollar savings, and income (if a fee is to be charged to students). Extrapolating the spreadsheet out three to five years will give the institution a better understanding of the long-term effects of the investment. Additional cost figures for any anticipated expansion of the system should be included chronologically at the appropriate point.

If funding a touchtone registration system is an issue, separate cost/benefit analyses that represent the funding options should be made. These

funding options might include lease/purchase costs, rental fees, installment payments to the vendor, student fee assessments to students, or the use of a 900 telephone number. All of these options will affect the break-even point of the investment return, and each option considered will have advantages and disadvantages.

Initial costs include the acquisition costs for hardware (voice response unit[s], application processors, and so on) and software, installation costs of hardware/software and telephone lines, costs for the person who is the system voice, as well as the additional start-up costs for temporary or contracted personnel. (This latter cost can ordinarily be distributed over time, but must still be considered an initial cost.)

Recurring costs may include costs for staff, hardware and software maintenance, script maintenance, telephone lines, supplies, repairs, etc. required to operate the system on an ongoing basis.

First-year costs include the initial cost added to the annual recurring cost.

A sample breakdown of costs appears below:

Initial Costs:

1 Voice Response Unit	$ 75,000
1 Application Processor	$ 15,000
1 Speech Development Software	$ 10,000
Installation of 48 telephone lines	$ 10,000
Worksheet Printing	$ 5,800
Wiring/Electrical	$ 2,000
Data Line Installation	$ 900
Total	$118,700

Recurring Costs:

Maintenance ($1000/month)	$ 12,000 annually
Telephone Line Charges ($1000/month)	$ 12,000 annually
Total	$ 24,000 annually

First-Year Cost:

Initial Costs + Annual Cost =	$142,700

Benefits

Savings may be identified in the form of "hard" or real dollars and "soft" or nonbudget reducing savings, values, or advantages. Depending on the type of registration system currently in place, hard dollar savings may be realized by reducing or eliminating forms costs, hourly wages, overtime, costs for moving, and set-up for registration. Soft dollar savings may be realized as the institution takes advantage of the flexibility resulting from the use of this technology to improve its efficient use of resources (e.g., service to students, reallocation of staff/physical space/computing resources, the competitive edge it may gain over other colleges and universities in recruitment and retention, especially if its campus is the first in a geographical area to implement TT/VR registration).

Examples of estimated savings in a registrar's office include the following:

Tangible Benefits:

1. No rewrite required of existing on-line registration system.

2. No central, large registration site required.

3. System is not labor intensive.

4. Equipment configuration allows for expansion at minimal cost.

5. Release of 5,000 square feet of valuable space needed for academic programs in the central campus. At $60 per square foot, equivalent space would cost $300,000.

6. Reduction or elimination of recurring expenses, such as part-time registration assistants (savings of $50,000 annually), preparation of registration site (savings of $2,500 annually), and production of registration forms (savings of $7,500 annually).

7. Fewer course add/drop transactions because students are confirmed in classes as they register.

Intangible Benefits:

1. Convenient and easy for students to use.

2. Stabilizes classroom enrollment and thus educational quality.

3. Makes course enrollment data available sooner for decision makers and advisors.

4. Confirms students' classes immediately or gives students feedback as to why course is not available.

5. Eliminates noninteractive early registration system.

6. Reduces student frustration in not obtaining requested classes.

7. Improves advising system by maintaining required link between the student and the advisor.

Funding the TT/VR Registration Project

If all presidents said, "I want touchtone telephone registration on this campus by next fall. You have $200,000 to do the job and get whatever you need to complete the project on time," every registrar and computer center director would realize his or her goals for TT/VR registration. However, when money is a problem, the TT/VR registration team can try several approaches to obtain funding.

Given administrative approval for a TT/VR registration system but no money for design and implementation, one university's project team went directly to the students. Each student was asked to pay a maximum of $6 per year in additional fees ($2 per student for the fall and spring semesters and $1 for each of two summer sessions) to support the system. The student senate and student fee review committee unanimously approved this fee increase, thus allowing the design and implementation of TT/VR registration to move forward.

Concluding that the implementation of TT/VR registration was a quality of life issue for students and not an administrative issue, another university team developed a proposal to seek student financial support for the project. A multimedia package, consisting of a video (borrowed from another university and used with its permission), 11 overhead slides, and an executive summary handout, presented the mission and defined the project (its background, goals, resources needed, and projected timelines). The commentary as well as the choice and order of slides were modified to fit each audience. The presentation was delivered in its entirety to the student fee advisory committee and to the chancellor and senior officers. The student fee advisory committee voted to allocate the funds for all start-up costs; the registrar agreed to divert the expected savings from the elimination of a drop/add session to underwrite the ongoing costs (e.g., telephone lines, software maintenance agreements); and the chancellor issued the approvals necessary for ongoing maintenance of the TT/VR registration system.

Assessing the On-Line Registration System Interface

The key to the success of a TT/VR registration project is institutional analysis, planning, and assessment of risk. Some institutions have successfully installed TT/VR registration without going through on-line registration via terminals or optical mark read equipment. The college or university currently operating in a batch processing environment most likely will have either an on-line mainframe course scheduling (registration) application in place to which the voice response side of the process can be added, or a scheduling application process that resides entirely on some voice processor platforms, to which information can be uploaded to the mainframe for batch processing.

The first step in identifying the necessary system interfaces is to evaluate the current course scheduling processes and the various phases that exist (i.e., early registration, regular registration, new student registration, late registration, drop/add), and special groups that must be considered (e.g., those with disabilities, athletes, nursing students, law students). The project team should also go through each step of the current scheduling processes and determine if the TT/VR registration system needs to perform a particular manual function (e.g., verifying that each student's entry time is appropriate or checking for academic advising approval). Those processes in registration that are being performed manually will have to be included in the application program logic to prevent students from bypassing the control process, e.g., advisor permission. Other processes such as purchase of a yearbook, car pool registration, or the selection of a fee payment plan can be added as options.

Depending on the sophistication of on-line registration at a college or university, different approaches to developing the computer programs needed for TT/VR registration can be considered.

1. The screen emulation approach can use an existing on-line registration program, with only minor changes. This process sends an existing screen full of information to the voice unit all at one time. It does not require that a separate mainframe registration program be written, and thus reduces initial implementation task time and future maintenance effort. It does require that the voice application processor accept all the data, sort out what is needed, and put it into a format acceptable for voice response processing. Most vendors, however, are willing to write this type of conversion program.

2. The program can be broken down into individual functions. Existing transactions may be separated into individual components and a

new transaction screen developed for each "new" voice response function. The "add" feature is separated from the registration program as a distinct module; the drop transaction becomes yet another, and so on.

3. A separate mainframe application can be designed specifically for touchtone registration to stress host response time considerations that affect the voice processor. This approach is usually more desirable if the institution's mainframe resources are at a premium and the goal is to maximize response time on both platforms.

Weighing Hardware and Software Issues

The computing and telephone service environments are seldom identical from one campus to another. Therefore, mainframe, voice hardware and software platforms, and telephone service connectivity must each be considered carefully.

THE COMPUTER ENVIRONMENT

Minimally, on the host side a college or university needs to consider the type of mainframe (e.g., IBM-compatible versus a DEC VAX), operating system, and communication protocol used on campus. On the voice response vendor side of the equation, hardware options will include, but are not limited to, small-line-capacity personal-computer-based systems; larger capacity proprietary systems; and industry-standard-less-proprietary components that can be assimilated to meet customer specifications. Many of these systems can operate in networks, a factor to be considered if expansion and redundancy are major issues. Regardless of how the system is packaged, voice system hardware must support basic functions. These functions include:

➤ communicating with one or more host computers;

➤ running the voice side of the registration application;

➤ sending instructions to the voice processor; and

➤ managing the telephony processes related to incoming calls and storing and speaking messages.

See Figures 5.2 and 5.3 for sample hardware configurations from the University of Wisconsin-Madison, and The Ohio State University, respectively.

The voice hardware components may be packaged as a single unit or separated into different physical units. Regardless of the configuration, an interactive voice processing system usually contains several microprocessors that perform specialized functions in what may appear to be a true multi-tasking environment. A system that functions well with a low volume load may demonstrate delayed or broken speech, slurred words, and overall poor response time during heavy processing periods.

A personal computer (PC) based system may result in greater redundancy than either mini or mainframe based systems. It also may offer greater ease of development, a much flatter learning curve, and a familiar technology and language depending on the technical expertise of in-house programmers. (Some institutions choose the PC option because it utilizes numerous units that can back up each other in case one fails.) Additionally the PC option may offer script writing software that allows college and university personnel, rather than the vendor, to alter the script. Personal computers operate independently when mainframe resources are not required and offer a cost efficient way to expand the system on campus to satellite campuses, to branch campuses, and to college and university centers.

The software is closely tied to the hardware as the two often share management roles in the system. With so many processes occurring, throughput (the time it takes for the telephone to be answered, a message to be spoken, input received, and a response completed) is a function of

Figure 5.2. Touchtone Hardware Configuration, University of Wisconsin-Madison

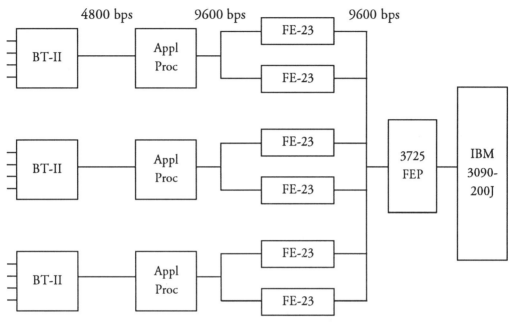

Note: Figure represents three fully redundant Perception Technology 48 line VOCOM V units.

Figure 5.3. BRUTUS Hardware Configuration, The Ohio State University

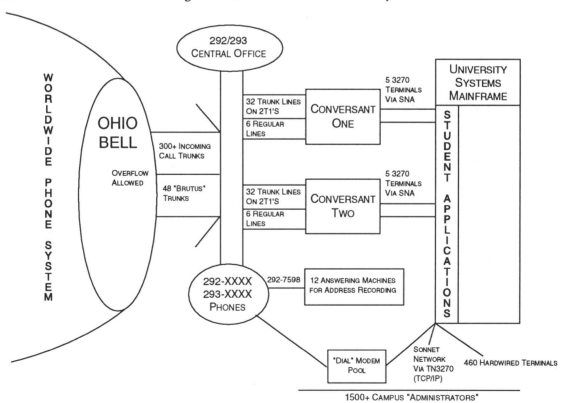

Source: Office of the University Registrar, The Ohio State University, December, 1992

processing power (i.e., how well hardware and software components work together simultaneously) and the host interface.

Software on a voice system will include an operating system, which may be DOS, UNIX, a vendor's proprietary version of UNIX, or even customized software; an application program, perhaps written in BASIC, C, COBOL, or some other programming language or a combination. In addition, an application generator, which is a specialized scripting language or graphical user interface designed to make the development of the application programs easier, and various communication protocol drivers may be included.

Other voice system features that can affect hardware and software considerations and price are FAX capability, text-to-speech capability, call progress handling, outdialing, voice mail or messaging options.

Detailed requirements for planned application(s) will determine whether these features are needed. Does the college or university plan to have multiple voice applications? If so, what are the expansion options and associated costs? Does the college or university plan to record its own speech? Is a separate recording unit needed, or will a telephone be utilized?

There are hardware and software feature issues associated with telephone service connectivity. The best sources to help pinpoint campus concerns are the person in charge of campus telecommunications and a technical representative from the local telephone company.

Hardware and software issues will be different for the institution that plans to purchase a turnkey system and have the vendor make all future changes and maintain the system, and the institution that plans to buy a system, develop and maintain its own voice applications. Regardless of the intent, these questions should be asked: How will we maintain the system if the vendor is bought out and maintenance is no longer available or if the vendor is not in business at some point in the

future? Will the vendor provide the source code? What is our disaster recovery plan?

TELEPHONE SERVICE INTERFACES
Local Telephone Company Interface

Some colleges and universities operate independent on-campus telephone exchanges linked to local telephone exchanges by leased lines. For example, one university's TT/VR registration lines were linked to both its on-campus AT&T Dimension AIS/System 85 exchange (with an on-campus telephone number) and to the local Southern Bell exchange (with an off-campus telephone number). The off-campus TT/VR telephone number was incorporated into the ESSX switching system owned by the university but operated by Southern Bell. The on-campus number was restricted from receiving off-campus calls and the off-campus number was restricted from receiving on-campus calls.

Initially, the majority of the lines were allocated to the off-campus number because most of the university's students lived off-campus. The registrar soon realized, however, that students who lived off campus tended to call while on campus, so the number of on-campus lines was increased. As a courtesy, Southern Bell was informed about the university's use of the ESSX lines. However, since Southern Bell had recently upgraded switching software, no problems were experienced. In retrospect, dividing the TT/VR registration numbers between two exchanges was an economically sound move that reduced the demand on any one switching system. Additionally, as the registrar's office gained more experience in scheduling TT/VR registration, the strain of busy signals on both exchanges was reduced.

Telephone Interface With Trunk Cards

Vendors usually provide support for a standard telephone line connection. Some vendors also offer what is known as trunk service which allows additional signaling over the telephone line. Trunks are the kind of service the telephone company sets up between its own switches.

In recent years, however, telephone customers with a large volume of calls have used trunks between the telephone company switch and a local site switch (private branch exchange). Instead of running one pair of wires between the user and the telephone company office for each phone, trunk service allows the institution to run fewer circuits, by installing another switch in between that tells the trunk to route the call to a specific telephone.

With trunk service, the college or university pays the telephone company for fewer tie-ins to the central office. By extending this application, colleges and universities can send a call over the same set of wires to the machine, and, using the switch to identify the number called for the TT/VR equipment, bring up the script corresponding to the number entered.

Another valuable trunk feature is "call supervision," a signalling facility provided on the trunks that allows the switch closest to the originating telephone to notify the next one along the way that the call has been terminated, i.e., the caller hung up the telephone.

Determining the Number of Telephone Lines

Determining how many telephone lines are needed initially is best made by informed decision. Providing the script to potential vendors as part of the RFP process will give a college or university an indication of how many telephone lines it needs. Enough institutions with similar implementations and equipment scheduling patterns now use TT/VR technology to doublecheck the recommendations of vendors. Phasing implementation so capacity can be checked and adjusted may prove to be the safest course.

As a rule, the number of telephone lines can be based on a formula recommending at least one line per 500 students, and on the configuration of the hardware of the system. Thus, for an enrollment of

25,000 students, a minimum of 50 lines will be needed. Voice response vendors can also provide more details on how to determine the number of lines needed.

PHYSICAL LOCATION OF THE VOICE RESPONSE SYSTEM

Physical location of the hardware and software is another consideration. System administrator terminals and recording equipment may be located in separate locations from the voice response system. Because TT/VR is a communications-oriented technology, the campus communications center is a possible site. Generally, however, the voice response system will be housed in the computer center. The most obvious advantage to the computer center location is its proximity to support personnel who have the expertise to handle any hardware or software problem. In addition, the computer center is most likely a secure site with appropriate environmental controls, and, at many institutions, around-the-clock supervision.

Some administrators may be reluctant to surrender direct control of program areas to the computer center. One university addressed this concern by providing remote access to the system; the administrator responsible for a particular area was issued a security code that enabled calls made from any touchtone telephone to activate or deactivate any portion of his/her area. The registrar, thus, could call from a home telephone and shut down the drop and add modules of the TT/VR system. The director of educational support services could call and record a new message on an information bulletin board.

Developing a Timeline and Project Management Plan

The timeline must consider the depth of in-house expertise and resources and the adaptability or viability of the preceding registration system. Institutional circumstances, defined in the needs analysis process and in contractual agreements with the vendor, will determine the target date for TT/VR registration implementation in a production environment. Some institutions have successfully installed production systems without going through a smaller pilot project to resolve potential problems. The wisdom and level of willingness to accept this kind of risk must be evaluated by the project team and a decision reached at the appropriate administrative level. The timeline will drive the decisions to be made and the processes to be followed to successfully implement the TT/VR registration project.

The first step in developing a timeline is to establish a target "start-up" date, whether it is for a pilot group or for the entire student body. If the start-up date is set for the middle of a fall semester, development of the timeline should start with this date.

The next move is to work backwards through each stage and identify key dates for major steps or milestones in the project. Milestones for which dates must be set will include:

> policy decisions that must be made;
> publication of course schedules; mass mailings and any other marketing communications or videos targeted for students, faculty, and staff;
> hardware and software installation dates;
> deadlines for new computer programs that must be written;
> deadlines to determine interface requirements and program changes;
> training schedules for staff and academic departments;
> testing dates necessary at various stages of the project; and
> script development and refinement deadlines.

The contract with the vendor should clearly outline which parts of the project are the institution's responsibility, the vendor's, the telephone company's, and any third-party contractors involved.

While many of the tasks associated with a TT/VR registration project can be run simultaneously, the third step requires a critical path analysis to identify the "progression" relationships or interdependencies that exist between various project components. A progression relationship means that one event cannot begin until another is complete. A voice response program cannot be written until the script is finalized. Host communication links cannot be established until the voice system is installed, and software cannot be fully tested until it is loaded on the system and preliminary testing is completed. Students cannot be informed about the use of the system until the schedule of course offerings is developed and in print. Failures to meet critical progression dates affect the likelihood of meeting the targeted start-up date.

The fourth step is to identify all tasks to be completed for each major date associated with the project. This may be accomplished as a part of a single document or prepared by various members of the project team or work groups who will develop sub-plans that define these detailed tasks; estimate work hours, weeks, or months needed for completion; and assign personnel to complete specific tasks. The more details included, the less opportunity to overlook a critical element.

The last step, which will be repeated many times after a commitment to the project is made, calls for the project team to review deadlines, identify tasks yet to be accomplished and their effect on progression relationships, and the completion date. If necessary, adjustments can then be made to the project management plan. Time can be built in to the schedule for contingencies that may otherwise spell defeat for the project. Several reasonably priced project management software packages to document the timeline are available on the market. Harvard Business Review, Quick Schedule, and InstaPlan are a few examples. Changes may take the form of added staff resources, further negotiations with the vendor to perform additional tasks, or modifications to the progression dates or the targeted completion date.

The communication, monitoring, and management of the overall plan that are critical to the success of the project are the responsibilities of the project team. The team should meet regularly, probably once a week or more, and include appropriate ad hoc members. A sample TT/VR registration plan documented at the milestone or major event level follows:

TT/VR Registration Timeline

June - October
> Thinking, learning, planning occurs

November - December
> Needs/cost/benefit analysis plan developed

January
> Plan "sold"/funding solicited

February
> Approvals secured
>
> Design team meetings begun

March
> RFP process initiated

April
> RFP sent to vendors

May
> Vendor selection completed

June
> Purchase order submitted

July
> Equipment received

August
> Equipment installed, training from vendor scheduled
>
> Software design and programming completed

September
> Video and information session materials produced

October
> Campus education begun
>
> Test groups identified

November
> Live test conducted

December
> Final preparations for full implementation begun

January
> TT/VR registration for all students implemented

See Table 5.1 for the teleregistration planning document from the University of North Texas and Table 5.2 for the timeline developed at the University of Wisconsin-Madison.

Naming the System

Naming the TT/VR registration system is important to marketing the system and creating ownership for users on campus. It can be a good way to get students, advisors, and faculty involved with the TT/VR registration system. A contest to name the new touchtone telephone registration system can be an informational and advertising tool to acquaint students with this new way to register. A contest flooded with catchy names can be an effective way to create interest and increase anticipation for the wonders of the new system. The bottom line is how well touchtone registration works. If it does not work well and students are not satisfied, the name that results from so much effort will be the least of an institution's or registrar's worries.

The name of the TT/VR registration system may be more the result of serendipity than a systematic naming process. Some colleges and universities use a descriptive acronym that doubles as the touchtone telephone access number. The acronym should be brief and memorable and a mnemonic device.

Names and acronyms (where developed) used by colleges and universities include:

ALBERT (Alabama's Best Ever Registration Technique)
> *The University of Alabama*

B.R.U.T.U.S. (Better Registration Using Touchtone Phone for University Students)
> *The Ohio State University*

CAPTURE (Cal Poly Touchtone User Registration)
California Polytechnic State University

CLASSLINE (Classline)
Lane Community College, Eugene, Oregon

CU CONNECT
University of Colorado, Boulder

INTOUCH
Arizona State University

RBT (Registration by Telephone)
University of California, Santa Barbara

REGI (Registrations Exceptionally Great
Innovation)
Central Washington University

SCOTS (Student Computerized On-line
Touchtone Systems)
Daytona Beach Community College

STAR (Student Telephone Assisted Registration)
University of Washington
Bowling Green State University
Miami-Dade Community College

STARS (Student Telephone Assisted Registration
System)
(Name of athletic teams)
Florida Community College at Jacksonville

STARS (Southern's Telephone Assisted Registration
System)
University of Southern Mississippi

TELUS (Telephone User System)
Community College of Rhode Island

TIPS (Telephone Information Processing System)
University of South Carolina

TOUCHTEL
*Gonzaga University,
Spokane, Washington*

TRACS (Telephonic Registration Access to
Computerized Scheduling)
North Carolina State University

TRS (Telephone Registration System)
University of Utah

TUTOR (Tulane University Telephone
Registration)
Tulane University

VIPS (Voice Interactive Phone System)
University of South Alabama

VRR (Voice Response Registration)
California State University, Long Beach

Table 5.1. Teleregistration Planning Document, University of North Texas

NAME	ESTIMATE	START	END
+ TELEREGISTRATION PLAN	919ed	01-01-87	07-07-89
+ TELEREGISTRATION PRETEST	98ed	12-01-87	03-07-88
- DEVELOP INSTRUCTIONS FOR STUDENTS	4ed	12-01-87	12-28-87
- SET UP FOR PRETEST IN THE COLISEUM	2ed	12-29-87	01-11-88
- CONDUCT PRETEST	9ed	01-12-88	01-20-88
- EVALUATE PRETEST	5ed	01-21-88	01-25-88
- DEFINE PHASE I&II CHANGES	4ew	01-26-88	02-22-88
- MAKE PHASE I CHANGES	2ew	02-23-88	03-07-88
+ CONTRACT	14ed	12-01-87	12-14-87
- SIGN	2ew	12-01-87	12-14-87
+ CREATE PROJECT TEAM	14ed	12-15-87	12-29-87
- NAME PROJECT MANAGER	2ew	12-15-87	12-28-87
- CONDUCT WEEKLY PROJECT TEAM MEETINGS WITH SIMS	18em	01-08-88	07-07-89
+ PHASE I TEST	101ed	01-08-88	04-10-88
- DEFINE TEST GROUP	30ed	01-01-88	01-30-88
+ TEST PLAN	65ed	01-21-88	03-25-88
- CLEAN UP EDUC MAJOR CODES	12d	01-21-88	02-05-88
- CLEAN UP ADDRESSES	12d	01-21-88	02-05-88
- ADD EUND MAJOR CODE TO DIC	1ed	01-29-88	01-29-88
- LIST OF EDUC CODES TO DON B	2ed	01-28-88	01-29-88
+ SET EDUC MAJOR CODE FLAGS	0ed	02-06-88	02-06-88
- 2 SETS PRESENT ADDRESS LABELS	0d	02-06-88	02-06-88
+ 10 LISTS OF TEST GROUP MEMBERS	0ed	02-06-88	02-06-88
- ALPHA WITH SS# INCLUDED	0d	02-06-88	02-06-88
- STUDENT AFFAIRS IN EDUC	0d	02-06-88	02-06-88
- ALL EDUC DEPARTMENT OFFICES 8??	0d	02-06-88	02-06-88
- RO-NANCY'S AREA	0d	02-06-88	02-06-88
- GRAD DEAN	0d	02-06-88	02-06-88
- PULL PDF FILE FOR EARLY REG	0d	02-06-88	02-06-88
+ DETERMINE SYSTEM AVAILABILITY	0ed	02-04-88	02-04-88
- 7AM-10PM, M-SU, 2/23-3/13	0d	02-04-88	02-04-88
+ DETERMINE TRAINING TAPE SCHEDULE	0ed	02-02-88	02-02-88
+ CONFIRM TRAINING TAPE DELIVERY	0ed	02-02-88	02-02-88
- 2/12/88 6 COPIES TO BE DELIVERED	0d	02-02-88	02-02-88
- EDUC,MED LIB,DAL CEN,RO,UNION,1 EXT	0d	02-02-88	02-02-88
+ SET TRAINING TAPE SCHEDULE	0ed	02-02-88	02-02-88
- 2/15—3/13	0d	02-02-88	02-02-88
- MATTHEWS HALL RM 349 8-5,EXC 12-1	0d	02-02-88	02-02-88
- MEDIA LIBRARY AFTER 5 PM & WEEKENDS	0d	02-02-88	02-02-88
- OTHER SHOWINGS AS REQUESTED	0d	02-02-88	02-02-88
- EXCLUDE EDUC MAJORS FROM ALL PDF'S	2d	02-12-88	12-15-88
+ RESTRICTED EDUC CLASSES	43ed	01-29-88	03-11-88
- IDENTIFY RESTRICTED CLASSES	5d	01-29-88	02-04-88
- REVIEW WITH DON B. & BETTY M.	1d	02-09-88	02-09-88
- ASSIGN RANDOM APPROVAL CODES	3d	02-10-88	02-12-88
- PROVIDE EDUC DEPTS WITH APP CODES	5d	02-15-88	02-19-88
- STUDENTS OBTAIN RES COURSE APP CODES	15d	02-22-88	03-11-88

(continued)

NAME	ESTIMATE	START	END
+ MODIFY TELEREG PROGRAM	17ed	02-01-88	02-17-88
- TERM IN ASSIGNMENT STATUS	13d	02-01-88	02-17-88
- LET EDUC MAJORS ONLY USE TELEREG	13d	02-01-88	02-17-88
- SPE RECORDS WILL BE ADDS	13d	02-01-88	02-17-88
- STF RECORD FLAG TO DENOTE TELEREG	13d	02-01-88	02-17-88
- CLASS FILE NOT AVAIL UNTIL AFTER ER REG	13d	02-01-88	02-17-88
- HONOR CAPACITY LIMITS	13d	02-01-88	02-17-88
- CONDUCT LOAD TEST	1d	02-16-88	02-16-88
+ MAIL 1ST LETTER TO TEST GROUP	0ed	02-08-88	02-08-88
+ TRAINING FILM SCHEDULE	0ed	02-08-88	02-08-88
- MATTHEWS HALL RM 349	0d	02-08-88	02-08-88
- MEDIA LIBRARY GAB 235	0d	02-08-88	02-08-88
+ MAIL 2ND LETTER TO TEST GROUP	38ed	02-17-88	03-25-88
+ INSTRUCTIONS/CONTENTS	0ed	02-17-88	02-17-88
- OVERLOADS	0d	02-17-88	02-17-88
- OPTIONAL TUITION PAYMENT	0d	02-17-88	02-17-88
- RESTRICTED COURSES	0d	02-17-88	02-17-88
- PARKING	0d	02-17-88	02-17-88
- TELEREG	0d	02-17-88	02-17-88
- BLOCKS	0d	02-17-88	02-17-88
- EXTENDED COURSES	0d	02-17-88	02-17-88
- MULTIPLE SEMESTERS	0d	02-17-88	02-17-88
- PIN	0d	02-17-88	02-17-88
- BILLING	0d	02-17-88	02-17-88
- WORKSHEET	0d	02-17-88	02-17-88
- EVALUATION FORM	0d	02-17-88	02-17-88
- ALPHA SCHEDULE	0d	02-17-88	02-17-88
- RETURN ENVELOPE	0d	02-17-88	02-17-88
- ADDRESS UPDATE AND PHONE #	0d	02-17-88	02-17-88
+ CONTACT FOR OPTIONAL TUITION	19ed	03-07-88	03-25-88
- RETURN BY MAIL	15d	03-07-88	03-25-88
- OPERATOR TRAINING FOR TMS	1d	02-10-88	02-10-88
- RESOLVE LINE PROBLEM	0d	02-11-88	02-11-88
+ SET UP ADMIN SYSTEM	0ed	02-17-88	02-17-88
- ELIMATE FALL 87 & SPR 88	0d	02-17-88	02-17-88
- SET DATE RANGE FOR CLASSIFICATIONS	0d	02-17-88	02-17-88
- SET ALPHA RANGE BY CLASSIFICATIONS	0d	02-17-88	02-17-88
- PIN--REVERSE YEAR TO MM/DD/YY	0d	02-17-88	02-17-88
- TEST WHOLE SYSTEM FOR DATA FLOW	2d	02-24-88	02-25-88
- MOVE TELREG FROM TEST TO PRODUCTION	1d	02-26-88	02-26-88
+ PHASE I ACCEPTANCE BY NTSU	0ed	02-08-88	02-08-88
- USER	0d	02-08-88	02-08-88
- ADMIN	0d	02-08-88	02-08-88
- SPECIAL FEATURES	0d	02-08-88	02-08-88
- PHASE I PROBLEMS TO BE CLEANED UP	5d	02-22-88	02-26-88
- PRESENTATION/DEMO FOR FACULTY SENATE	0d	02-10-88	02-10-88
- CONDUCT PHASE I TEST	10d	02-29-88	03-11-88

NAME	ESTIMATE	START	END
- EVALUATE PHASE I TEST	30ed	03-11-88	01-10-88
+ PHASE II REQUIREMENTS	212ed	01-01-87	07-31-87
- DEFINE AND DOCUMENT	90ed	01-01-87	03-31-87
- REFINE PHASE II REQUIREMENTS	30ed	04-01-87	04-30-87
- PROGRAM PHASE II REQUIREMENTS	3em	05-01-87	07-31-87
+ PHASE I BILLING	130ed	03-31-88	08-07-88
- MAIL SS I BILLS	18ed	03-31-88	04-17-88
- RECEIVE SS I PAYMENTS	21ed	04-18-88	05-08-88
- MAIL SS II BILLS	15ed	06-01-88	06-15-88
- RECEIVE SS II PAYMENTS	11ed	06-16-88	06-26-88
- MAIL FALL BILLS	18ed	07-03-88	07-20-88
- RECEIVE FALL PAYMENTS	18ed	07-21-88	08-07-88
+ PHASE I TRAINING	87ed	01-01-88	03-27-88
- DEVELOP TRAINING GUIDES	30ed	01-01-88	01-30-88
- CONDUCT TRAINING	30ed	01-31-88	02-29-88
- SELF HELP TRAINING	27ed	03-01-88	03-27-88
+ PHASE II TEST	152ed	07-01-88	11-29-88
- DEVELOP PHASE II TEST PLAN	8ew	01-01-88	08-25-88
- CONDUCT PHASE II TEST	30ed	10-01-88	10-30-88
- EVALUATE PHASE II TEST	30ed	10-31-88	11-29-88
+ PHASE II TRAINING	183ed	05-01-88	10-30-88
- DEVELOP TRAINING GUIDES	60ed	05-01-88	06-29-88
- CONDUCT TRAINING	30ed	09-01-88	09-30-88
- SELF HELP TRAINING	30ed	10-01-88	10-30-88
- INSTALL UCAP	30ed	11-31-87	12-29-87
- INSTALL 20 PHONE LINES	14ed	01-01-88	01-14-88
+ PHASE I INSERVICE	44ed	10-01-88	11-13-88
- USE PHONE FOR EARLY REG SPRING 1989	30ed	10-01-88	10-30-88
- EVALUATE PHASE I INSERVICE	14ed	10-31-88	11-13-88
+ PHASE I INSERVICE BILLING	18ed	11-14-88	12-01-88
- MAIL SPRING 1989 BILLS	18ed	11-14-88	12-01-88
- RECEIVE SPRING 1989 PAYMENTS	0d	12-01-88	12-01-88

The above document is output from A Project Planning and Presentation System software package from InstaPlan.

Table 5.2. University of Wisconsin-Madison, Registration Development Plan 1985-1988

1985	Feb.	Initial Staffed-Terminal Automated Registration Proposal Rejected.
	Nov.	Two New Automated Registration Committees Formed With a New Charge.
	Dec.	Attendance at Touchtone Workshop Hosted by Georgia State University.
1986	May	Touchtone Telephone/Voice Response Registration Proposed.
	June	* Proposal Approved by the Chancellor.
		* Attendance at Touchtone Workshop Hosted by Brigham Young University.
	Aug.	1st Discussion Paper Distributed.
	Sept.	Discussion Paper Reviewed with Each College/School Dean and Staff.
	Oct.	Revised Discussion Paper Distributed.
	Oct.-Dec.	Study Team Meetings with All Academic Departments and Administrative Offices.
1987	Feb.	Governor Included Funding for Developing TT/VR Registration in Budget Message.
	April	Project Definition Paper Distributed to All Colleges, Academic Departments, and Appropriate Administrative Offices.
	May	Written Reactions Received.
	May-July	Joint Application Design (JAD) Process Conducted.
	June	Attendance at Touchtone Workshop Hosted by Brigham Young University.
	July-Nov.	Hardware Acquisition Bid Developed.
	Oct.	Begin "Keeping in Touch", an Informative Newsletter Distributed to All Faculty, Advisors, and Other Appropriate Registration Support Staff.
	Dec.	Hardware Bid Awarded; Begin Responding to Protest from Unsuccessful Bidder.
1988	Feb.-April	Meetings with Colleges and Other Units by Invitation.
	March	* Hardware Received.
		* Information Materials About the System and the Pilot Mailed to Colleges and Academic Departments.
		* Information Materials Mailed to Pilot Students (Departments and Colleges Copied).
		* Voice Response Script Submitted.
	April	* Begin Departmental Orientation Workshops.
		* Students Begin Plans for Fall Pilot.
	April-July	Fall Timetable Preparation.
	May	* Vendor-recorded Script Received.
		* Meetings with Wisconsin Bell, Inc.
	June	* Telephone Lines Installed.
		* Attendance at Touchtone Workshop Hosted by Brigham Young University.
	June-July	Load Test of Hardware by ADP, Registrar.
	July-Aug.	Test of System and Resolution of Problems.
	July 22	Last Date for Receipt by Registrar's Office of Traditional Hold Information.

July 24-29	Testing by Registrar, Dean's Offices, Departments, Administrative Offices.
July 30	Eligibility File of Data for Touchtone Registration Materials Established.
Aug. 4	Touchtone Registration Materials Available for Distribution.
Aug. 15-24	Touchtone Telephone Pilot Registration (16,000 students eligible; 12,925 registered by touchtone).
Aug. 25	Celebrate.
Aug. 26	* Starter Rosters Delivered to Departments
	* Begin the Process of Modifying, Fine Tuning, and Adding Features.

Design and
Development

MICROBIOLOGY

COMMUNICATION

ENGLISH

FINANCE

CERAMICS

GEOMETRY

ARCHITECTURE

NEUROSCIENCE

PSYCHOBIOLOGY

PRIMARY AUTHORS:

Melanie Moore Bell
Gonzaga University

Earl W. Hawkey
University of Nebraska

SUPPORTING AUTHORS:

Robert F. Askins
University of South Carolina

James H. Bundy
North Carolina State University

Lou Ann Denny
Arizona State University

Jack Demitroff
University of Rhode Island

Janice Garcia
Arizona State University

T. Luther Gunter
University of South Carolina

John W. Orwig
The Ohio State University

William L. Salter
University of South Carolina

R. Eugene Schuster
The Ohio State University

Genene Walker
Arizona State University

Some simple suggestions can greatly increase a college or university's success in developing a touch-tone telephone/voice response (TT/VR) registration system. Discussion on the specifications overview in this chapter is reprinted from "Developing an Application ... A How To Guide" (1992) with permission from Perception Technology.

Creating the Specifications Overview

The first step in designing and developing a TT/VR registration system is to create a specifications overview that clearly defines the objectives of the TT/VR system and the requirements needed for application. A major group to consider is the audience: current users, typical users and future users. In setting these parameters a college or university can design and develop a TT/VR registration system that will best serve students and the institution.

SCENARIO

Once the specifications overview is completed, the flow of the call or the scenario can be determined. The scenario script should describe the operation of the TT/VR registration system in nontechnical terms. The best approach is to create some typical scenarios using real students' registering. A useful technique is to include an outline of the call flow that reflects the course of the conversation between the student and the TT/VR registration system and the defaults that serve as guidelines for each entry. The scenario script turns the abstract system design into something real.

These scenarios should be recorded and tested with two people, two telephones, and a recorder and telephone patch. One person speaks the scenario script while the other person enters the responses using the telephone keypad. Someone uninvolved in development should enter the responses and monitor the reactions and difficulties.

Seeing a message and hearing it provide two different ways to evaluate the message's effectiveness (the problem most often identified is that the messages are too long). Thus, the scenarios set up an opportunity to identify and resolve problems early and can contribute to a shorter development period. See Exhibit C for a sample scenario from the University of Washington.

VOCABULARY

Creating the vocabulary is time intensive but important. The vocabulary of the TT/VR registration system has two parts: the phrase, which is a continuous flow of speech, and the variable, which is caller-specific data. Breaking down messages into common phrases which can be used in many different messages promotes consistency in the messages and eliminates unnecessary words, e.g., "press Y" and "enter Y." Phrasing minimizes the amount of text that will be recorded. A common phrase can be used in more than one message, even though it may need to be recorded using different voice inflections, depending on its placement in the message.

It is important to number each individual phrase so that the location and identity of the phrase can be tracked at all times. It is also important not to lump phrases and variables together when numbering. They are, in fact, two separate pieces of script and should be defined as such. In developing generic but informative vocabulary, redundancy should be avoided, vocabulary should be kept short and simple, and the caller's attention span should be remembered when commands are created.

FUNCTIONAL SPECIFICATIONS

The next step in the process is to revisit the scenario and introduce the technical components or technical instructions, known as the functional specifications. The functional specifications consist of various aspects of the application such as call length, system length in hours, standard timeouts, error handling, and any error messages. When creating a specification (known more commonly as a spec), a college or university should set up general instructional guidelines that will be used throughout the application. Any changes or variances in these established guidelines (e.g., changes in defaults) should be identified and recorded within the functional spec. See Exhibit D for final specifications, including flow charts and transaction paths, from the University of Washington.

FLOW CHARTS

At this stage of development, flow charts that illustrate the vocabulary and sequence of events occurring during a telephone session with a student should be created. Flow charts are diagrams that use boxes, squares, circles, lines, and arrows, each representing a function, phrase, or command to show step-by-step progression through the script. They are visual overviews of the script that represent the logical flow of action and speech that are essential to understanding an institution's vocabulary and are recommended when developing the script. Flow charts assure that no "dead ends" or "loops" develop; they create a "road map" for the system's programming. See Figure 6.1. See also Exhibit D for a flow chart developed by the University of Washington.

Several steps are involved in developing a flow chart.

➢ Identify points in the sequence of events that require a Prompt message, an Error message, an Instruction message, or just a simple Statement message.

➢ List the messages to be spoken. Most computer personnel are familiar with computer-based systems that are designed in terms of screen messages; difficulties arise when visual screen messages must be translated into audio telephone messages. In developing the message, remember that telephone messages must be as informative and understandable as possible since they are the only feedback the student has at the time. Decide on the length of the call and whether the information should be spoken

or written. Consider how specific it needs to be. Does the college or university want the spoken message to say, "A hold has been placed on your record," or "A hold has been placed on your record by the Traffic and Parking Department." In general, being more specific is desirable. Specific responses are more user friendly; students may feel the TT/VR registration system is responding to them rather than the reverse (i.e., students are responding to the system). The only drawbacks are the additional processing needed to determine the specific message to be spoken and the extra text phrases required for each possibility.

➢ Separate the messages into the four categories (prompt, error, instruction, statement).

➢ Assign a code to each, and then insert these message codes into the flow chart. Keep the actual message apart from the transaction flow so it can be reworded without affecting the flow chart.

➢ Keep a list of these messages and the conditions that will produce the text response. Try to be specific on responding to entries that are in error. Since it is not possible to know exactly which keys were pressed, the caller may not know why the entry was in error. If the student's entry is repeated back as part of the response, many second time errors can be eliminated.

DATA TRANSACTIONS FORMAT

Having developed the scenario, vocabulary and functional specifications, it is now time to decide what type of format will run the TT/VR registration system. Two options are available to develop a host transaction format: a screen-oriented/transactional system, or a human interface/conversational system. A host transactional interface system that creates its own format is strongly recommended for the college or university. Using a set of transactions allows greater functionality and, if necessary, is more easily altered than a human host interface system.

A host screen format uses the "pictures" or "snapshots" of the screen to identify fields of definition and location. System developers using this sort of system must always remember to specify those screens that are being referred to or highlighted in commands or messages. The location of the screen and the screens themselves can then be easily identified when in use. Some institutions supply their vendor with a numbered listing of data definitions rather than "snapshots" of their screens, but still manage to reflect their format in an easily understood manner. Both methods are suitable, as long as the information appearing on the screens is identifiable.

Developing the Script

The first step in developing the script is to create a processing flow chart (described earlier) with a list of all possible error codes and their corresponding messages. Messages prompt for each piece of needed information. Error messages are developed for each error condition. Consider the sequence of prompts and responses and determine what to ask the student first, e.g., student identification, personal access code, date of birth, term/year, etc. TT/VR response time may be affected by the order of data entry. For instance, if a large number of calls is expected, minimizing the number of voice response hardware transactions with the host computer is desirable.

Once the student identifies the registration and identification data, this information is passed to the host computer for confirmation that the student is eligible to register. The computer gathers the needed data from the student's computer record and passes this back to the voice response hardware for processing. Understanding this "serial" processing and determining how to make it work effectively is key to the efficiency of TT/VR registration.

Careful consideration of error conditions and how much time to allow a caller to spend on any one function and for all functions is necessary because of the serial nature of data entry and hard-

ware constraints. Set limits for each process and establish a "time-out" for each response. The system will "time-out" and treat the response as an error entry when the specified response time runs out. The exact number of seconds that determines a "time-out" can be changed and varied depending on the complexity of the response.

Verify each of the error conditions on the flow chart. Decide how many times a particular error can be allowed and what action must be taken when the number is exceeded. Choosing three to four attempts is adequate, depending on the type and complexity of the required response. A different response to a repeated error may be used. For example, if the first or second entry to a prompt was in error, a simple "please re-enter . . . social security number is invalid." If the required entry is more complex (i.e., there are more alternatives), respond to the third or fourth error with a "menu" giving the list of alternatives. Any subsequent error to that prompt could lead to terminating the function or telephone session and a referral to written instructions.

Consider the amount of security to use. The opening of any script usually deals with determining who the caller is, whether he or she is eligible to register, and what transactions he or she wants to perform. The more checks included at this point, the more secure the system; however, the telephone session lengthens. Since this process occurs on every call, take care to balance the security and the length of calls.

Using a functional approach in system design after the sign on and security screening, the student is able to enter requests for courses, hear a list of his or her schedule, and various other transactions based on the college or university's TT/VR registration features. A series of messages may be included to help students respond correctly, thus, complementing the functional approach. Explanatory messages, therefore, are available to those callers who need assistance but do not become a barrier to others.

The script may be maintained using word

Figure 6.1. Flow Chart of a Touchtone Conversation, University of Wisconsin-Madison

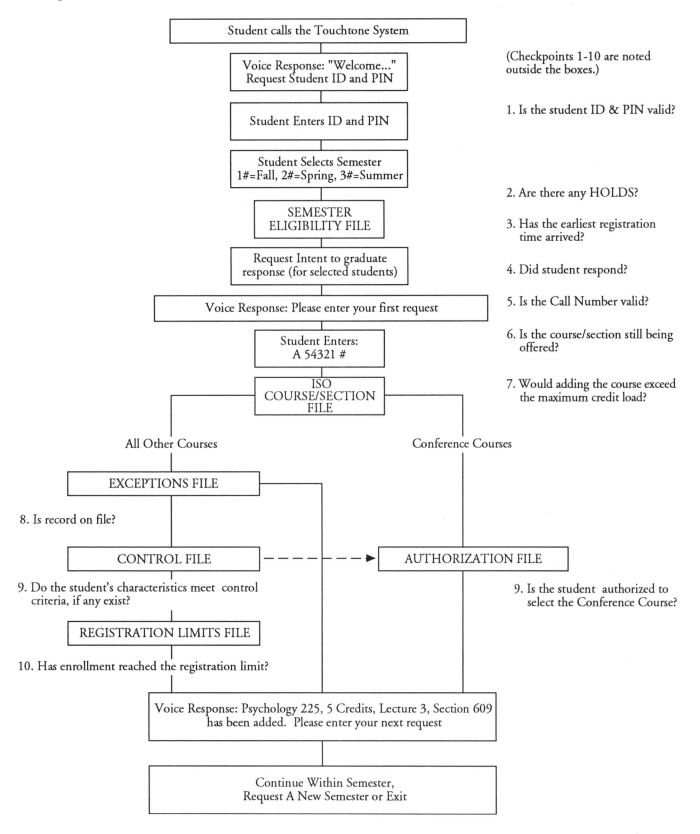

processing software, such as Word or WordPerfect. If the TT/VR registration project is implemented in stages, the changes that are made for subsequent phases can be shaded in the document until the next phase is implemented. This may be helpful when testing phases two and three, for example, since colleges and universities may prefer to concentrate only on areas where modifications have been made. Do not forget, however, to test the complete script!

A script committee will find that determining the appropriate message for each transaction is difficult and time consuming. Although the task becomes easier and faster as more experience is gained, the time spent developing the script is usually much greater than anyone had anticipated. Every effort must be made to keep the messages concise yet informative enough to prevent confusion for the student. See Exhibit E for a sample script developed by the University of Wisconsin-Madison.

The script should be completed by the time the Request for Proposal is forwarded to vendors for the bid process. The vendors will then know the speech needs and can furnish appropriate hardware and software quotations that will reflect the needs for the TT/VR registration system. Although modifications to the script may be necessary as more is learned about how the TT/VR registration application generator works, the effort put into the script before the voice response application is developed helps make TT/VR registration successful.

Determining Student Access . . . Who, When, and How?

One of the first factors to consider in developing a TT/VR registration system is the type of access to grant students who use the system. Because the choices made will fundamentally determine the whole structure of a system and the path of future enhancements, the beginner should be

aware of a number of different nuances. Most colleges and universities, for example, that begin using voice response technology for registration quickly recognize that additional applications are possible. Demands to add additional functions can often be overwhelming. An institution needs to consider not only where it wants to be tomorrow, but also where it hopes to be in five years. This process involves several steps:

➢ Review the various levels of access that could be granted to students.

➢ Examine the advantages and disadvantages of those levels of access.

➢ Discuss the classes of students to be accommodated in a TT/VR registration system and when each will be accommodated.

➢ Consider the question of security that designers should consider to prevent fraudulent use of the system.

EARLY REGISTRATION

Colleges and universities have traditionally used a two-tiered registration system which gives continuing students an opportunity to register for classes several weeks or months prior to the beginning of a term. Two common approaches to early registration are course request and confirmed registration. With the course request variant, students do not know whether they will receive the courses they are requesting; that decision is usually made when all of the registration requests are prioritized and final course assignment takes place. In a confirmed registration system, students are given immediate feedback and told up front whether they are confirmed in the course.

Generally, the first step in implementing TT/VR registration systems is to allow students access to a voice response unit for early registration. The advantages of focusing first on early registration are obvious. First, a much larger volume of students can be accommodated in a very short period of time than could be accommodated using any other registration method.

Second, because students can usually get immediate confirmation on their course sections, they can make schedule adjustments at that time and reduce the add/drop activity that takes place during the first weeks of instruction.

However, the use of voice response technology for early registration raises the first major access question. Despite its speed and efficiency, voice response technology is still a finite resource bound by the number of students who can access the system in a given period of time over a limited number of telephone lines. For example, if the TT/VR registration equipment has 24 telephone lines and each registration takes an average of five minutes, that means only 288 registrations (5 minutes divided by 60 minutes multiplied by 24 lines) can be accommodated in an hour. If 2,000 eligible students try to register on the system at the same time, some will have to wait over six hours on the telephone before a line is free. This is an unacceptable delay for any student. Thus, registration priorities must be built into the system and student access controlled in some manner from the very beginning.

Some colleges and universities have already dealt with such questions; they've identified the students who may register early. For example, most institutions give seniors priority over juniors, and juniors priority over sophomores. Unfortunately, such priorities may be too general and probably should not be the only criterion restricting access to the TT/VR registration system during early registration. Such simple prioritization may, in fact, allow too many students access to the TT/VR registration system at one time. Further refinements known as "pacing" are almost always necessary to move students through the registration system in an orderly manner without overwhelming the system.

Pacing Factors

There are three reasons for pacing students through the early registration process. First, access to the system at any particular time must be restricted to avoid overloading the voice response equipment, the computer, and the telephone system. Voice response equipment has a limited number of telephone lines and a limited potential for processing calls. The computer system into which all of these registration requests stream can comfortably process only a certain number of transactions in a given period. Finally, the telephone system can be overloaded to the point of collapse if the volume of calls is not controlled in some manner. While the advancements made in computer and telephone switching hardware over the years are impressive, real limits on various system capacities cannot be ignored.

Second, since not everyone can be accommodated at the same time, some known and agreed upon scheme must be put in place so that students feel they are being treated fairly in the registration process. It is a fact of life that certain popular courses close very early in the registration process. It is important that students feel they are getting a fair chance to enroll in these courses to reinforce their immediate embrace and support of the system. If this is not done, system acceptance will be poor from the very start.

Third, advising resources are a scarce commodity during early registration. The advising period must be spread across a reasonable period of time so students have an opportunity to see an advisor in the event of scheduling problems. If students can be paced through the registration process in an orderly manner, advisors will be better able to deal with their advising workload and scheduling problems in a timely manner.

The Pacing Plan

In developing a pacing scheme, it is important to remember that beyond an optimum number of appointments peak efficiency and easy access will be difficult. One university began with the premise that a student spends approximately six minutes on the telephone during an initial registration session. Therefore, optimum use of the resource would mean no more than ten students per hour per line could be accommodated. From there, it was a simple matter of calculating the number of students who could be handled by the number of lines available for registration and the number of hours of system operation per day. If the TT/VR registration system was available eight hours per day, the system could handle 4,000 students per day with minimal risk of overload or occurrence of busy signals. Five days of early registration at this rate could accommodate 20,000 students. To provide unobstructed access to more students, more lines or a greater number of days would be required.

Some colleges and universities assign a specific appointment date and time for each student eligible to register early for the upcoming term. The student is allowed access to the system only after that appointed date and time. In addition, certain limits are sometimes placed on how long this registration window is left open for the student to access. This is probably the ultimate in flow control; the institution can precisely control student access to the system at any particular time.

Unfortunately, there is also a downside to this type of precise control. Assigning appointments each term and reliably communicating this appointment to all students can be difficult. It would be ironic to eliminate registration lines only to create appointment lines. Such pacing procedures inject a great deal of rigidity into a process that is of necessity amorphous. It makes the system less friendly and accessible to students, and complicates rather than simplifies the process.

To offset the frustrations such highly constricted systems can create when students accessing the system are confronted by busy signals, some colleges and universities have gone back to setting up appointments. One university assigned students registering in the early period an "appointment" time determined by the total number of credits they had completed and their grade point average. This system had worked well for previous on-line registrations, but, as TT/VR registration call traffic steadily increased, freshmen had difficulty accessing the TT/VR registration

system and load degradation on the campus telephone exchange resulted. To counter the "building wave" effect, the university instituted a 72-hour registration "window," set computer controls to separate graduate and undergraduate early registration periods, and spread early registration scheduling over a greater number of days.

To pace students through the system, other universities have created another subdivision to control competition for the system just enough to avoid overloading any critical phase. They have controlled access, for example, based on the student's last name, the last digit of the student number, a randomly determined priority number or the school in which the student is enrolled. This scenario calls for extreme caution so that priorities can rotate from term to term or can be assigned in some sort of random fashion. Thus, no group is permanently disadvantaged in its order of access to the registration system.

This strategy makes it possible to leave the registration window for each group open for a longer period of time. The registration system becomes less restrictive and more available at the time and place of the student's choosing. Dissatisfaction, as some form of priority is imposed, will always come from certain groups who feel they are at a disadvantage in being able to access high demand classes.

ADD/DROP PERIODS

Just as important as early registration via telephone voice response systems is the use of telephone technology to provide registration services during the course adjustment period when students can add or drop course sections. The course adjustment period has always been a problem for registrar's offices. The time restrictions for schedule adjustments and the large number of changes students make generally require hiring large numbers of part-time employees. Fortunately, TT/VR registration systems are ideally suited for this period since they can perform multiple transactions in a short period of time. Any institution implementing telephone registration today would be hard pressed not to allow student access to the system for this purpose.

Because add/drop activity is more sporadic in nature, it can be less restrictive than early registration, where student pacing is very important. Peaks of activity will still occur but generally transactions will be spread fairly evenly throughout the time students are allowed access to the system for add/drop adjustments. In addition, not all students will use this opportunity to adjust their schedules. The only real questions to consider then are the days of the week and the times of day to make the system available for student use.

In dealing with this access question, two competing requirements need to be balanced. The first of these calls for extending the hours of operation as much as possible. After all, the major advantage of TT/VR registration is that the system is available at the student's convenience rather than just during normal business hours. Just as bank card machines have greatly expanded access to banking services in this country, TT/VR registration should provide service at the student's convenience. However, some practical considerations cannot be ignored. Chief among these is the need to set aside a period of time each day for system backups and production data processing, normally when access to the computer system is shut down. Added to this is the fact that many colleges and universities cannot provide 24-hour staffing in the computer machine room, and thus may further restrict the times when telephone registration can be made available.

In the final analysis, although expanded hours of availability are important and can be accomplished at almost all institutions, what is most important is that students know when the system is available. It is much better to define a set schedule each day of the week than it is to vary availability from day to day. See the Exhibits to find out how different institutions define systems availability for their end users.

SECURITY CONCERNS

Most colleges and universities that initially allow limited access to registration functions via telephone soon expand the services students may access as well as the time periods that students can access the system. For this reason alone, the security arrangements designed for a TT/VR registration system are very important.

The purpose behind TT/VR registration security protocols is to make sure that persons performing transactions on the system are who they purport to be. Just as with bank cards and computer accounts, some sort of password or access number is normally built into the system. The caller is asked to enter some student identifier into the system. This is analogous to an individual's being asked to key in a computer account number or log-on ID. In addition, the system user also supplies a second "secret" code the system can use to confirm the caller identity. The development team thus needs to decide what the secret code will be and how it will be distributed to students.

A number of colleges and universities require telephone callers to enter their student number and the last six digits of their social security numbers (SSNs). The assumption is that student numbers and SSNs are not the same; students normally keep their SSN private. A variation on this approach for institutions that use the SSN as the student ID number is to use the student's birth date as the password; an unscrupulous person, it is assumed, would need both pieces of information and at least one of them would be difficult to obtain. Either scheme requires only that the institution teach its students how to use the system since students already know both pieces of information. And the college or university thus avoids having to generate and distribute these secret and random PINs (personal identification numbers) to students. The disadvantage is that, while such security schemes may deter the casual prankster, it does not prevent someone with detailed information about the student from fraudulently accessing the system. For this reason, institutions often opt for more elaborate security systems.

The most obvious scheme for a more secure system substitutes the already known pass code or PIN for one randomly assigned by the institution. Regardless of how much one student knows about another, the chance of guessing what the pass code may be is nearly impossible. Counterbalancing this advantage, however, the college or university must find a reliable and secure way to communicate these secret numbers to students. Since students do not choose the PIN themselves, they are less likely to memorize it and may well keep it in written form where it can be discovered.

One methodology which avoids most of these problems and provides a more secure system combines the best aspects of the two schemes previously discussed. In this scenario, students first access the TT/VR registration system with a predefined PIN such as their birth date or SSN. At this point the system asks students to define a new secret PIN which they choose for themselves. The system can prevent them from choosing an obvious pass code and allows them to change their pass codes whenever they desire. Such a system is highly secure and lets students determine how safe they wish their records to remain. From an administrative viewpoint, time, money, and staff are conserved since no special communication with students is necessary whenever they access the system. From the students' standpoint their institutions are truly working on their behalf.

In summary, when designing a TT/VR registration system questions of student access and security arrangements are central to how well the system will work and how friendly the system will appear to users. The more restrictive the institution is in granting access to students, the less well received it will be in the campus community. On the other hand, the more expansive the procedures become, the less secure and controlled the telephone environment. In the final analysis each institution must arrive at some compromise acceptable to all parties. Campus traditions and desires will play the largest role in determining exactly where that point will be. The possibility of being an agent for positive change in the campus community should not be dismissed. Implementing TT/VR registration systems should make life easier, not more complicated for everyone.

Easing Special Registration

Convenience and ease of registering are among the primary advantages of TT/VR registration. It is self-defeating, therefore, to require paper forms for advisor approval of registration or permission forms to access courses for any number of reasons (e.g., overloading closed course sections, overriding course restrictions, checking for prerequisites).

COURSE PERMISSION

In the days of batch registration systems or arena registration, permission to enroll was granted for specialized courses through signed permission cards or some other sort of specialized form. Unfortunately, no matter how hard a college or university tries, it is virtually impossible to verify the signatures on permission cards over the telephone using the TT/VR system. For this reason a basic decision on how to deal with these courses must be made when the TT/VR registration system is being developed.

Colleges and universities currently employing voice response technology use three approaches:

1. Exclude registration for these special types of courses from the TT/VR registration system. Continue in-person or departmental registration for these courses and TT/VR registration for general admission course registration. This type of arrangement greatly simplifies the design of the telephone registration system and avoids a major campus re-education campaign.

2. Use entry codes as a substitute for permission cards. In this scheme, permission to enroll in a restricted course is granted by giving the student a special randomly generated, one-time-use code. The telephone registration system verifies the

code is valid for that particular course before allowing the student entry. Entry codes are distributed to departments prior to the start of registration and are available for use during both early registration and regular registration periods. Students can perform all of their registration activities by telephone and do not have to attend any form of mass registration. While it may require more effort and time to design this feature into the telephone registration system, it will more than pay for itself in student goodwill and crowd reduction at the beginning of each term.

3. Enable departments to maintain special permission and course restriction controls without unnecessarily inconveniencing the student. A course authorization screen allows the controlling department to "pre-authorize" a student for a particular course, usually during the advisement process. The program contains three levels of authorization: special permission, override of departmental enrollment limit, and override of room capacity. A course- and section-specific schedule code is entered along with a student's social security number or 9-digit student number and the level of permission to be granted. Another screen allows the student's dean to restrict or extend the number of credits in which the student may enroll in a given semester. By entering these authorizations in advance, students are spared the hassle of submitting forms for approval. The enforcement of special permissions is returned to the deans and departments where it belongs. The amount of paperwork in the registrar's office is reduced considerably, and perhaps, most importantly, the convenience of TT/VR registration is preserved.

For those colleges and universities that wish to eliminate in-person registration but do not wish to move completely to TT/VR registration for restricted course offerings, compromises are possible. For instance, an institution might allow academic departments to register students for restricted courses through the on-line registration system. While the thought of departmental

personnel performing registration activities may cause consternation for some, the decentralization of entry activity with proper control is usually positive. Certainly if a college or university trusts its students to master the intricacies of TT/VR registration, academic departments can master registration as well.

ADVISOR PERMISSION AND ACADEMIC ADVISING

Somewhat similar to the problem of limited access courses is the question of how student advisement is enforced in a TT/VR registration system. This is especially important for new students who should see their advisors before starting on their academic careers. Much as before, institutions are of two minds when it comes to this problem. The first school of thought simply relies on a required orientation program to take care of the problem. The second restricts TT/VR registration for new and possibly continuing students until they have seen their advisor. Several different mechanisms can be implemented to accomplish this task.

1. Give advisors new pass or PIN codes each term. Without the pass codes students cannot access the TT/VR registration system. As a high tech variant on this idea, allow advisors to release students for registration with on-line transactions. Without this release, students cannot access the TT/VR registration system.

2. Set up voluntary advisement appointment dates before registration. In this way, an institution communicates the idea that advising is strongly recommended, but does not force students to participate if they feel they are capable of self-advisement.

3. Allow telephone registration only for continuing students. New students would be registered in courses by their advisor or by some other mechanism which avoids telephone technology completely.

One institution devised a procedure referred to as "advisor review." Students were allowed basically unlimited access to the TT/VR system. Each time a student made a schedule adjustment that might be of interest to his or her advisor, a switch was set in the student's computer record. A facility (or corresponding program) enabled advisors to identify themselves to the computer and access their advisees' records to review schedule changes. Since most students sought advice or handled their own self-advisement reasonably well, very few problems occured. When they did, advisors simply contacted the students to discuss the situations. If timing was a problem, the school or college allowed the advisor to make adjustments for the student, trusting he or she would inform students of the changes. Schedule changes were also reported to the student via the routine schedule/billing mailing.

This viable alternative unfortunately suffers from a number of difficulties. First, it deprives students of one of the great benefits of telephone registration—the ability to determine the schedule of courses which best fits their needs rather than the convenience of the institution. Second, it communicates to students that they are not being treated as adults and are not trusted to make the right choices on their schedules. Third, it simply postpones the inevitable learning curve (usually short) for students discovering how to use the telephone system in an efficient and routine manner. Finally, it retains manual registration methods which are inherently inefficient and waste human resources.

Students are strongly encouraged to discuss their educational objectives and their progress toward completion of academic requirements with an academic advisor even though advisement may not be mandatory. In some colleges and universities, academic advisors are housed in a central location. Advising on other campuses is handled by faculty members in schools, colleges, and departments, many of whom do not have access to a computer. Each academic department may devise its own procedures for getting advisement

information into the system. Often, when computers are not readily available, the advising signatures and course restriction overrides are issued on forms. The student is directed to a central area, usually within the department office, to have the form keyed into the database. Since on-line registration may still be an option for some students, advisor signatures and course overrides can still be processed at the registration sites. As students and faculty become more familiar with TT/VR registration and its functionality, the need for on-site registration will decrease.

Telephone advising may increase, however, depending on the complexity of the advising session. And the student may be asked to schedule an in-person appointment before being cleared to register.

In summary, TT/VR registration systems require colleges and universities to rethink some of their current registration procedures and develop alternatives that make sense from an institutional perspective. This may require challenging old perspectives and assumptions on advising, but it also opens up opportunities for change and evaluation. What must be remembered is that the goal of TT/VR registration is to make the registration process simple and relatively painless from the user's (student's) perspective. The important point is to avoid hobbling the promise of telephone technology by insisting on grafting the old with the new. While this may seem the most expedient method for the short term, from a strategic perspective it is likely to be the most expensive alternative.

Design Factors for the College and University Community

SERVICES FOR THE STUDENT

The TT/VR system allows students to handle as many registration transactions as possible over the telephone. Students can add courses, drop courses, add courses for audit grading, change a course that is already in the schedule to audit, and change a course from audit to regular grading. Students can select a student insurance plan, contribute to student lobby organizations by adding the charge to their billing statement, place their names on "wait lists" if academic departments offering the courses have created them (TT/VR should not allow students to add courses that meet at the same time as ones they have wait listed), list their confirmed course schedules, and access a search function to see if certain sections of courses are available without adding the courses. If the section of a course is full, TT/VR registration can search for an open section offered at the same day and time or for an open section closest to the original request.

TT/VR registration should not allow students to register for more than one section of a course, nor permit them to add a course that creates a time conflict with a course already in their schedule. TT/VR should also restrict students so that they cannot exceed the maximum credits allowed for their classification.

SERVICES FOR THE ACADEMIC DEPARTMENT

Academic departments can place multiple scheduling restrictions on any course to stop ineligible students from registering. For example, the chemistry department may place a restriction on a course that requires students to be juniors majoring in chemistry before they can successfully add the course. Departments can also set up a prerequisite prompt message that reminds students a course prerequisite exists but does not prevent them from adding the course. Voice messages to inform ineligible students that they cannot register for courses without authorizations from departments offering the courses can be instituted. Departments can change the seat counts for their courses on-line. If a department wishes to allow more students to register for a course

that has reached its seat limit, it can simply raise the seat count on-line and immediately make space available.

OPTIONS FOR THE BURSAR'S OFFICE

Because registration and tuition and fee payment activities go hand in hand, modules for optional services with charges (student health insurance, meal plans, parking plans, yearbook) can be adapted to voice response technology along with registration functions. Similarly, tuition can be calculated at the time of registration based on the number of credits scheduled and the current tuition and fee structure. Students can then access a transaction from the registration menu to inquire about the amount due on their accounts.

Typically, during early registration periods tuition and fees are not calculated instantly, but are computed by batch calculation prior to the end of the term in session. Bills for the upcoming term are then produced and mailed to students who generated schedules during the early registration period. Once the batch calculation job has been run, students can inquire about the amount due on their student accounts for the term via the TT/VR registration system. The registration crunch is eased; students and administrators are free to work on other projects.

A credit card tuition and fee payment feature can be added to the TT/VR system. Some colleges and universities report that about 10% of the student population pay tuition and fees with a credit card during the first year of operation. Tuition and fee payment can be made interactive: the student waits for the system to verify the transaction with the credit card processing center. If the verification transaction is successful, the TT/VR registration system gives the student a number which serves as a receipt should questions arise later. All TT/VR registration lines can be available for fee payment and verification of credit. Payment is immediate, and monies can be deposited directly to the institutional account.

PLUSES FOR THE OFFICES OF ADMISSIONS AND FINANCIAL AID

Voice response technology offers a partial solution to problems of high numbers of student inquiries. Adding more telephone lines may not help if there are too few staff to manage an increased load and adding staff is not feasible. Students, however, can be offered a number of options. They may request application forms, inquire about admission or loan/scholarship status, or authorize the use of their financial aid funds to pay registration tuition and fees. They may opt to speak to an operator or leave a message on a voice mail system, and, having given their student identification numbers and explained the nature of their requests, expect to have their calls returned within one working day.

Programming can enable the system to handle concurrent years of admission and financial aid information. Integration with TT/VR registration may also give callers the capability to key in institutional application information via telephone.

INTERFACES WITH THE COMPUTER CENTER

The computer center is essential to a TT/VR registration project from the beginning. A good working relationship between the computer center staff and the registrar's office must exist. A college or university may decide that the voice response hardware will reside in the computer center where air control conditions and the expertise and resources for continuous monitoring are available 24 hours a day, seven days a week. One university reports having monitoring equipment in several locations within the computing areas and in the registrar's office.

Concern over a remote site removed from the registrar's office may not be a problem if rapport exists between the computer center and the registrar. In practice, the arrangement has worked well at many colleges and universities. There may be occasional differences of opinion over issues such as system access, but these are minor.

Choosing
a Vendor

JOURNALISM

GEOGRAPHY

FRENCH

GREEK

THEOLOGY

PHOTOGRAPHY

SHAKESPEARE

NUCLEAR ENGINEERING

ISLAMIC STUDIES

PRIMARY AUTHORS:

Melanie Moore Bell
Gonzaga University

Sally Hickok
*University of California,
San Diego*

Developing a Request for Proposal

Developing a successful Request for Proposal (RFP) requires a full understanding of available technology and how it may be adapted to an evolving registration system. The RFP should be written broadly enough to allow vendors to bid on either a totally mainframe-based system or a personal computer-based system linked to the mainframe.

The RFP may ask for proposals on several systems: one that will allow the college or university to develop its own software and programing tools (i.e., application generators) for multiple voice response applications; another that may require turnkey applications software; a third that might combine the features of the first two. Refer to Exhibit B for a sample RFP from The Ohio State University.

PROPOSAL COMPONENTS

Start by organizing the various components for the proposal. The first section should include the scope of the proposal, i.e., the institution's requirements and instructions. Most of this section of the proposal will probably be written by the principal buyer from the purchasing division who will follow institutional policies and guidelines for making major purchases of this type. The components should include, but not be limited to:

➤ Proposal submission instructions
➤ Oral presentations
➤ Contacts
➤ Definitions
➤ Specifications
➤ Exceptions
➤ Delivery schedule
➤ Acceptance test procedure
➤ Final acceptance of system after delivery and installation
➤ Payment schedule
➤ Seller's express warranty
➤ After sales service and support

➤ Installation
➤ Customer references
➤ Requirements for equipment demonstration
➤ Applicable terms and conditions
➤ Bid evaluation criteria/basis for award
➤ Right to negotiate
➤ Termination/cancellation
➤ Request for published price list
➤ Price reasonableness question
➤ State and OSHA standards
➤ Freight-on-Board point
➤ Extended acceptance period
➤ Insurance requirements
➤ Late proposals
➤ Business classifications
➤ Right to audit
➤ Certificate of current cost or pricing data
➤ Listing of employment openings

The component listing of institutional voice processing system specifications and the format for the vendor proposal is the charge of the project team. Team members should not be called together until they have had a draft to review that will form the basis for discussion. The registrar and staff should take a "first cut" to outline specifications for discussion by the project team. The first draft should be as comprehensive as possible and should include specifications for team review, even if they are later deleted.

Two questions apply in preparing this component of the proposal:

1. What is required?
2. What is preferred?

The draft should follow a question and answer outline that will accommodate detailed, itemized descriptions of the hardware, software, and service support. When each "requirement" is listed separately in the form of a question, vendors can explain in detail how their system can accommodate each specification. Preferred specifications should be organized as questions in a logical pattern. Separate sections for Host Environment, Vocabulary, Telephony, Application Generation, System Migration,

Training, Vendor Requirements, and Costs should be included.

Listed below are guidelines intended to help colleges and universities develop a complete and comprehensive RFP and evaluate voice response solutions. Since the impact of voice response is campuswide, it is important to factor in the needs and concerns of all of the departments involved. The information collected will give institutions general information on technologies, equipment, service, and other critical elements required for successful implementation.

The Introduction in an RFP

The following is a sample introduction for a Request for Proposal:

The (college/university) expects to install a touchtone telephone registration system by (month/year). When the system is installed, students will be able to call a telephone number and communicate directly with the (name of computer hardware) computer to register for classes. Currently, the (college or university) registers (number) students each term on a combination batch and on-line registration system that utilizes optical scanning and terminal input of data. On a designated date, the sectioning algorithm generates confirmed course schedules which are then mailed to students. A disadvantage of this course requests/sectioning mode of registration is that students must wait to learn what courses they are confirmed into for the term. Another disadvantage of the current mode of registration is that (number) square feet of valuable space is needed for registration. This space could better be utilized by academic programs. Touchtone telephone/voice response registration offers a very sound alternative for a more efficient, cost-effective, and appealing form of registration.

The hardware being purchased will consist of a voice response unit and an application processor that will handle the interface between the (computer) and the voice response unit. Software to handle the calls and communicate with the mainframe will be developed by the systems development staff.

The system must be capable of handling (number) lines initially. It must be modular to allow for necessary expansion. About (number) seconds of digitized voice storage will be required. The voice response units will operate in the (college/university) telephone environment. The processor will connect to the mainframe using bisynchronous communication protocol.

This system will be installed by (date) to permit release of space in (name of building/gym/hall), presently used for registration. A saving in hourly registration expenses is expected over the long term.

Qualified vendors must have successfully installed a system in an institution with a similar registration transaction environment. The vendor must demonstrate, by a corroborating letter from an institution similar to (college or university), that the vendor's equipment has been successfully installed, tested, and implemented in an on-line telephone registration system.

Detailed Specifications

Detailed specifications should cover system architecture, telephony, vocabulary, voice messaging, application development capabilities, application development, debugging, and monitoring capabilities, host environment, and maintenance. Examples of detailed specifications, suggested by Perception Technology, are provided below.

SYSTEM ARCHITECTURE

1. The proposed system must include one or more dedicated voice processing units (VPUs). Each VPU must be capable of expansion to a 96-line capacity.

2. Line expansion to support as many as 96 lines with a single VPU must be accomplished by

installation of additional line cards within the voice processor, rather than by installation of additional voice processors and/or Local Area Network (LAN) hardware/software. Materials and labor required to add lines to a voice processor must be described in detail.

3. The voice processing module must be capable of supporting all lines simultaneously with no degradation of voice quality or response time attributable to the voice processing unit hardware or software.

4. The proposed system must include a dedicated UNIX application processing unit (APU). The APU must be capable of controlling one or more voice processing units. The voice processing unit(s) may be located at the APU site and/or remote locations.

TELEPHONY

5. The VPU must be capable of simultaneously supporting a combination of telephone line/trunk interfaces. The mandatory interfaces include analog loop and ground start, ear and mouth leads (2 and 4 wire) which carry signals between trunk equipment and a separate signalling equipment unit, as well as T-1, i.e., digital transmission links and connections. T-1 interfaces must connect directly to the VPU without the use of channel bank equipment.

6. The VPU must accommodate simultaneous combinations of analog and direct T-1 interfaces.

7. In-band Dialed Number Information System (DNIS)/Automatic Number Identification (ANI) signalling must be supportable by the proposed system.

8. The system must be able to automatically terminate a call upon receipt of a far-end disconnect signal by the voice processing unit.

9. The proposed system must be capable of call transfer to another telephone number or extension. This feature must be available upon demand (Dual-Tone Multi-Frequency [DTMF], i.e., push button or touchtone, entered by caller), as a result of caller or host response time outs, and/or if triggered by a command from the host. The call transfer feature must support call progress tone detection.

VOCABULARY

10. The VPU must provide a minimum of 30 hours of hard disk-based voice storage capacity. Expansion to over 600 hours of voice storage per VPU must be available.

11. The college or university may choose to develop its own vocabulary for use on the interactive voice response system. A speech development work station must be available for the recording, digitizing, editing, and downloading process. The work station must accommodate both microphone and tape recorder inputs. Downloading to the voice processor(s) must be supported by a serial port connection.

12. The college or university must be given the option of locating the speech development work station at the VPU location or at a remote site.

13. The proposed system must also support remote dial-up changes to system vocabulary.

14. The proposed system must allow the system manager to make changes or additions to existing vocabulary without interruption of service on any portion of the production system.

15. The voice processing system (VPS) must allow the system administrator to make a backup copy of vocabulary files. In order to simplify the backup procedure, a tape device must be included.

16. Vocabulary must be automatically preserved during a power failure and ready for immediate access once power is restored. Requiring operator intervention to achieve this function is unacceptable.

17. Automatic reload after power failure and tape backup capability must be included in the basic price of the VPS.

VOICE MESSAGING

18. As a standard feature, the VPU must support voice message recording and retrieval on all lines.

APPLICATION DEVELOPMENT CAPABILITIES

19. The application generator must support both audio-text-only and host-interactive applications.

20. The proposed system must allow the user to make changes to existing applications, test those changes, and/or develop new applications without interruption of service on any portion or module of the VPS.

21. Installation of a separate "development work station" must not be required to perform on-line development or changes.

22. The system must be capable of simultaneously supporting multiple applications. There must be no system-imposed restriction on the number of applications requiring a specific feature, such as host database access, voice messaging, etc.

23. There must be no arbitrary limitation on the number of supportable applications. The application accessed by an individual telephone call must be controlled by caller use of touchtone menus, the line used, and/or the Data Network Information Service digit feed from the Public Switched Telephone Network (PSTN) which is the worldwide voice telephone network accessible to all those with telephone and access privileges.

APPLICATION DEVELOPMENT

24. The proposed system must include application development software running under an industry standard multi-tasking, multi-user, operating system.

25. The development software must include a high level scripting language able to provide the run time environment that controls voice processors and application processors and communicates with external host computers.

26. The development language must allow program development by any editor capable of producing ASCII files, e.g., a personal computer and word processing application.

27. The development software must include a full array of computation functions, including addition, subtraction, multiplication, division, and modulo (the remainder of a division).

28. The development software must include a display function used to output selected data to the management console for debugging and monitoring purposes.

29. The development software must include a "go to" command. This command must support transfer of program control to another label or module within the same scenario (application program) and/or to another scenario.

30. The development software must include the ability to check for multiple logical conditions within one command and cause the execution of a true or false procedure. These procedures must be able to accommodate more than one command and physically reside immediately after the check without use of branches or "go to" commands.

31. The development tools must include a log command to send data to a system log file. Once stored in the file, the system manager must be able to download the data for use by other applications, such as Lotus 1-2-3 and dBASE.

32. The development of an application must result in a compiled machine-executable program and not an interpreted program that allows the utility to maximize the power of the system without wasting processing power on the interpreter.

DEBUGGING AND MONITORING CAPABILITIES

33. The proposed system must be able to perform real time monitoring of system status. Call processing cannot be impacted by operation of these functions.

34. Monitoring functions must be menu driven and must require programming knowledge for their operation.

35. A real time window must allow the administrator to monitor the status of each telephone line. Each line's operational status must be indicated as the number of calls currently in process and the accumulated totals for calls answered and calls transferred.

36. A real time window must allow the administrator to monitor the status of each voice processor, displaying the unit number, the number of telephone lines installed, and the processor's operational status.

37. A real time window must allow the administrator to monitor the status of each host to which the VRU is interfaced, displaying the host name, number of logical units configured, and its status.

38. A real time window must allow the administrator to monitor the status of each host session, displaying the session number, host name, status, screen display of host sessions, log-on ID used, and password ID used.

39. A real time window must allow the administrator to monitor the status of each application, displaying the application program name, the current cumulative accesses completed, and the application program status (UP, DOWN, application file update pending and about to be loaded, or application program shutdown pending and waiting for all calls to complete).

40. A real time window must allow the administrator to monitor the contents of the system TRACE (shows the communication between two devices) log. This log must be configurable by the application developer to include any desired data gathered during execution of the call scenario, including conditional comments and annotations used by the application developer as debugging aids.

HOST ENVIRONMENT

41. The voice processing system (VPS) must be capable of communication rates as high as 19.2K BPS (bits-per-second) to the host computer.

42. The VPS must be capable of simultaneously supporting synchronous and asynchronous data communications.

43. The VPS must be capable of accommodating as many as twelve asynchronous communication ports, connected to one or more physical hosts.

44. Systems Network Architecture (SNA, an IBM product)/Synchronous Data Link Control (SDLC, a bit-oriented synchronous communications protocol developed by IBM) interfaces must be capable of supporting as many as 64 LUs (logical units that support sessions with a host-based system), and one or two physical connections.

45. Binary Synchronous Communication (BSC) interfaces must be capable of supporting as many as 64 sessions, and one or two physical connections.

46. The VPS must be capable of simultaneously supporting two separate SNA/SDLC or BSC host interfaces.

47. The VPS must be capable of automatically polling the host computer. Should a host-down condition occur, the VPS must recognize that state and automatically perform the appropriate call processing, such as playback of a special message or call transfer to an attendant. The VPS must support the ability to perform alternate actions based upon time of day, day of week, etc. Host-down processing must be configurable by the application designer.

MAINTENANCE

48. The VPS supplier's warranty and maintenance plans must include both on-site and 24-hour telephone support.

49. The proposed system must include remote diagnostic capability. When diagnostics are in process, call processing must not be interrupted.

Identifying Vendors

The project team may be the best resource for identifying possible vendors for the purchasing division because it is usually aware of the market. A Request for Proposal should be sent to vendors who can best meet the college or university's specifications. Project members should be assigned to call various colleges and universities to obtain information about vendor accountability.

Evaluating a Vendor's Bid

The project team should establish firm guidelines for review of vendor responses and the selection process. Whatever method is decided should be applied consistently and fairly to each vendor review. It is important to weigh the bids on the "required" specifications, with a lower weight given to the "preferred" specs. If two or more vendors are tied in meeting the "required" specifications, then the "preferred" specifications should be included. The purchasing division may want to take the lead in checking references.

OPTION 1

The project team should evaluate and individually score each vendor's proposal on the eight factors listed below in order of importance:

1. Conformance of proposal to mandatory requirements. Any proposal not meeting all mandatory requirements should be disqualified.

2. Conformance of proposal to optional requirements.

3. Performance of the vendor at other locations.

4. Technical expertise of vendor employees assigned to the project.

5. Vendor's maintenance and support services.

6. Vendor's proposed training plan.

7. Financial stability of the vendor.

8. Total cost of the proposed system including five times the present annual maintenance rate, less warranty.

Within each category the vendors' scores are totalled and averaged. The eight averages are added for an overall evaluation score. The highest score wins the contract.

OPTION 2

A vendor's bid may also be evaluated according to the criteria listed below (reprinted with permission from Perception Technology).

System Architecture and Technical Design

➤ Independent computer processors for the application and for handling the telephone lines
➤ Minicomputer or microcomputer based
➤ Self-generating software or custom code
➤ Extensiveness of telephony capabilities

System Compatibility

➤ Software compatibility from 4 lines to hundreds of lines
➤ Private Branch Exchange (PBX) compatibility
➤ Ability to install system without any changes to host system's application of software
➤ Ability to install system without any changes to PBX
➤ Common carrier interface capability

System Reliability

➤ Component reliability
➤ Total system reliability

Growth and Expansion

➤ Maximum number of telephone line expansion in the same cabinet
➤ Maximum number of telephone lines available in the network
➤ Maximum amount of speech available in the same cabinet
➤ Maximum amount of speech

Vendor's Voice Recording Capabilities

➤ Professional recording studio and personnel
➤ Ability to change voice available in the network on site

Vendor's Manufacturing Capabilities

➤ USA-manufactured
➤ Vendor's own manufacturing staff

Vendor's Experience and Financial Strength

➤ Number of systems installed
➤ Number of telephone lines installed
➤ Number of applications installed
➤ Balance sheet and long-term financial strength
➤ Record of research and development expenditures
➤ Experience in complicated telephony situations

System Reports

➤ Application-dependent reports
➤ Phone system reports
➤ Standard data storage formats
➤ Ability for college or university to change and create reports

System Implementation Procedures

➤ Vendor-provided implementation support
➤ On-site technical support in scenario development
➤ Project management teams
➤ Centralized project management and direction
➤ Project status reporting
➤ System acceptance criteria

Personnel Requirements

➤ Experience required by person defining application
➤ Experience required by person generating application
➤ On-going staffing requirement

Training Procedures

➤ Self-study training materials
➤ Training classes at vendor's office
➤ On-site training classes

Documentation

➤ Technical
➤ Nontechnical
➤ Implementation plan

Costs and Expenses

➤ Hardware cost
➤ Application cost
➤ Delivery and installation charges
➤ Monthly maintenance charges
➤ Expenses/expense reductions due to telephony capabilities
➤ Expense to modify host computer application software

Site Requirements

➤ Normal office environmental conditions
➤ Ability to be installed in telephone room environment

Installation Support

➤ Turnkey solutions
➤ Ability for the college or university to make software and voice changes
➤ On-site engineering support

Field Service

➤ Vendor's own field service organization
➤ Four-hour response time
➤ Remote diagnostic capabilities

Warranty and Installation Charges

➤ Length of warranty
➤ Period of free on-site maintenance
➤ Hardware installation charges

Chapter 8

Implementing TT / VR Registration System

ECONOMICS

SPACE SCIENCES

JAPANESE

POETRY

GEOLOGY

DESIGN

PALEONTOLOGY

GENETIC ENGINEERING

MYTHOLOGY

Primary Authors:

Robert F. Askins
University of South Carolina

Melanie Moore Bell
Gonzaga University

Lou Ann Denny
Arizona State University

Janice Garcia
Arizona State University

T. Luther Gunter
University of South Carolina

William L. Salter
University of South Carolina

Genene Walker
Arizona State University

Elaine Wheeler
University of California, Irvine

The script has been written and the hardware and software are installed. Now it is time to continue the process for implementing touchtone telephone/voice response (TT/VR) registration which includes selecting a voice to record the script, designing a registration worksheet, developing statistical reports, training staff, and testing the new system in preparation for the project start-up date.

Selecting a Voice

The college or university involved in voice selection has several options. It may consider an artist with a trained voice, someone with experience or, most importantly, someone who will be available to record future additions and modifications to the script. It may find the broadcast professional in journalism, communications, or in the instructional center who becomes the "voice" has access to a recording studio on the campus. One university saved money by using a member of the registrar's staff to record the script.

Colleges and universities may also weigh the purchase of voice production service from a vendor or an off-campus broadcast professional and pay a fee for each voice recording session.

One university provided a studio in its instructional media center and taped a portion of the script read by talent auditioning for the "voice" of the TT/VR system. The registrar provided the script. Several sample voice tapes supplied by the vendor were also used during the testing. Campus personnel (22 advisors, administrators, and students) were invited to listen to each of the anonymous voices at the media center throughout the day. The scoring sheet issued included the scorer's name and the criteria to consider:

➢ Presents a good voice image for the university
➢ Good delivery
➢ Good delivery of short sentences and phrases
➢ Voice commands attention

➢ Voice is pleasant to the ear
➢ Voice is clear
➢ Speech is well paced
➢ Words are clearly enunciated
➢ Voice is well modulated

Each voice was assigned a number and each scorer rated the voices on a scale of 1 to 5 with 1 being excellent and 5 being poor. An overall ranking of 1 was judged "best" and 5 indicated "not acceptable." Judges were permitted to add additional comments about each voice. Comments for the same female voice ranged from soft voice, to mature sounding, appealing to students, too formal, distant, low, crisp, clear, nice, a little mechanical, and not as upbeat. Comments for the same male voice included good, more conversational pace, a bit impersonal, deep voice, good inflection, good speed and well articulated, not attention keeper, some slurring, friendly, needs work, and no coherent ending.

The top three scorers were asked to record another portion of the script. Judges then ranked these and selected a male TT/VR voice. Because the three finalists' voices were so similar, the two runners up were asked to be backup voices for the project.

Recording the Script

Recording and editing with a voice development system makes the script conversion process fairly painless. Some systems require only a touchtone telephone and vendor software to record script. An artist with a professional "voice" records each word, number, phrase, and sentence in the TT/VR registration script. The vendor then digitizes the initial script from a recorded voice process in the campus studio. Subsequent recordings are completed on campus using voice development software purchased by the college or university. However, a professional voice recording does not make the speech recorded at one time sound exactly the same as speech recorded in a different session. Keeping up with the script changes that occur on a college or university campus requires the script to be adjusted periodically. Indeed, shortly after using TT/VR systems, many colleges and universities revise and add some messages in response to suggestions from wide-spread use. Sooner or later the speech will sound different enough that a college or university may need to re-record the entire vocabulary.

Software makes recording and editing the script a fairly simple process. A tape deck is connected directly to a microcomputer. Each phrase is introduced by typed commands. The software converts the recorded voice to a digital representation, and, for editing purposes, returns a graphic representation of the script showing the peaks and valleys of inflection in the speech. With a little practice, selecting words within a line of speech becomes easy. Phrases or sections of phrases can be replayed, deleted, or copied for inclusion in another phrase, thereby reducing the need for re-recording. One university reported a few students had difficulty distinguishing between the spoken "B" and "D" in the grades section; such complaints, however, may have been prompted by wishful thinking.

According to Perception Technology, the following points are important for the institution recording the script in a studio.

➤ Use a high quality 1/4-inch magnetic audiotape.
➤ Use a 7-inch reel from which a 1/4- or 1/2-track MONO recording at 7-1/2 inches-per-second (ips). Do not use Dolby or other on-tape signal processing.
➤ Use a professional quality microphone. Do not substitute microphones during the recording session, because different microphones—even high quality microphones—produce different sounds at different levels.
➤ Set the playback machine for 1/4 track. A 1/4-track recording that is played back on a 1/2-track machine will not reproduce the output quality necessary for encoding.
➤ Use the following settings for the equipment:

tape recorder—0 decibels (dB) at 1000 Hertz (Hz), microphone—75 Hz bass rolloff.
➤ Make three copies of the complete TT/VR registration script: one each for the recording artist, the recording supervisor, and the recording engineer. Use a highlighter to indicate exactly what is to be spoken. This is especially helpful if the script also contains notes on program logic, or other comments not to be recorded.
➤ Have the recording artist speak each script message three times in succession. Do not read numbers that are assigned to messages.
➤ Listen for variations in the recording artist's performance. These variations include:

• Sound. Is the volume level of the artist's voice constant? The sound engineer can compensate for variations to some degree, but the range of volumes should be fairly narrow (-6 to -3VU).
• Pronunciation. Is the pronunciation of key words correct? Use phonetic spellings if necessary.
• Presence. Does the recording have an echo? Be sure the microphone is properly placed. Notice if the artist speaks "off mike."
• Enunciation. Are words spoken clearly and distinctly?
• Voice Modulation. Does the artist resist the urge to be overly conversational or monotonous? Some monotone is required for small bits of speech that will be strung together.
• Pitch. Does the voice get lower or higher in tone as the recording proceeds?
• Phrasing. Do pauses occur naturally in the script?
• Pace. Does the artist speed up or slow down as he/she speaks?
• Inflection. Are words or phrases spoken naturally and do they sound natural in the context of the recording?
• Tone. Is the voice direct and friendly? This can be achieved if the artist smiles while recording.

Designing a Registration Worksheet

The design of a registration worksheet grows almost naturally out of the development of registration scenarios and flow charts. As with script development, colleges and universities can study what others have produced and both adopt and adapt ideas to suit the needs of their TT/VR registration system. Each design can then be circulated among the project team, academic advisors, and registration staff who can check on accuracy, and among students who will check the clarity of the worksheet and its ease of use.

The criteria for rating the worksheet—on a scale of 1 to 5—may include the following questions: Are the worksheet instructions easy to understand? Does the worksheet appear uncomplicated? Is the worksheet clear about the transactions to be entered? Is the worksheet easy to follow? Comments on the strengths and weaknesses of the worksheet and suggestions for improvement may also be solicited in the evaluation. See Figures 8.1 and 8.2 for the registration worksheets developed at Arizona State University and the University of Washington, respectively. See also Exhibits F.1 and F.2 for additional worksheets developed for TT/VR registration at The Ohio State University, and the University of North Texas, respectively.

Developing Statistical Reports

A variety of standard statistical tracking reports are usually available from the vendor. These reports range from overall system performance information to details about each telephone line activity. The most beneficial reports are summary, procedure, and transaction reports. Summary reports show the number of calls within time increments. Procedure reports indicate where in the touchtone application calls are terminated. Transaction statistics provide the number of times callers choose an option (e.g., add course, drop course, fee payment, specific function such as initial PIN changes) or receive a

specific error condition. Figure 8.3 shows a daily summary report for Arizona State University.

Other data items have proved helpful and might require selective capture. Counts on the number of times instructions are repeated or certain transactions taken in the script can be reviewed to improve the script itself. Tracking the number of calls being serviced within five-, ten-, or fifteen-minutes periods allows the development of a usage pattern for planning how to adjust the equipment loading schedule. It also can document service outages for follow-up, especially if unattended operation is contemplated.

In addition to the information provided by standard system statistical reports, selective activity can be captured with data logging. These data files can be used in microcomputer applications to generate customized reports, process credit card payments, provide backup in case of system problems, meet disaster recovery requirements, and resolve questions from students.

A report-generating facility can log all calls and every touchtone entry. A mainframe operating system can track the number of times each program module is accessed and, therefore, is a useful and readily accessible source of raw numbers on TT/VR registration usage. During the initial testing of telephone registration, the logging feature is especially helpful to programmers as an analytical tool. Some colleges and universities later discontinue the logging feature because the volume of information written to files during heavy usage consumes valuable time and disk space. They may opt for a less comprehensive report-generating feature which records the number and duration of calls on each line, the number of busy signals and hang-ups, and the number of input errors and system errors. These numbers, combined with transaction counts, provide a good picture of the type of activity on the system and alert TT/VR managers to potential problems. The recorded data from an on-line, cumulative transaction screen that records all add, drop, and withdrawal actions as well as other transactions provides useful documentation and helps resolve students disputes over when transactions were made. These data may be transferred to microfiche periodically.

Training Staff

TECHNICAL STAFF

Technical staff training begins immediately after installation of the hardware and software. Staff must learn the voice response application and mainframe computer application as well as how to add and change speech.

THE REGISTRAR'S STAFF

Colleges and universities strengthen the in-house sales and support team by allocating resources to train campus and registrar's staff who have frequent contact with the students; by keeping staff members informed; and by providing them with many opportunities to ask questions, voice concerns, and build their confidence in the TT/VR registration system. Registrar staff become particularly effective in helping the design team head off potential problems. Their questions and concerns often reduce the potential for error or misunderstanding. Their perspectives reflect the diverse interpretations students can bring to the material. Refinements to the instructions before they are published can then be made easily and effectively so that the instructions and worksheet remain virtually unchanged from the originals.

A few staff, trained to answer a helpline installed as a precautionary measure, can answer basic questions that might arise. A "trouble shooting" form can be designed to track complaints or problems of each helpline caller. Anomalous situations, error messages, and misunderstood script messages recorded on the forms and given to the technical staff can lead to timely refinements of both the script and the application. Relying upon what the machine shows in its audit trails, the accuracy and reliability of the system can be established immediately with great confidence. "Registrar error" can

quickly become a relic of the old system as students perform the operator transactions themselves.

Staff in the registrar's office should be involved from the outset. Keeping them informed of major decisions and implementing the system in phases minimizes the amount of intensive, last minute training they may need. Those participating on the project team can keep other staff informed of decisions, solicit their input, and involve them with the project throughout all phases. They can provide statistics, prepare development and production test cases, help with testing, and furnish complete written documentation and a quick reference guide that summarizes the more critical changes and provides instructions on accessing new screens developed to support the TT/VR application. Staff will be confident answering questions from students because of the background and knowledge gained from their continual involvement and training throughout all phases.

ACADEMIC DEPARTMENT PERSONNEL

One university allowed academic departments on-line access to curriculum resource files for up-to-the-minute enrollment information. By accessing a separate telephone number and using a personalized access code, departmental personnel were able to get the enrollment information for any course. Information available included notification of course cancellation, the open or closed status of any class, the seating capacity of the room, the number of enrolled students, and the number of spaces still available.

Three important goals were accomplished by communicating the enrollment information. First, by encouraging department personnel to use the system, staff gained a firsthand knowledge of how easy the TT/VR system was to use. Second, departments without on-line terminal connections could still have access to accurate and timely enrollment data whenever they needed it. Finally, registrar personnel who normally fielded these questions could turn their attention to higher level tasks while the machine responded to the mundane looking up and reporting of enrollment data.

Figure 8.1. Registration Worksheet, Arizona State University

PLEASE FILL IN THE SHADED AREAS OF THIS WORKSHEET BEFORE CALLING INTOUCH.

INTOUCH PHONE NUMBER: (602) 350-1500

INTOUCH FUNCTIONS:	Registration System:	Initial Registration (for students not pre-registering) Drop/Add Unrestricted Course Withdrawal List Classes (Quick or Complete List)
	Fee Payment System:	Payment by VISA/MasterCard Payment using Financial Aid Request Refund Itemized List of Fees Fee Instructions Add or Remove Insurance

ACCESS DATES: See the Schedule of Classes.

TIMES: 7AM - 9PM (MST) Monday - Friday
7AM - Noon (MST) Saturday
Noon - 6PM (MST) Sunday

ASU ID: _____ - _____ - _____

PIN: Initially your personal identification number (PIN) will be set to the month and day of your birth (e.g., June 2 = 0602). You will be prompted to select a new 4-digit PIN the first time you access InTouch. THE NEW PIN YOU SELECT WILL BE YOUR PERMANENT PIN. If you need assistance with your PIN, call the Registrar's Office at (602) 965-3124 or Computer Accounts at (602) 965-1211.

YEAR/TERM: _____ _____
(year) (term)

Valid Term Codes: 1 = Spring.
3 = 1st Summer Session.
5 = 2nd Summer Session.
7 = Fall.

REGISTRATION SYSTEM

HEALTH INSURANCE DESIRED: _____ 1 = Yes   If you elect insurance coverage, the insurance premium will be included
2 = No   in the total registration fee when you select the InTouch Fee Payment System option.

YEARBOOK DESIRED: _____ 1 = Yes   If you elect to obtain a yearbook, the fee for the yearbook will not be
2 = No   included in the registration fee that InTouch calculates. This $35 fee will be billed separately.

TRANSACTION CODE*	SCHEDULE LINE NUMBER	TRANSACTION CODE*	SCHEDULE LINE NUMBER
____	_____	____	_____
____	_____	____	_____
____	_____	____	_____
____	_____	____	_____
____	_____	____	_____
____	_____	____	_____
____	_____	____	_____

*Valid transaction codes:
1 = Add
2 = Drop
3 = Unrestricted Course Withdrawal
4 = Audit
0 = To signal the end of your entries

Schedule/Billing Statements will not be produced by InTouch. A complete list of your classes with days, times and locations can be obtained by selecting option 5 from the Registration System available options. Please use this area to record information from your InTouch session.

SCHEDULE OF CLASSES

Course	Line #	Days	Times	Building	Room

FEE PAYMENT SYSTEM

Select the InTouch Fee Payment System to hear information about your registration charges and payment deadlines. Payment of fees is critical to hold your classes. Schedule/Billing Statements will not be produced by InTouch, but you may use this area to record information from your InTouch session.

ITEMIZED LIST OF CHARGES

Registration _____   BALANCE DUE _____
Tuition _____
Insurance _____   DUE DATE/TIME _____
Special Fees/Deposits _____
Late Fees _____
Music Fees _____
Student Rec Center Fees _____
FA Trust Fund Fee _____

TOTAL CHARGES _____

HOW TO PAY:

● Use InTouch to pay with VISA/MasterCard. Have the following information available:
  Card # _____
  Expiration Date _____
  Daytime Phone # (_____) _____ - _____

● Use InTouch to acknowledge your intent to pay fees with financial aid.

● Mail your payment in time to ensure receipt by the fee payment deadline date (see Schedule of Classes for actual date). Use the remittance form included in the Schedule of Classes.

● Pay in person at the Student Fee Payment Office, Student Services Building, Room B235. Use the remittance form included in the Schedule of Classes.

For questions about fee payment, call (602) 965-4347, Monday - Friday, 8:15AM - 4:30PM (MST).

Figure 8.2. STAR Worksheet, University of Washington

University Of Washington
Student Telephone Assisted Registration (STAR)

Spring Quarter 1993 STAR Work Sheet

I. Always access STAR with these four steps:

1. Call STAR [5][4][8]-[S][T][A][R] (If calling long distance, precede STAR number with 1- 206) (On UW campus call, 9-548-STAR)
   7 8 2 7
2. Enter Quarter Code [2] 2 = Spring
3. Enter your Student ID number: [ ][ ][ ][ ][ ][ ][ ]
4. Enter your birth date or assigned Private Access Code as six digits, followed by [#] Example: 04 16 70 # for April 16, 1970. *For security of your record, do not write your date of birth or Private Access Code on this work sheet.*

[1] [ABC 2] [DEF 3] [GHI 4] [JKL 5] [MNO 6] [PRS 7] [TUV 8] [WXY 9] [*] [OPER 0] [#]
Star Key — Number Sign Key

II. You will only be asked to provide this information during your first call each quarter. Make your entry after the STAR voice asks for each selection.

1. Student Health Insurance [ ] INSURANCE OPTIONS (For descriptions, refer to Student Insurance section of the Time Schedule. Press zero for no insurance.)
   0 (zero) = No Insurance
   1=Student Quarterly Insurance
   2=Student and Spouse Quarterly Insurance
   3=Student, Spouse and Children Quarterly Insurance
   4=Student and Children Quarterly Insurance
   5=Student Annual Insurance
   6=Student and Spouse Annual Insurance
   7=Student, Spouse and Children Annual Insurance
   8=Student and Children Annual Insurance
2. ASUW membership [ ] Y = Yes N = No
3. Contribute to Washington Student Lobby [ ] Y = Yes, add $1 for WSL to my bill N = No
4. Contribute to WashPIRG [ ] Y = Yes, add $2 for WashPIRG to my bill N = No

Address to use for Official UW mailings: (updated at time of call)

5. Registration Confirmation/ID Card [ ] L = Local Address P = Permanent Address
6. Statement of Account (Tuition and Fee Bill) [ ] L = Local Address P = Permanent Address
7. Grade Report [ ] L = Local Address P = Permanent Address

Be sure your current address is on file with the Registrar's Office. Call 543-3868 24 hours a day, seven days a week to update your address.

III a. To add courses NOT requiring Entry Code:

[A] [ ][ ][ ][ ] (Schedule Line Number) [#]
You will be prompted to enter credits if course has variable credits.

III b. To add closed courses or courses requiring Entry Code:

[A] [ ][ ][ ][ ] (Schedule Line Number) [*] [ ][ ][ ][ ][ ] (Entry Code Number) [#]

Even if you receive an Entry Code from the department, you will not be able to add if the course is already overloaded to 115% of room capacity.
You will be prompted to enter credits if course has variable credits.

IV. To drop courses:

[D] [ ][ ][ ][ ] (Schedule Line Number) [#]
You will be prompted to enter Entry Code if required to drop.

V. To list your schedule:

[L] [#]
Includes meeting days and times, building and room.

VI. To check course status: (Open/Closed)

[S] [ ][ ][ ][ ] (Schedule Line Number) [#]
Includes available alternate sections if requested section is closed.

VII. To list your grades:

[G] [#]
Includes officially recorded grades for the most recently completed quarter.

VIII. Student Account and Loan Status Inquiries:

- [1][1] [#] To list current student account balance.
- [1][2] [#] To list summary of disbursed financial aid and aid check availability.
- [1][3] [#] To determine if outside lender loan funds are available.
- [1][4] [#] To list the latest recorded student account payment.
- [1][5] [#] To list this quarter's selected optional charges (WashPIRG, WSL, Insurance.)

IX. To discard any partial entry and repeat previous message:

[*] [#]

X. To exit STAR (terminate call) and receive information on Registration Confirmation and ID Cards:

[T] [#]

7/31/90

Table 8.1. Daily Summary Report, Arizona State University

STARTING 08-10-92   GROUP "INTOUCH"
Printed 00:01 08-11-92

	CALLS RECEIVED	MODUOLE DISCONNECT	CALLER DISCONNECT	CALL TRANSFERRED	AVERAGE CALL LENGTH
00:00 - 00:30	34	16	18	0	0:22
00:30 - 01:00	13	4	9	0	0:22
01:00 - 01:30	5	2	3	0	0;25
01:30 - 02:00	7	3	4	0	0:25
02:00 - 02:30	11	3	8	0	0:17
02:30 - 03:00	5	1	4	0	0:19
03:00 - 03:30	0	0	0	0	0:00
03:30 - 04:00	3	1	2	0	0:22
04:00 - 04:30	5	3	2	0	0:23
04:30 - 05:00	4	3	1	0	0:26
05:00 - 05:30	4	0	4	0	0:22
05:30 - 06:00	8	4	4	0	0:23
06:00 - 06:30	46	14	32	0	0:21
06:30 - 07:00	112	27	85	0	0:31
07:00 - 07:30	554	318	236	0	4:48
07:30 - 08:00	367	185	182	0	4:18
08:00 - 08:30	438	222	216	0	4:13
08:30 - 09:00	394	191	203	0	4:18
09:00 - 09:30	451	216	235	0	3:39
09:30 - 10:00	417	210	207	0	3:58
10:00 - 10:30	400	198	202	0	3:48
10:30 - 11:00	346	179	167	0	3:42
11:00 - 11:30	325	159	166	0	3:47
11:30 - 12:00	303	145	158	0	3:34
12:00 - 12:30	307	161	146	0	3:54
12:30 - 13:00	276	140	136	0	3:40
13:00 - 13:30	294	135	159	0	3:44
13:30 - 14:00	275	134	141	0	3:54
14:00 - 14:30	255	107	148	0	3:43
14:30 - 15:00	242	103	139	0	3:23
15:00 - 15:30	250	118	132	0	3:52
15:30 - 16:00	229	116	113	0	3:49
16:00 - 16:30	236	117	119	0	3:32
16:30 - 17:00	200	94	106	0	3:47
17:00 - 17:30	171	84	87	0	3:37
17:30 - 18:00	118	57	61	0	3:25
18:00 - 18:30	139	79	60	0	3:39
18:30 - 19:00	125	43	82	0	2:50
19:00 - 19:30	59	19	40	0	2:20
19:30 - 20:00	47	13	34	0	2:04
20:00 - 20:30	76	34	42	0	2:07
20:30 - 21:00	35	12	23	0	2:17
21:00 - 21:30	25	9	16	0	0:39
21:30 - 22:00	11	5	6	0	0:27
22:00 - 22:30	8	3	5	0	0:24
22:30 - 23:00	6	2	4	0	0:24
23:00 - 23:30	5	3	2	0	0:27
23:30 - 24:00	5	2	3	0	0:24
TOTAL	7646	3694	3952	0	3:43

Testing the System

The institution ready to develop a test plan must remember to be consistent in its testing, using clear and concise language and an organized method of inventory. When developing the test data, the project team needs to correlate the data and the data related to those students (a description of student A would include such relevant information as the student's name, student number, previously registered classes, etc.). A snapshot of the screen in use or tables can highlight the connection. Completing a thorough and well organized test is a preview to the future success of a TT/VR registration system.

SAMPLE INVITATION TO TEST

To solicit participation in testing the TT/VR registration system, the following invitation can be issued.

On Tuesday, May 31, from 3:00 p.m. to 3:30 p.m. we will be conducting the first high-volume test of the TT/VR registration system. For those of you who would like to take part in the test, registration testing materials are attached. We would like to get students, faculty, advisors, and administrators to call in simultaneously to see how the system handles a heavy load of telephone calls. That is why the test is scheduled for a specific short period of time. Forty people will test a system that can handle 24 callers at once, so do not be surprised if you get a busy signal. Keep trying until you get through.

The test is being conducted before the system has been completely debugged, so if you get a response that does not seem appropriate, note it and let us know. The digitized speech for some messages has not been finalized; what you hear will not be as good as the message you will hear when the system is implemented July 1. This is especially true of the response to the "List Schedule" and "Add Course" transactions.

SAMPLE EVALUATION FORM FOR TESTING

Please complete the following form and return it by 5 p.m., May 31, to the registrar, mailstop 1234.

Name_____

Campus Address/Phone_____

Does the system respond promptly?

Does the system always do what you expect it to do?

Is the voice response speed adequate?

Are the voice response messages clear and concise?

Do the voice messages provide adequate direction as to what to do next?

Is there any voice response that is confusing? Please identify the content.

Is the worksheet easy to follow as you input the transactions on the telephone keypad?

What are the BEST features of the TT/VR registration system?

What are the features that need improvement?

List overall comments.

Thank you for giving us your time and efforts.

SAMPLE TEST REGISTRATION INFORMATION

A portion of the spring announcement of courses is attached. We suggest you limit yourself to the courses on these pages.

Test system telephone number: 439-3444
(Not 542-9999 as on work sheet)

Registration term: 2 (Spring)

Your student ID: 8726888

Your Date of Birth: 11/30/64

You may use these Entry Codes to register for these courses which require departmental permission:

SOC 346 A, Schedule Line Number 2345, Entry Code = 17856

ENG 423 A, Schedule Line Number 1555, Entry Code = 12345

Conclusion

There are no foolproof methods for designing and developing a TT/VR registration system. A detailed test plan identifying transactions or functions may be followed throughout development of TT/VR registration.

Simulated registration tests may use a development version or the student information system database. These tests may include load testing all the telephone lines. Once the system is ready to go, personnel from the registrar's office may conduct a small scale test. Programmers and systems analysts should monitor the system during testing.

Communication Strategies

MUSICOLOGY

RELIGION

CREATIVE WRITING

WEAVING

PHYSICS

DANCE

PORTUGUESE

SOCIAL SCIENCES

ART THERAPY

Melanie Moore Bell
Gonzaga University

Fred Dear
University of Southern California

Edna Brinkley
University of Cincinnati

Elaine Wheeler
University of California, Irvine

Inaugurating Promotional Activities

Approximately one year prior to implementation of the touchtone telephone/voice response (TT/VR) registration system, the project team and the office of the registrar should begin planning communication strategies. The first step is to contact other colleges and universities that have implemented TT/VR registration and request copies of their course schedules and any promotional material developed for their system. The second step is to develop promotional plans tailored to the institution's needs and resources. A variety of approaches can be used to inform students about TT/VR registration. Promotional plans may include developing a logo, a video, a skit, and a campus advertising campaign with newsletters, posters, brochures, and student newspaper advertisements. Students should be involved. Capitalize on the fact that if students are funding the project, it belongs to them.

Produce a short, inexpensive video to call attention to a "Name the System/Design a Logo" contest. Play the video while students wait in line to adjust their course schedules. During an average 15-minute wait, students will watch a three-minute video at least once, but no more than twice. The video may explain what TT/VR registration is, what benefits students can expect, and the prize for the winner . . . the number one slot to use TT/VR registration.

Word-of-mouth advertising should be encouraged. TT/VR registration is generally well received from the start. Students are very vocal in their praise of the new system and the registration system is usually a tremendous public relations boon to any college or university.

Students in advertising and design classes may compete to develop a logo and a poster. The logo may be featured on the cover of the master schedule of classes the first term students are permitted access to TT/VR registration.

Start a teaser ad campaign by using the logo and an invitation to watch for more information in the Schedule of Classes, in the campus newspaper, in memos, and on status reports. Use newspaper advertisements, flyers, and small posters designed to feature the logo.

The poster developed for on-campus promotion can be featured prominently in student newspaper advertising.

Contact the editor of the campus newspaper and persuade him or her to run feature articles highlighting student involvement.

The registrar's office and the division of student affairs may cosponsor a similar competition among script-writing classes in the college or university's school of media arts to develop a promotional video. Involving students as much as possible gets students to participate, gives them valuable "practical" experience, and provides an economical solution to developing these materials. The latter may be an important factor when state-imposed budgetary constraints force some colleges and universities to scale back plans.

Develop educational materials to train students. Some colleges and universities do not allocate much time or money for educational materials or training for students although they may be just as important as all of the elements listed above. Instead, they put their efforts into designing simple and concise instructions that allow the TT/VR registration system to guide the student through the process. The instructions are usually published in the Schedule of Classes, and give all students access to the information before they attempt to register. A special instructional insert with worksheets should be included in the first master schedule. Extra copies of this insert can double as brochures promoting the system.

Developing Information Sessions

Essential to the successful implementation of TT/VR registration is the development of information sessions throughout the university community. All individuals responsible for student services and academic advisement must be involved in these sessions. Separate meetings may be scheduled with larger organizations, such as the council of academic advisors, the student affairs council, and the student senate. Subsequent to these meetings, smaller sessions may be arranged with student affairs directors and advisors from each school and college within the college or university.

Each session may include the following materials:

1. The Touchtone Telephone/Voice Response Registration Proposal. The TT/VR registration proposal should emphasize the primary benefits of the system. A brief overview and description of student usage of the system should be included.

2. Summary of the Script. The quality, accuracy, and thoroughness of the script is the single most important factor in obtaining the confidence and support of the community in implementing the new system. Consequently, at each information session, a detailed review and discussion of the script should be included.

3. Contingency Plans. In the event of a failure of the voice response system, a contingency plan for reverting to the previous registration system should be identified. The key to the success of a contingency plan is the absolute guarantee to students that the fairness and accuracy in the priority schedule will be followed.

An emergency mailing to all students should include a letter explaining the system failure and telling students how to register. Students should be assured that the published appointment times will still be honored. Registration staff will enter registrations as they are received following the strict order of the appointment schedule. Overtime hours will be established to accommodate the work flow. The overall goal will be to process all registrations by an established date. Registration confirmations will be produced in batched mode and mailed to students.

Getting the Word to Students

DEVELOPING LETTERS AND NOTICES

Repackaging the student registration packet and permit-to-register procedure may be the best way to let students know about the new TT/VR registration system at some colleges and universities. Boldface type in a redesigned packet may announce the new process. Repeating a student's registration appointment in a letter from the dean of academic records and registrar, and inserting a copy of the TT/VR registration worksheet in mailings to currently enrolled students two weeks before the first scheduled appointment time may be very effective.

FLOODING CAMPUS AIR SPACES

Displaying eye catching banners and signs that herald the implementation of the new system, repeat the campaign logo, and pose questions to stimulate campus curiosity are often effective strategies.

EXPLAINING HOW TT/VR REGISTRATION WORKS

Using a Question and Answer Approach

Anticipating questions on how TT/VR registration works, a question and answer listing of possible problems published in the student newspaper can offset student resistance. The University of Southern California (USC) used this approach very effectively (see Exhibit G.1).

Producing a Video

The video may be produced in-house by instructional/media services personnel with student participation for distribution to departments, colleges and student organizations within colleges and universities. It may be played in common areas such as the student union lobby, dormitory lobbies, and during walk-in registration activity where the lines that resulted from an "old-style" registration system produce an ideal captive audience. The videotape may be made available to student orientation leaders and to instructors as well. See Exhibits G.2 and G.3 for scripts used in videos produced at Boston College, and The Ohio State University, respectively.

Producing a Skit

A skit that will showcase touchtone telephone registration can also be an effective introduction to TT/VR registration. It can be presented to student and faculty groups and can be modified for any college or university (see Exhibit G.4 from the University of Washington).

Acknowledging Staff

PART-TIME STAFF

Part-time staff have been important to the registration function at most colleges and universities for many years. When TT/VR registration warrants elimination of part-time staff positions, acknowledgment of their contributions can be made in several ways.

➤ Honor them at an all-college or university reception and issue service certificates.
➤ Present a skit of how the TT/VR registration system works and encourage their continued "ambassador" role.
➤ Help them find part-time employment in other areas of the campus.

Some colleges and universities may decide to continue the in-person, on-line method of registration in use prior to touchtone telephone registration. Students can choose to register in-person or by telephone. Cuts in the part-time staff budget may occur since in-person registration activity slows with TT/VR registration.

KUDOS FOR EVERYONE

Acknowledging the value of each person's participation in the TT/VR project is of vital importance. People need to know that their ideas have been heard, understood, and incorporated into the discussion/process. Motivation at all levels occurs when feedback is given on a regular basis. Let people know it's coming, it's coming together, it's working, it's great! This is not to say that a Pollyanna attitude should be adopted. Instead, be honest. Encourage open discussion of problems so solutions can be found. Focus on the goals of the project. Be diplomatic. Be slow to point fingers, and quick to hear ideas.

Celebrating along the way allows success to grow. Nurture successes by using small rewards for the things well done. Do not wait until everything is completed before the team celebrates. Gatherings for breakfast, happy hours, and/or coffee breaks give people a chance to socialize in celebration of what has been accomplished.

Conversely, do not celebrate failure. If a deadline is missed, talk about how it was missed and structure the discussion around formulating action plans to ensure future success in meeting the approaching deadlines.

Early and effective communication is important for the successful implementation of a project of this magnitude. The basic tenet governing the structure of TT/VR registration implementation should be effective communication involving everyone.

TT / VR

Batch

Sectioning

Registration . . .

No Longer an

Either/Or

Decision

SOCIOLOGY

MILITARY SCIENCE

THEATER

CHINESE

COUNSELING

GEOCHEMISTRY

PHYSIOLOGY

ENGINEERING

PUBLIC AFFAIRS

William R. Haid
University of Colorado, Boulder

Pros and Cons Can Co-Exist

Most discussions of touchtone registration assume that the advent of this technology means replacing previous forms of registration. Using touchtone telephone/voice response (TT/VR) technology calls for a different form of contact with the student and sometimes involves an entirely new registration process. It does not always mean that traditional ways of handling registration have to be thrown out when the registration telephone number is published! Personal contact with students, for example, will not stop. The long lines of students negotiating their way through the registration process may be eliminated when students can register through the TT/VR registration system. Some institutions may combine arena and TT/VR registration (see the University of North Texas program, Exhibit F.2). Other institutions may still want their students to register on campus, particularly when in-person orientation and advisement are mandatory. Registration by telephone becomes simply the last step in an on-campus program.

Many schools provide phone banks where students can access the system in a supervised environment and at their convenience. Other students are happy to return to their dorm, home, or even the nearest pay phone to enter the system. Touchtone telephone technology gives students and administrators new options to complete a necessary process.

Whether to use touchtone registration in an on-line or batch mode needs careful consideration, especially if an institution is presently using a form of batch processing registration. Some colleges and universities use both on-line confirmation at the time of registration and batch sectioning (students submit their course requests and find out they are actually registered) in conjunction with TT/VR. Many people argue that this approach gives them the best of both worlds. Others are ardent proponents of one over the other.

Using TT/VR in a Course Requests Mode

When the TT/VR system is set for "course requests" mode, students who access the registration system are told they are not "enrolled" in any classes, but that their "course requests" are being logged. At the end of the course requests period, a master course request report is produced for deans and department chairpersons who look at the course demand statistics and then make course adjustments—add new course sections to meet student demand, cancel low enrollment sections, move course sections to classrooms with the appropriate number of chairs—before the batch sectioning algorithm is run. This review, typically referred to as "request analysis," is conducted in a large conference room with deans in residence and department chairs reporting in on a pre-set schedule. Some colleges and universities have found this process highly effective. Once all student demands for courses are identified, infinite adjustments can be made to meet the demand, and an excellent and efficient allocation of instructional resources is possible.

After all course adjustments are processed into the database, the sectioning algorithm begins. A series of programs is run to schedule student selections into requested, alternate, and available course sections. Registration confirmation notices are produced and mailed to students in preparation for the start of the term.

Success is measured in terms of completed course schedules for students and is dependent on the availability of courses. Academic administrators maintain that they have the highest probability of matching the instructional resources with the course demand when they view the demand for courses at request analysis sessions.

When students request courses, they are advised of the most successful ways to request courses. Usually they are assured that collecting all course requests before actual registration assignment yields the best set of offerings for each student.

Thus, waiting for all course requests to be identified is fair.

One of the drawbacks to course request registration is that new students leave campus after orientation sessions without being confirmed in courses; they leave with a false sense of security without realizing that if they do not get all their first-choice course requests, they may have only a partial schedule. On the other hand, students are less likely to abandon plans to attend a college or university when they are physically present for the start of a term and are more likely to accept course alternates suggested by academic advisors. Another drawback, however, is the amount of processing time required to complete the request analysis and sectioning steps because it is a sequential process, and running sectioning for all or even groups of students is a relatively large computer process.

Course requests can be collected during an early phase of registration via touchtone telephone/voice response technology. Request analysis can be conducted at the close of the phase. Course adjustments can be based on projections if the total demand for courses is not known. Additionally, an appropriate number of spaces in courses can be reserved, based on final statistics for prior course offerings. Then when the TT/VR confirmation phase begins, students can be confirmed in classes as they register.

This process combines the efficient batch sectioning mode with the effectiveness of the TT/VR registration on-line process, thus meeting the needs of the college or university as well as the student. The University of Colorado at Boulder and The Ohio State University have selected the best of both systems on their campuses, proving registration does not have to be an either/or proposition when it comes to the batch sectioning mode of registration.

Chapter 11

The Service Bureau Alternative

BUSINESS

MICROBIOLOGY

MUSIC

RUSSIAN

ECOLOGY

ZOOLOGY

GEOPHYSICS

DENTISTRY

ASTROPHYSICS

Charles L. Dowburd
Voice FX Corporation

The college or university committed to implementing touchtone telephone/voice response (TT/VR) registration can develop its own system or buy a system. It can also contract with a service bureau to develop and manage its registration with high capacity voice processing systems that support interactive voice response (IVR) applications.

By outsourcing registration, the college or university can test the feasibility of implementing a new procedure for registration on campus, and save on institutional resources (initial capital expenditures on hardware, software, and physical facilities; ongoing maintenance and updating costs; and staff).

One Vendor's Views

According to one vendor, the service bureau . . .

1. enables the college or university to test TT/VR registration, with no outlay for capital expenses. (See Chapter V for an example of equipment costs.) For start-up programs especially, the cost per transaction may be less than the cost an institution incurs to build its own system or purchase a turnkey system with programs or applications it has not tested. A service bureau has many voice response systems and its on-site storage, reports of results, and monitoring of systems are services it provides. Savings for services purchased in volume (e.g., lower telephone rates for all institutions serviced by the bureau) may be passed on to the institution as may sponsor-supported discounts, if and when available.

The services of a bureau can be packaged to the college or university as an operating rather than capital expense, which serves and enhances the bottom line for four budget centers: the registrar's credit side of course offerings, the continuing education director's noncredit offerings, the bookstore manager's inventory, and/or the security director's monitoring of parking decals and passes issued.

2. enhances the registrar's tools of the trade by giving the institution the ability to add TT/VR to the existing mail-in, walk-in, phone-in, and FAX-in registration methods.

3. houses state-of-the-art hardware and software and assumes the responsibility (and generally cost) for upgrading the system.

4. offers the expertise of highly trained and experienced technical staff, including complete operations, administration, and maintenance personnel who are familiar with a variety of applications. Tapping service bureau staff reduces staff workloads and minimizes the time each might devote to training, maintenance, troubleshooting the equipment, testing the effectiveness of an application, and debugging a program.

5. provides security with full redundancy. The service bureau's operations are supervised and monitored 24 hours a day, 365 days a year by specialists, auxiliary power sources, security, etc. to protect the college's voice response program.

6. allows other institutional areas (computer center/system, telephone system) to operate with little or no impact on their budget, staff time, equipment use, maintenance, space, utilities, security, insurance, etc.

7. eliminates the need to store backup system components because all equipment, including backup hardware and software, resides in the bureau location;

8. improves institutional service. The service bureau eliminates the downtime associated with equipment ownership for report generation, maintenance, redundancy file development, or simply unscheduled or unavailable staff. It responds quickly to college inquiries and concerns (short turnaround cycle) that may mean the difference between recruiting and retaining students and losing them.

9. can demonstrate how institutions can reallocate existing resources, save dollars, or break even. For those college or university administrators who view education as analogous to business,

the bureau can suggest how to make a "profit" to help offset realistic and growing student service costs that perhaps neither county, state, nor federal representatives adequately address. It can advise institutions of the funding options businesses employ that higher education may modify according to its own needs.

The service bureau, in addition, can mail follow-up written registration confirmation to students, and prepare or develop other features (hard copy summary reports, priority registration, etc., at the request of the college/university). It can offer features that, with one telephone call, permit a student to . . .

a. register for credit and noncredit courses,
b. be advised of co/prerequisites,
c. purchase associated course textbooks,
d. order a parking decal,
e. choose to pay by credit card, mail, in-person, and/or
f. be informed of "live" college operator availability.

In addition, the bureau can schedule student entry into the system by characteristics, such as class standing, credits hours completed, etc.

How It All Comes Together

The bureau's system operates easily and interfaces with most on-line systems. It can enhance on-line capabilities, so that minimal strategy is required for integrating with the institution's on-line system.

Typically, the registrant calls the service bureau's 800 toll free number directly into the voice response unit that holds the institution's individual program. The unit provides callers with the college's unique voice prompts that walk the student through the registration process. The call is billed to the service bureau.

Weighing the Costs

SERVICE BUREAU

Service bureau costs are user-driven. The college pays for the features it uses and the number of calls it receives without worrying about the capacity of the system, especially during peak "burst" periods (i.e., registration, and drop/add periods), or the need to stagger scheduling to prevent overloading the system. It pays the service bureau according to "per minute" pricing which addresses the issue for the part-time or add/drop student caller who requires less time than the full-time student caller who may charge the cost per call rather than per minute. The average service bureau charges $.23 per minute or less for each student call made to the voice response system during registration.

The $.23 per minute pricing can be made relevant in staff costs alone; this figure approximates the salary for a staff person earning $20,000 a year, with $6,660 in benefits (approximated at 33% of salary), working 37.5 hours a week, 50 weeks a year over 12 months. (Multiplying 37.5 hours x 60 minutes = 2,250 minutes x 52 weeks = 117,500 minutes per year; $26,660 personnel minutes divided by 117,500 minutes = $.23 per minute.)

SERVICE BUREAU VS. EQUIPMENT OWNERSHIP

The service bureau provides all the benefits of TT/VR registration cost-effectively with none of the ensuing costs and inconveniences associated with equipment ownership. Cost factors, estimated by a vendor, include the following:

1. capital budget expense at $25,000-$250,000 or more depending upon features, etc.,

2. hardware maintenance at 5%-10% annually of equipment purchase price,

3. software maintenance at 10%-15% or more annually of purchase price if not developed in-house,

4. upgrades at $7,000-$42,000 or more per upgrade,

5. staff training at $25,000-$200,000 or more,

6. equipment installation (varies extensively),

7. additional ports or telephone lines at a minimum of $200 per line for the one-time installation and a minimum of $300 per line annually for service plus additional line charges. A suggested ratio is four phone lines for every 2,000 students enrolled,

8. a long-term commitment with a three- to ten-year maintenance contract that may unknowingly include slow or unacceptable service which in turn may lead to college frustration, anxiety, and other intangible costs,

9. on-site expertise or consulting at $75-$200 per hour or more,

10. additional, temporary, overworked existing staff or technical support,

11. script development,

12. vocabulary encoding,

13. utilities, plus special wiring/electrical set-up,

14. air conditioning,

15. storage of backup system components,

16. moving,

17. insurance,

18. security,

19. space,

20. downtime,

21. high phone carrier rates as a single institution,

22. special financing expense associated with equipment purchases,

23. costs to tap into lines of credit or cash reserves for a capital expense, and

24. costs related to county, state, federal grants and/or regulations.

See also Chapter V for costs based on a needs analysis.

SERVICE BUREAU VS. IN-HOUSE SYSTEM DEVELOPMENT

According to one vendor, a service bureau, by its very nature, is able to install a TT/VR registration system faster (an institutionally developed system takes approximately six to 15 months to develop) and for substantially less up-front money. Not only does the college or university save the capital investment, but it earns income from the interest on funds not spent to purchase equipment.

In one scenario, it took 2,500 staff hours spread out over 15 months to develop an in-house system. If one $45,000 salaried staff person with an additional $15,000 (33% of salary) provided for benefits worked 2500 hours to develop an in-house TT/VR registration system, the institution would spend a minimum of $75,000 for just the one staff person ($60,000 divided by 12 months = $5,000 per month; $5,000 x 3 = $15,000 + $60,000 = $75,000). This figure does not factor in other costs, such as equipment, enhancements, software, installation and service of telephone lines, utilities, training, and other costs analogous to some of those associated with equipment purchase.

The service bureau may be the most logical, viable, and cost-effective means of delivering TT/VR registration for some colleges and universities. The direction an institution takes will be determined by its unique characteristics (see Chapter V).

Chapter

12

TT/VR ...

Other

Applications

MEDICINE

WOMEN'S STUDIES

FILM

BOTANY

SPANISH

CALCULUS

APPLIED ART

ANTHROPOLOGY

GEOGRAPHY

Melanie Moore Bell
Gonzaga University

James H. Bundy
North Carolina State University

Louise Lonabocker
Boston College

Erlend R. Peterson
Brigham Young University

R. Eugene Schuster
The Ohio State University

In recent years college and university personnel have not only been impressed with the development and sophistication of touchtone telephone/voice response (TT/VR) registration systems, but have also begun to see other applications. Once the investment in TT/VR computer equipment was made, software "wish lists" beyond registration began to emerge.

University representatives attending the 1991 summer seminar on "The Future of Touchtone Telephone Technology" hosted by Brigham Young University presented their "lists" of touchtone telephone enhancements—some of which they had already implemented on their campuses.

➢ ordering "will call" transcripts
➢ ordering "will call" verifications ofenrollment
➢ verifying enrollment and degrees from outside callers
➢ verifying addresses
➢ updating the personal access code (PAC)
➢ guaranteeing sequential course enrollment
➢ scheduling new student orientation
➢ processing student elections
➢ registering for extension/continuing education/self-support programs
➢ scheduling placement interviews
➢ collecting grades from faculty
➢ making credit card payments
➢ disbursing aid to bank accounts
➢ disbursing refunds
➢ transferring funds for tuition and fees from students' bank accounts
➢ determining how a student will pay for tuition, e.g., cash, check, credit card
➢ recording assessments
➢ determining admissions status
➢ buying meal plans
➢ ordering bus passes
➢ ordering textbooks
➢ ordering yearbooks
➢ accessing name of course instructor
➢ accessing course specific information
➢ registering for sports skills classes
➢ administering multiple choice tests

Ideas for applying TT/VR technology continue to multiply as college and university personnel gain experience.

Grade and GPA Inquiry

Students can access their grades and GPA (grade point average) from a touchtone telephone by entering their personal access codes and the term they wish to access. The TT/VR system will speak all grades, the term in which these grades were earned, and cumulative GPAs. During final exam week, only those grades that have been turned in by instructors are spoken. GPAs are not given until the final grade process is completed. Students can continue to track incomplete grades until instructors turn the actual grade into the registrar's office. This takes the pressure off the staff in grade recording offices to forward grade change notices to students.

Some colleges and universities implement the easier grade inquiry feature that is popular with students before registration. This gives systems personnel a chance to get used to voice response technology and experience successful implementation.

Student Account Inquiry

Students can call TT/VR systems to determine their current account balance, past due balance, last recorded payment (in the event a third party is responsible for payment), and optional charges. They can find out how much financial aid has been credited to their account, how much is available as a check or a deposit, and what offices have placed blocks preventing disbursement of aid. Students can also find out if outside lender loans (Stafford, Supplemental, etc.) are available for pickup.

Math, English, and Foreign Language Clearance

Because adequate preparation in math, English, and foreign languages is vital to many degree programs, extensive edits can be built in TT/VR systems for entry into these courses. The mainframe portion of the TT/VR system can verify that students attempting to take one of these courses have met the prerequisites. Students who do not meet the requirements can be directed to an advisor for course alternatives.

Guaranteed Sequence Course Registration

Academic departments can add a directional flag to any sequence course (e.g., chemistry, physics, foreign languages). This flag can ensure that students currently enrolled in a sequence course will be guaranteed registration in the next level of the following term as long as they register during the early registration period. Departments should use this flag with discretion because of the impact on department resources, course time/day scheduling, and public relations.

Recording Addresses

One feature common in most registration systems is the attempt to obtain up-to-date addresses from students. With the TT/VR environment this requires some ingenuity. Several institutions have scripted the spelling out of the address. Some TT/VR systems "read" the words or the Postal Service's 80+ abbreviations for street, road, etc. The residence hall names may be recorded, too. The script may contain about ten of the most frequent city names (usually 30%-40% of the addresses) so they can be spoken instead of spelled out. This reduces the average amount of time necessary to communicate the address. But better yet, the TT/VR equipment may be configured with an out-dialing facility.

When a student indicates an address is incorrect, the machine "conference calls" with a standard telephone answering machine. The answering machine message asks the student to leave his/her name, student ID number, new address, and telephone number after the tone. The staff use a dictation transcriber to input the addresses with the proper editing to conform to database standards. Text-to-speech capability recently available on the market promises to simplify address collection without requiring scripting.

Voice mailboxes are also available to collect address changes, and may be configured with TT/VR equipment. This technology allows students to report their correct addresses 24 hours a day, seven days a week.

Audio Text Messaging

Use of voice response systems to provide the caller with audio text messages or specific information from a database has increased dramatically in the past few years. Using a touchtone telephone, callers now can access weather reports, sports scores, financial information, soap opera updates, local/state/national news, and a myriad of other data.

Student Government Elections

With TT/VR systems, students can enter their personal access codes and then the appropriate code for the candidates or issues they wish to support. To ensure security, the TT/VR system then sets a flag that prevents another student from voting using the same student personal access code. The system tallies the counts and produces a statistical report identifying the election results.

Financial Aid Information and Tracking

With the increased state and federal governmental regulations on student financial aid, financial aid offices can use a voice response system to answer the more routine questions and free staff to deal with student caseloads. A financial aid voice response application can provide students with audio text information in such areas as how to apply for financial aid, what specific types of aid (e.g., Pell Grant and Stafford Loans) are available, and how to apply for a short-term loan. TT/VR can track a student's financial aid application against a table to make sure all required information has been submitted, inform the caller when a decision had been reached, and an award had been made. Students for whom awards cannot be made can be referred to a financial aid counselor. See Exhibit F.2 for the financial aid script from the University of North Texas.

Admissions Information and Tracking

TT/VR systems can provide callers with such information as how to apply for admission, how to apply for in-state residency status, and how to leave their names and addresses for admission application mailings. The host interactive application can track a student's admission application and inform the student if a particular item is missing. A pending or negative decision can be referred to an admissions counselor.

Touchtone Technology as Part of an Integrated Approach

Many institutions that capture data at the source have, when the source is the student, selected one method of capturing that data, like telephones. Boston College has adopted an integrated approach

for displaying and capturing information. The devices and systems available to students are U-VIEW, which can be accessed from Consumer Transaction Terminals and from terminals with a connection to the mainframe computer; and U-DIAL, the TT/VR registration system.

U-VIEW gives students access to their own academic, biographic, and financial information. The menu-driven system allows students to select transactions that display their class schedule, grades, grade point average, rank in class, final exam schedule, home and local address and telephone numbers, financial aid award, student account information, and vehicle registration. Other transactions let students know the status of their guaranteed student loan check; their advisor's name, office number, and telephone extension; their registration appointment time; their library account; and their financial clearance status. Degree audits can also be requested on U-VIEW.

The U-VIEW system first made use of IBM terminals and later added Consumer Transaction Terminals manufactured by Diebold. The Consumer Transaction Terminals, which look like Automated Teller Machines (ATMs) without a cash dispensing unit, have some attractive features including character graphics to simplify instruction; function keys for faster transaction selection; an 80-column high speed printer; durability; forced log-off to recapture the ID card; and the ability to retain lost, stolen, or invalid ID cards.

U-VIEW provides a fast, visual display to a limited set of functions and the devices conveniently serve a resident population. It is not a replacement, however, for other methods of distributing transaction processing to end users including TT/VR technology or microcomputers with connectivity to the host computer. Voice response technology is ideal for students transacting business from work or home, and for straightforward registration and drop/add procedures. Microcomputer terminals offer opportunities for conducting more involved transaction processing.

U-DIAL, the voice response system that resembles systems developed at other institutions, allows students to process registration by telephone by entering their student ID numbers, their Personal Identification Numbers (PIN) and a registration access code. Registration access codes are printed on students' registration forms, which are distributed to students' advisors. The release of the form by the advisor to the student replaces the advisor's signature.

The registration system contains all the edits of the previous on-line registration system for closed, restricted, and permission-of-department courses; time conflicts; registration holds; and attempts to log on before the registration appointment time. Registration appointment times are scheduled in 15-minute intervals, and students are instructed to complete a registration worksheet before calling. See Exhibit G.2 for the U-DIAL script.

U-VIEW Plus, an application developed on computer terminals when U-DIAL was made available to undergraduates, added registration as an additional feature to the U-VIEW menu. The application was named U-VIEW Plus since students could now view all of the information available on U-VIEW ATM terminals plus register for or drop/add courses.

Access to U-VIEW Plus is available on terminals in the student computing facility or via a dial-up connection if students have access to a computer and a modem either from home or from their dormitory rooms.

The terminal-based system has several advantages over the U-DIAL system. Terminals have both keyboards and display screens, which normally are not part of a telephone set. With terminals students can enter all their course selections at once; search for open sections of a course; display information about courses including titles, instructors, and meeting times; and simulate various options before finalizing a schedule. Thus, despite the advantages of the terminal-based system, the TT/VR registration system remains a

vital part of an integrated approach because it gives students the opportunity to construct or modify their schedule anytime, anywhere.

Summary

As college and university personnel become more familiar with TT/VR technology and the convenience it provides, they will take greater advantage of those capabilities. Most colleges and universities have expanded their applications of this process in a relatively short time. One leading university implemented touchtone telephone applications for financial aid analysis, financial aid application status, change of major, end of semester grade information, and advisement for graduation (university requirement deficiencies, general education deficiencies, major and minor requirement deficiencies, and applying for graduation).

A major step in the area of automated registration is the integration of student access terminals that resemble automatic teller machines. ATMs tie into the "front-end" of a TT/VR registration system; they allow students to extend the transactions they currently conduct over the telephone system.

Author Profiles

The value of this resource to those considering TT/VR registration can be laid right at the doorstep of the authors and sponsors who so generously shared their time, their expertise and the experiences of their institutions.

Robert F. Askins is the Director of Registration at the University of South Carolina/USC (Columbia). Mr. Askins has conducted research for a TT/VR project, developed communications strategies, vocabulary, and worksheets for a TT/VR project, and trained faculty and staff. He has produced a video, devised the appointment scheme, and overseen the administration of registration controls. Prior to joining the registrar's staff at USC in 1987, he taught English literature and composition and worked in magazine publishing and small business management.

Address:　Office of the Registrar
University of South Carolina
Columbia, SC 29208
Telephone: (803) 777-3533　FAX: (803) 777-6349
E-Mail: IRECO24@UNIVSCVM.CSD.SCAROLINA.EDU

Melanie Moore Bell is the University Registrar at Gonzaga University (Spokane, Washington). While not involved in implementing TT/VR registration at Gonzaga, she was project coordinator for the TT/VR project at the University of Washington (Seattle) throughout the University's implementation and expansion of the TT/VR system (1987-91). She serves as a consultant on TT/VR registration and related applications to more than a dozen colleges and universities and has been a member of review teams charged with recommending technological enhancements.

Address:　Administration Building, Room 229
Gonzaga University
Spokane, WA 99258-0001
Telephone: (509) 328-4220, ext. 6107　FAX: (509) 484-2818
E-Mail: BELL@GONZAGA.EDU

James H. Bundy has served as University Registrar at North Carolina State University (Raleigh) since 1971. He has also been assistant director of registration, assistant registrar and associate registrar at North Carolina.

Address: Box 7313
North Carolina State University
Raleigh, NC 27695-7313
Telephone: (919) 737-2576　FAX: (919) 737-2376
E-Mail: NCSUJHB@NCSUADM.BITNET

Donald D. Carter is the Registrar at Texas A&M University (College Station).
Address: Texas A&M University
College Station, TX 77843-0100

Fred Dear has been Associate Registrar at the University of Southern California, Los Angeles since 1966. He created the Touch-Tone proposal for the senior administrator, wrote the touchtone telephone voice response script introduced on the UCLA campus.
Address: University Park, Registration 104
University of Southern California
Los Angeles, CA 90089-0912
Telephone: (213) 740-5306   FAX: (213) 74-8710

Jack Demitroff has been the Registrar at the University of Rhode Island (Kingston) since 1975. He was responsible for all aspects of planning and development of URI's TT/VR registration system, from drafting the grant proposal through implementation.
Address: 11 Carlotti Administration Building
University of Rhode Island
Kingston, RI 02881-0806
Telephone: (401) 792-4468   FAX: (401) 792-2910
E-Mail: RFJ101@URIACC.URI.EDU

Lou Ann Denny is the Registrar at Arizona State University. She has been a co-project manager on the project team, and a co-chair on the advisory committee.
Address: Arizona State University
Tempe, AZ 85287
Telephone: (602) 965-7302   FAX: (602) 965-2295
E-Mail: ISTLAD@ASUACAD

Charles L. Dowburd is Director of the Telephone Registration Network, Voice FX Corporation in Conshohocken, Pennsylvania. He has over ten years of higher education experience in administration as a department chairperson, director, and dean for both credit and noncredit programs. His education background combined with several years in business provide the relevant experience necessary for developing a viable TT/VR registration system through a service bureau.
Address: Voice FX Corporation
Lee Park Office Complex
1100 E. Hector Street, 4th Floor
Conshohocken, PA
Telephone: (215) 941-1000   FAX: (215) 941-9544

Janice M. Garcia has served as Systems Analyst at Arizona State University (Tempe) since 1990. She has worked on the TT/VR registration script, on test cases and testing, on statistical reporting from data logging, and on the interface with admissions. Ms. Garcia had worked for more than twenty years in private industry, supporting and organizing computer systems.

    Address: Office of the Registrar
          Tempe, AZ 85287-0312
    Telephone: (602) 965-7302   FAX: (602) 965-2295
    E-Mail: ICJMG@ASUACAD.BITNET

T. Luther Gunter has served as University Registrar at the University of South Carolina/USC (Columbia) since 1977. He originated and designed a TT/VR project. He served also as USC's Director of Administrative Data Processing and Computer Services.

    Address: University of South Carolina
          Columbia, SC 29208
    Telephone: (803) 777-3871   FAX: (803) 777-6349
    E-Mail: IRECO11@UNIVSCVM

William R. Haid is the Registrar and Director of Enrollment Services at the University of Colorado, Boulder.

    Address: Regent 105-CB 20
          University of Colorado at Boulder
          Boulder, CO 80309
    Telephone: (303) 492-1130   FAX: (303) 492-4884
    E-Mail: HAID_W@CUBLDR.COLORADO.EDU

Joneel J. Harris has been the Registrar at the University of North Texas (Denton) since 1981. She served as project manager of the TT/VR registration project on campus.

    Address: P.O. Box 13766
          University of North Texas
          Denton, TX 76203-3766
    Telephone: (817) 565-2748   FAX: (817) 565-4913
    E-Mail: HARRISJ@ABN.UNT.EDU

Earl W. Hawkey is the Director of Registration and Records at the University of Nebraska-Lincoln. He served as a member of the project team at the University of Washington and later maintained the voice response equipment and managed voice recordings.

    Address: University of Nebraska-Lincoln
          Lincoln, NE 68588-0416
    Telephone: (402) 472-2025

Sally Hickok was the Associate Registrar and Admissions Officer at the University of California, San Diego until her retirement. She had been an admissions and records professional for twenty-eight years.

Address: 9500 Gilman Drive
La Jolla, CA 92093-0021
Telephone: (619) 484-4813   FAX: (619) 534-5723

Edna Brinkley Jones is the Associate Registrar and Director of Registration and Scheduling at the University of Cincinnati (Ohio). She has worked in various positions in the University since 1959.

Address: 430 Teachers College
University of Cincinnati
Cincinnati, OH 45221
Telephone: (513) 556-6510   FAX: (513) 556-3838

Louise Lonabocker has been University Registrar at Boston College since 1979. She has been involved in the planning, development, implementation, and evaluation of the TT/VR project on BC's campus.

Address: Lyons Hall 106
Boston College
Chestnut Hill, MA 02167
Telephone: (617) 552-3318   FAX: (617) 552-4975
E-Mail: LOUISE@BCVMS

John W. Olwig is the Coordinator — Systems Development at The Ohio State University (Columbus). He served as the voice response coordinator at Ohio State.

Address: 1800 Cannon Drive, 1210 Lincoln
The Ohio State University
Columbus, OH 43210-1230
Telephone: (614) 292-3947   FAX: (614) 292-7199
E-Mail: ORWIGL@OSU.EDU

Erlend D. Peterson is the Dean of Admissions and Records at Brigham Young University (Provo, Utah). He assisted in the design and implementation of the first TT/VR registration project in the United States.

Address: A-185 ASB
Brigham Young University
Provo, UT 84602
Telephone: (801) 378-2539   FAX: (801) 378-4264
E-Mail: EDP@ARLAN.BYU.EDU

William L. Salter is Publications Editor at the University of South Carolina (Columbia). He edits the master schedule of classes, the primary source of TT/VR registration information for students, each semester.

Address: Office of the Registrar
Tempe, AZ 85287-0312
Telephone: (803) 777-3549   FAX: (803) 777-6349
E-Mail: IREC019@UNIVSCVM.CSD.SCAROLINA.EDU

R. Eugene Schuster is the University Registrar at The Ohio State University (Columbus). He spearheaded the development of TT/VR registration at Ohio State.

Address: 1800 Cannon Drive, 1250 Lincoln
The Ohio State University
Columbus, OH 43210-1230
Telephone: (614) 292-1556   FAX: (614) 292-7199
E-Mail: SCHUSTER.3@OSU.EDU

Genene C. Walker is the Manager, Computer Information Systems, at Arizona State University (ASU). She has spent the past seven and one-half years at ASU Computer Services in support of Student Records Computer Systems.

Address: Computing Services - 0101
Tempe, AZ 85287-0101
Telephone: (602) 965-2284   FAX: (602) 965-8698
E-Mail: KAGCW@ASUACAD.BITNET

Donald J. Wermers is the Registrar at the University of Wisconsin-Madison. He led the TT/VR project campus-wide, initiating the idea and carrying it through to implementation. He chaired the Chancellor's Committee on Automated Registration, a campus policy and procedures committee.

Address: 750 University Avenue
University of Wisconsin-Madison
Madison, WI 53706
Telephone: (608) 262-3964   FAX: (608) 262-6002
E-Mail: DON.WERMERS@MAIL.ADMIN.WISC.EDU

Elaine Wheeler is the Statewide Associate Director, California Alliance for Minority Participation at the University of California, Irvine. She served as project manager for the TT/VR project at the University of California, Irvine, and continues as a consultant to the Registrar, advising on new applications.

Address: Administration 600
University of California, Irvine
Irvine, CA 92717
Telephone: (714) 725-2937   FAX: (714) 725-3048
E-Mail: ejwheele@uci.edu

Institution Profiles

Contributing authors submitted voice response system profiles for their institutions. When information was unavailable, categories were not included. Note that contact names in such specific areas as telecommunications, voice response, or student information system have been included, along with addresses, telephone and FAX numbers and e-mail addresses. Further information on vendors cited in the profiles is available either in the sponsor profiles section or in the directory of vendors.

Arizona State University
Boston College
Brigham Young University
Gonzaga University
North Carolina State University
The Ohio State University
Texas A&M University
University of California, San Diego
University of California, Santa Barbara
University of Cincinnati
University of Colorado, Boulder
University of Lincoln at Nebraska
University of North Texas
University of Rhode Island
University of South Carolina
University of Southern California
University of Washington
University of Wisconsin-Madison

ARIZONA STATE UNIVERSITY

Address: Tempe, Arizona 85287

Author(s) Represented: LOU ANN DENNY, JANICE M. GARCIA, GENENE C. WALKER

Enrollment: 42,626

Funding Source: State

Institution Type: Four-year with master's, and doctoral programs

Academic Calendar: Semester

Voice Response Applications: Registration, Class Listing, Fee Payment, Credit Card Authorization, Class Status, Financial Aid Acknowledgement (authorize financial aid to be used for fee payment)

Future Goals: Grade Inquiry, Financial Aid Status Inquiry

Current # of Telephone Lines: 120 (24 lines added to original 96 when fee payment system was added to application)

Host Computer: IBM 3090 Model 500E, Cray X-MP/14se, IBM 3081, VAX 6000 Model 430

Operating System: MVS/ESA on the IBM 3090

Memory Size: 128 Megabytes and 256 Megabytes extended memory

Disk Size: 315 Gigabytes

Database Used: IDMS/R

Persons Supporting Student Information System: 23

Student Information System Software: Developed in-house

Voice Response Software: Syntellect, Inc. -Infobot, Gateway 1 Monitor

Voice Response Hardware: Syntellect, Inc. - Infobot/Emperor

Interface: IBM 3745 Controller

First Application: Fall 1991

Weeks TT/VR Is Available Each Term: Continually available, although each function within application has begin and end dates (e.g., registration and drop/add function Fall is mid-April through August, Spring is late November through January, and Summer is February through June.

Implementation Time: One year for first pilot; available to all students two years from start of project

Student Security Control(s): ASU ID and PIN (initially set to month and day of birth; student must assign a new PIN on first call)

Gender of Voice Used: Female voice of Associate Registrar Mary M. Neary

Name of TT/VR System: Touch-Tone Telephone Registration and Fee Payment

Acronym: InTouch

Unique Features: Record script over the telephone in-house; modular hardware design results in only 12 lines impacted if hardware problems occur (versus 32, 48, etc.).

Primary Contact: Janice M. Garcia

Title: Systems Analyst

Address: Arizona State University
Office of the Registrar-0312
Box 870312
Tempe, AZ 85287-0312

Telephone: (602) 965-7302

FAX: (602) 965-2295

E-Mail: ICJMG@ASUACAD.BITNET

Student Information System Contact: Same as Above

Voice Response Contact: Genene C. Walker

Title: Manager, Computer Information Systems

Address: Arizona State University
Computing Services-870101
Tempe, AZ 85287-0101

Telephone: (602) 965-2284

FAX: (602) 965-8698

E-Mail: KAGCW@ASUACAD.BITNET

Telecommunications Contact: Dave McKee

Title: Manager, Data Communication

Address: Arizona State University
Telecommunications Services
Box 870201
Tempe, AZ 85287-0201

Telephone: (602) 965-4016

FAX: (602) 965-0963

E-Mail: ICSDMM@ASUACAD.BITNET

Notes of interest to readers:

Voice response application uses in-house developed Access Control subsystem to determine avaiability of various functions. These functions and dates and times of availability are updated on-line by Registrar's Office. Functions can also be temporarily disabled on line by Registrar's Office.

BOSTON COLLEGE

Address: Chestnut Hill, Massachusetts 02167

Author(s) Represented: LOUISE LONABOCKER

Enrollment: 14,500

Funding Source: Church-Jesuit

Institution Type: Four-year master's and doctoral programs

Academic Calendar: Early semester

Voice Response Applications: Registration

Current # of Telephone Lines: 27

Host Computer: IBM 3090

Operating System: MVS/ESA

Memory Size: 64 MB

Disk Size: 37 MG

Persons Supporting Student Information System: 3

Student Information System Software:

Developed in-house

Voice Response Software: IBM VRU9274

Interface: Channel

First Application (Term/Year/Name): Fall 1990

Weeks TT/VR Is Available Each Term:
    Beginning registration through drop/add

Implementation Time: 2 months

Student Security Control(s): Student ID and PIN

Gender of Voice Used: Female

Name of TT/VR System: U-DIAL

Acronym: U-DIAL

Primary Contact: Louise Lonabocker

Title: University Registrar

Address: Lyons Hall 106
    Chestnut Hill, MA 02167

Telephone: (617) 552-3318

FAX: (617) 552-4975

E-Mail: LOUISE@BCVMS

Student Information System Contact:
    Joe Harrington

Title: Director, Management Information Systems

Address: Boston College
    Chestnut Hill, MA 02167

Telephone: (617) 552-8510

E-Mail: HARRING@hermes.bc.edu

Voice Response Contact: John Springfield

Title: Technical Support Programmer

Address: Boston College
    Chestnut Hill, MA 02167

Telephone: (617) 552-4969

E-Mail: SPRING@BCVMS

Telecommunications Contact: Jeff Jeffers

Title: Director, Network Services

Address: Boston College
    Chestnut Hill, MA 02167

Telephone: (617) 552-8507

E-Mail: JJEFF@hermes.bc.edu

BRIGHAM YOUNG UNIVERSITY

Address: Provo, Utah 84602

Author(s) Represented: ERLEND D. PETERSON

Enrollment: 28,890

Funding Source: Church

Institution Type: Four-year with master's, doctoral,
    and professional programs

Academic Calendar: Semester

Voice Response Applications: Registration,
    Financial Aid Status, Grade Reporting to
    Students, Admission Status

Future Goals: Class Status to Faculty

Current # of Telephone Lines: 72

Host Computer: AMDAHL 5880

Operating System: IBM MVS

Disk Size: 3380 and 3350

Database Used: CA/DATACOM

Persons Supporting Student Information System: 10

Student Information System Software: Developed
    in-house

Voice Response Software: Developed in-house

Voice Response Hardware: Perception Technology

Interface: Screen-based, specific to voice response application

First Application (Term/Year/Name): Registration, Fall 1983 for all students

Weeks TT/VR Is Available Each Term: Fall (21 weeks), Winter (14 weeks)

Implementation Time: 6 months

Student Security Control(s): Social Security # and PIN

Gender of Voice Used: Male

Unique Features: Speaks current schedule to students, checks open/closed status of sections, gives available sections if initial course requested is not available.

Primary Contact: H. Garth Rasband

Title: Assistant Dean

Address: BYU Box 280 ASB
Provo, UT 84602

Telephone: (801) 378-4254

FAX: (801) 378-5278

E-Mail: HGR@ARLAN.BYU.EDU

Student Information System Contact: H. Garth Rasband

Voice Response Contact: H. Garth Rasband

Telecommunications Contact: Farrell Mallory

Title: Manager, Communication Systems

Address: 1206 SFLC, BYU
Provo, UT 84602

Telephone: (801) 378-7412

GONZAGA UNIVERSITY

Address: Spokane, Washington 99258-0001

Author(s) Represented: MELANIE MOORE BELL

Enrollment: 5,200

Funding Source: Independent

Institution Type: Four-year with master's, doctoral, and professional programs

Academic Calendar: Semester

Voice Response Applications: Registration

Future Goals: Grade Inquiry, Billing Inquiry, Application Status

Current # of Telephone Lines: 12

Host Computer: Hewlett Packard, Model 947 Spectrum

Operating System: MPE/IX

Memory Size: 192 Megabytes

Disk Size: 6.0 Gigabytes

Database Used: Turbo Image

Persons Supporting Student Information System: 3

Student Information System Software: In-house

Voice Response Software: Applied Voice Technology

Voice Response Hardware: Applied Voice Technology

Interface: Applied Voice Technology

First Application (Term/Year/Name): Fall 1989

Weeks TT/VR Is Available Each Term:
Fall (24 weeks), Spring (9 weeks)

Implementation Time: 2 months

Student Security Control(s): Social Security #and PIN

Gender of Voice Used: Male

Name of TT/VR System: Touchtel

Primary Contact: Melanie Moore Bell

Title: University Registrar

Address: Gonzaga University
Spokane, WA 99258-0001

Telephone: (509) 328-4220, Ext. 6107

FAX: (509) 484-2818

E-Mail: BELL@GONZAGA.EDU

Student Information System Contact: John Bujosa

Title: Director, Computing and Information

Address: Gonzaga University
Spokane, WA 99258-0001

Telephone: (509) 328-4220, Ext. 2244

FAX: (509) 484-2818

E-Mail: JB@GONZAGA.EDU

Voice Response Contact: Kaihehau Uahinui

Title: Computer Programming Supervisor

Address: Gonzaga University
Spokane, WA 99258-0001

Telephone: (509) 328-4220, Ext. 2245

FAX: (509) 484-2818

E-Mail: KAI@GONZAGA.EDU

Telecommunications Contact: Joan Allbery

Title: Assistant Director, Computing and
Information, Campus Network Manager

Address: Gonzaga University
Spokane, WA 99358-0001

Telephone: (509) 328-4220, Ext. 2243

FAX: (509) 484-2818

E-Mail: JOAN@GONZAGA.EDU

NORTH CAROLINA STATE UNIVERSITY

Address: Raleigh, North Carolina 27695-7313

Author(s) Represented: JAMES H. BUNDY

Enrollment: 26,500

Funding Source: State

Institution Type: Four-year with master's, doctoral, and professional programs

Academic Calendar: Semester

Voice Response Applications: Registration

Future Goals: Grade Inquiry, Student Address Changes, Financial Aid Inquiry, Admissions Inquiry, Career Planning and Placement, Job Interview Schedule, Jobline

Current # of Telephone Lines: 64

Host Computer: IBM 3090-180J

Operating System: IBM-MVS 2.20

Memory Size: Real-32 MB (central), 64MB (expanded) Virtual-201MB

Disk Size: 37.5 Gigabytes

Database Used: IDMS

Persons Supporting Student Information System: 15

Student Information System Software: Developed in-house

Voice Response Software: Developed in-house

Voice Response Hardware: Perception Technology (VOCOM BT III)

Interface: Screen-based, specific to voice response application

First Application (Term/Year/Name):Registration, Spring 1989 for all students

Weeks TT/VR Is Available Each Term: Fall (23 weeks), Spring (10 weeks)

Implementation Time: 14 months

Student Security Control(s): Student ID # and PIN

Gender of Voice Used: Male

Name of TT/VR System: Telephonic Registration Access to Computerized Scheduling

Acronym: TRACS

Unique Features: Checks prerequisites, speaks current schedule to students, checks open/closed status of sections, gives available sections if initial course requested is not available, gives classroom building and room location.

Primary Contact: James H. Bundy

Title: University Registrar

Address: Box 7313, NCSU
  Raleigh, NC 27695-7313

Telephone: (919) 737-2576

FAX: (919) 737-2376

E-Mail: NCSUJHB@NCSUADM.BITNET

Student Information System Contact:
  Craig McQueen

Title: System Analyst, ACS Office

Address: Box 7209, NCSU
  Raleigh, NC 27695-7209

Telephone: (919) 737-2794

FAX: (919) 737-3787

E-Mail: N906855@NCSUADM.BITNET

Voice Response Contact: James H. Bundy

Telecommunications Contact: Miriam Tripp

Title: Director of Telecommunications

Address: Box 7217

Telephone: (919) 515-7046

FAX: (919) 515-6237

E-Mail: MIRIAM_TRIPP@NCSU.EDU

THE OHIO STATE UNIVERSITY

Address: Columbus, Ohio 43210-1230

Author(s) Represented: JOHN W. ORWIG, R. EUGENE SCHUSTER

Enrollment: 60,589

Funding Source: Public

Institution Type: Four-year with graduate and professional programs

Academic Calendar: Quarters

Voice Response Applications: Registration

Future Goals: Wait Lists, Grades, Address Changes and Enrollment Verifications

Current # of Telephone Lines: 64

Host Computer: Amdahl 5890-300E-administrative

Operating System: MVS/CICS

Memory Size: 192 Megabytes

Disk Size: 43 Gigabytes

Database Used: Mainframe SIS uses IMS. TT/VR statistics are kept with ORACLE

Persons Supporting Student Information System: 6 FTE

Student Information System Software: Developed in-house

Voice Response Software: Co-developed with AT&T

Voice Response Hardware: Initially implemented on AT&T Model 80; now running on CVIS platform for ease of operation, reduced mainte nance costs and new development feature avail ability

Interface: Initially asynchronous, now SNA

First Application (Term/Year/Name): May 1987

Weeks TT/VR Is Available Each Term: Third week of preceeding quarter through the first Friday of the quarter (about 40 weeks per year).

Implementation Time: About 9 months after vendor selected

Student Security Control(s): Access code assigned quarterly

Gender of Voice Used: Male

Name of TT/VR System: Better Registration Utilizing TouchTone phones for University Students

Acronym: BRUTUS (after the University's mascot)

Unique Features: Collects both course requests for demand registration and handles registrations-add/drop thereafter; checks/enforces pre/corequisites and course repeatibility; collects optional fees infor mation; "reads" billing address and collects changes for later operator entry. The system is set up so it does not require delimiter entry by the student (every entry is not followed by the #) but does allow additional application/scripts to be triggered by calling different phone numbers (no menus).

Primary Contact: R. Eugene Schuster

Title: University Registrar

Address: 1800 Cannon Drive, 1250 Lincoln
Columbus, OH 43210-1230

Telephone: (614) 292-1556

FAX: (614) 292-7199

E-Mail: schuster.3@osu.edu.

Student Information System Contact: Henry Lee

Title: Associate Registrar/Senior Computer
Specialist

Address: 1800 Cannon Drive, 1210 Lincoln
Columbus, OH 43210-1230

Telephone: (614) 292-3947

FAX: (614) 292-7199

E-Mail: henry.lee@osu.edu.

Voice Response Contact: John Orwig

Title: Coordinator - Systems Development

Address: 1800 Canon Drive, 1210 Lincoln
Columbus, OH 43210-1230

 Telephone: (614) 292-3947

FAX (614) 292-7199

E-Mail: ORWIG.1@OSU.EDU

Telecommunications Contact: Barry Hayes

Title: Senior Telecommunications Specialist

Address: UNITS
320 W. 8th Avenue
Columbus, OH 43201-2331

Telephone: (614) 292-5215

FAX: (614) 292-9350

E-Mail: hayes.11@osu.edu.

Notes of interest to readers:

System also utilized by students on distant regional campuses. Built as integrated part of terminal registration to allow improved targeting of advising. Allows differential registration practices by college/campus.

TEXAS A&M UNIVERSITY

Address: College Station, Texas 77843-0100

Author(s) Represented: DONALD D. CARTER

Enrollment: 41,171

Funding Source: State

Institution Type: Four-year with master's, doctoral, and professional programs

Academic Calendar: Semester

Voice Response Applications: Registration, Class Room Assignment, Grades

Future Goals: Student Billing, Grade Inquiry, Bulletin Board, Scheduling Student Orientation Appointments, Financial Aid Inquiry

Current # of Telephone Lines: 96

Host Computer: IBM 3090-600E

Operating System: MVS/ESA

Memory Size: Real-256 MB, Virtual-128M

Disk Size: 1920 MB

Database Used: ADABAS

Persons Supporting Student Information System: 14

Student Information System Software: Information Associates (see Systems & Computer Technology Corporation inSponsor Profiles; modified in-house)

Voice Response Software: Information Associates (modified in-house)

Voice Response Hardware: Perception Technology

Interface: Conversational

First Application (Term/Year/Name): Registration, Spring 1987. Began with preregistration in November 1986 for all students.

Weeks TT/VR Is Available Each Term: Fall (15 weeks), Spring (9 weeks), Summer (3 weeks) each session

Implementation Time: 6 months

Student Security Control(s): Social Security # and PIN

Gender of Voice Used: Male

Name of TT/VR System: Touchtone Telephone Registration

Primary Contact: Willis Ritchey

Title: Assistant Registrar

Address: TAMU, Mail Stop 0100
    College Station, TX 77843

Telephone: (409) 845-7117

FAX: (409) 845-7117

Student Information System Contact: Larry Malota

Title: Manager, SIMS

Address: TAMU, Mail Stop 1119
    College Station, TX 77843

Telephone: (409) 845-5830

FAX: (409) 845-2074

E-Mail: K119LM@TAMVM1

Voice Response Contact: Larry Malota

Telecommunications Contact: Walt Magnussen

Title: University Telecommunications Manager

Address: TAMU, Mail 1371
    College Station, TX 77843

Telephone: (409) 845-5588

UNIVERSITY OF CALIFORNIA, SAN DIEGO

Address: 9500 Gilman Drive
    La Jolla, California 92093

Author(s) Represented: SALLY HICKOK

Enrollment: 22,000

Funding Source: Public

Institution Type: Four-year public

Academic Calendar: Quarter

Voice Response Applications: Enrollment, Add/Drop, Holds, Grades

Future Goals: Admissions, Financial Aid Information, Student Accounts

Current # of Telephone Lines: 48

Host Computer: IBM ES 9021 Model 580

Operating System: MVS/ESA Enterprise System Architecture

Memory Size: 256 MB - 128 MB Extended Storage

Disk Size: 138 GB

Database Used: IDMSR

Persons Supporting Student Information System: 4 in-house plus programming and computer assistance as required. In-house staff also responsible for all system work.

Student Information System Software: SCT Custom Designed

Voice Response Software: Perception Technology

Voice Response Hardware: Perception VOCOM 40

Interface: IBM 37-25 Front End Processor/Comm Controller

First Application (Term/Year/Name): Winter Quarter 1987

Implementation Time: Daily and weekends

Student Security Control(s): Custom designed including double passwords

Gender of Voice Used: Female

Name of TT/VR System: Telephone Enrollment Student Services

Acronym: TESS

Unique Features: System supports advisor/depart ment restrictions

Primary Contact: Myra Webb

Title: Assistant Registrar and Admissions Officer

Address: 9500 Gilman Drive
La Jolla, CA 92093

Telephone: (619) 534-0071

FAX: (619) 534-5723

E-Mail: MWEBB@UCSD

Student Information System Contact: Myra Webb

Voice Response Contact: Myra Webb

Telecommunications Contact:
David Cupp

Title: Assistant Systems Manager

Address: 9500 Gilman Drive
La Jolla, CA 92093

Telephone: (619) 534-0082

FAX: (619) 534-5723

E-Mail: DCUPP@UCSD

UNIVERSITY OF CALIFORNIA, SANTA BARBARA

Address: Santa Barbara, California 93106

Author(s) Represented: ELAINE WHEELER (now at University of California, Irvine)

Enrollment: 18,000

Funding Source: State

Institution Type: Four-year with master's, and doctoral programs

Academic Calendar: Quarter

Voice Response Applications: Registration, Grade Inquiry, Transcript Ordering

Future Goals: Financial Aid Status

Current # of Telephone Lines: 40 (36 for registration + 4 for test and development)

Host Computer: IBM 3090

Operating System: MVS

Memory Size: Mainframe

Disk Size: Mainframe

Database Used: ADABAS/Natural/Complete

Persons Supporting Student Information System: 3 to 6

Student Information System Software: ADABAS

Voice Response Software: Syntellect -Infobot

Voice Response Hardware: Syntellect -Infobot

Interface: SNA

First Application: Winter 1991 Registration

Weeks TT/VR Is Available Each Term: Continuous

Implementation Time: One year of planning, 3 months of implementation

Student Security Control(s): PIN

Gender of Voice Used: Female voice of graduate student also involved in application programming.

Name of TT/VR System: RBT (pronounced RiBiT)

Acronym: RBT-Registration By Telephone

Unique Features: Programming changes can be installed immediately; no reprogramming of existing applications required

Primary Contact: Patrick McNulty

Title: Assistant Registrar

Address: UCSB Office of the Registrar
Santa Barbara, CA 93106

Telephone: (805) 893-4165

FAX: (805) 893-2985

E-Mail: rg00psm@ucsbvm.bitnet

Student Information System Contact:
Virginia K. Johns

Title: Manager, Student Systems Group

Address: UCSB Information
Systems and Computing
Santa Barbara, CA 93106

Telephone: (805) 893-3858

FAX: (805) 893-8016

E-Mail: is00vj@ucsbvm.bitnet

Voice Response Contact: Patrick NcNulty
(see Primary Contact)

Telecommunications Contact: Vince Sefcik

Title: Director of Communication Services

Address: UCSB Information
Systems and Computing
Santa Barbara, CA 93106

Telephone: (805) 893-4182

FAX: (805) 893-8016

E-Mail: comlvs@ucsbvm.bitnet

Notes of interest to readers:

Menu driven programming

UNIVERSITY OF CINCINNATI

Address: Cincinnati, Ohio 45221

Author(s) Represented:
EDNA BRINKLEY JONES

Enrollment: 36,078 Autumn

Funding Source: State of Ohio

Institution Type: Four-year through doctoral and
professional (Law and Medicine) programs

Academic Calendar: Quarter

Voice Response Applications: Registration, Student
Elections, Course Availability

Future Goals: Grades, Student Accounts and
Financial Aid

Current # of Telephone Lines: 48

Host Computer: 5890/300E

Operating System: MVS/ESA

Memory Size: 256 Megabytes

Disk Size: 127.5 Gigabytes

Database Used: IMS

Persons Supporting Student Information System: 12

Student Information System Software: In-house

Voice Response Software: Periphonics, Inc.

Voice Response Hardware: Periphonics, Inc.

Interface: CICS

Registration: August 1989 (test for 2,000 students),
Winter 1989 (live for everyone)

Weeks TT/VR is Available Each Term: 16 weeks (4
to 5 weeks each term except summer, when
TT/VR is available for 2 weeks)

Implementation Time: 1 year, 7 months from
vendor selection to system up

Student Security Control(s): Social Security # and
Month/Date of Birth

Gender of Voice Used: Female

Name of TT/VR System: UC Express

Acronym: Same

Primary Contact: Edna Brinkley Jones

Title: Associate Registrar and Director of
Registration and Scheduling

Address: 430 Teachers College
Cincinnati, OH 45221

Telephone: (513) 556-6510

FAX: (513) 556-3838

Student Information System Contact: Thomas C. Koerner

Title: Assistant Director, Center for Information Tech Services

Address: 2900 Reading Road
Cincinnati, OH 45221-0149

Telephone: (513) 556-9103

FAX: (513) 556-2100

E-Mail: Thomas Koerner @ UC. EDU

Voice Response Contact: Rudy Cammerer

Title: Area Systems Manager, Center for Information Tech Services

Address: 2900 Reading Road
Cincinnati, OH 45221-0149

Telephone: (513) 556-9056

FAX: (513) 556-2199

Telecommunications Contact: James Champlin

Title: Director of Communication

Address: 217 Edwards Center
University of Cincinnati
Cincinnati, OH 45221

Telephone: (513) 556-2066

FAX: (513) 556-2042

UNIVERSITY OF COLORADO, BOULDER

Address: Boulder, Colorado 80309-0020

Author(s) Represented: WILLIAM R. HAID

Enrollment: 24,364

Funding Source: State

Institution Type: Four-year with master's, doctoral, and professional programs

Academic Calendar: Semester

Voice Response Applications: Registration

Future Goals: Call Attendant-Audio Library system for registration, records and admissions, selection of optional fees

Current # of Telephone Lines: 48

Host Computer: Hitachi Data Systems AS/XL60

Operating System: MVS/XA

Memory Size: 192 Megabytes

Disk Size: 52 Gigabytes

Database Used: IDMS

Persons Supporting Student Information System: 15 approximately

Student Information System Software: Information Associates

Voice Response Software: Perception Technology

Voice Response Hardware: Perception Technology

Interface: Conversational

First Application (Term/Year/Name): Registration, Fall 1988 for all students

Weeks TT/VR Is Available Each Term: Fall (24 weeks), Spring (12 weeks), Summer (14 weeks)

Implementation Time: February 1985 to Spring 1988

Student Security Control(s): Social Security # and PIN

Gender of Voice Used: Male

Name of TT/VR System: CU Connect

Unique Features: Speaks current schedule to students, checks open/closed status of sections, gives alternatives if initial course request is not available, allows wait listing and adding a course for pass/fail or no credit. UC-Boulder uses a combination course request and confirmed registration system for fall semester.

Primary Contact: William R. Haid

Title: Registrar and Director of Enrollment Services

Address: Regent 105-CB 20, UC-Boulder
Boulder, CO 80309-0020

Telephone: (303) 492-1130

FAX: (303) 492-4884

E-Mail: HAID__W@CUBLDR.COLORADO.EDU

Student Information System Contact:
Barbara J. Ross

Title: Associate Registrar

Address: Regent 105, Campus Box 20 UC-Boulder
Boulder, CO 80309-0020

Telephone: (303) 492-8669

FAX: (303) 492-4884

Voice Response Contact: Nancy Martin

Title: Systems Analyst

Address: UMS, One Pearl Plaza
Boulder, CO 80309-0050

UNIVERSITY OF NEBRASKA-LINCOLN

Address: Lincoln, Nebraska

Author(s) Represented: EARL W. HAWKEY

Note: See University of Washington's Profile. Earl W. Hawkey was Assistant Registrar for Data Management at the time of touchtone tele phone/voice response technology implementation and subsequently moved to the University of Nebraska at Lincoln to serve as Registrar.

UNIVERSITY OF NORTH TEXAS

Address: Denton, Texas 76203

Author(s) Represented: JONEEL J. HARRIS

Enrollment: 27,020

Funding Source: State

Institution Type: Four-year with master's, and doctoral programs

Academic Calendar: Semester

Voice Response Applications: Registration, Financial Aid, Campus-wide Emergency Notification and Message System

Future Goals: Grade Inquiry, Service Options for Students (SOS)

Current # of Telephone Lines: 48

Host Computer: IBM ES 9000, Model 9121-440

Operating System: MVS-ESA

Memory Size: 128 MB

Disk Size: 48 GB

Database Used: ADABAS

Persons Supporting Student Information System: 6

Student Information System Software: Information Associates with many in-house modifications

Voice Response Software: Touch-Talk

Voice Response Hardware: NCS Application Processor, Perception Technology BT III's

Interface: Bisync, SNA-SDLC

First Application: Fall 1987 Registration (test), Spring 1988 Registration (production), Spring 1992 (installed new system)

Weeks TT/VR Is Available Each Term: 4-5 weeks Fall and Spring

Implementation Time: 1st system, 9 months; 2d system, 30 days

Student Security Control(s): Social Security # and PIN

Gender of Voice Used: Female

Name of TT/VR System: Teleregistration

Unique Features: Billing due date, address to which bill will be sent, alternate courses, advising clearance, co-requisites, fee payment plan, year book, car pool registration, registration for up to three terms, schedule revision period after grades but before Coliseum registration. Selected new students may use the system as well as continuing students.

Primary Contact: Joneel J. Harris

Title: Registrar

Address: University of North Texas
P.O. Box 13766
Denton, TX 76203

Telephone: (817) 565-2748

FAX: (817) 565-4913

E-Mail: HARRISJ@ABN.UNT.EDU

Student Information System Contact: Don Butler

Title: Student Records Team Leader

Address: P.O. Box 13495
Denton, TX 76203

Telephone: (817) 565-2324

FAX: (817) 565-4060

Voice Response Contact: Nancy Fisher

Title: Voice Response Analyst

Address: P.O. Box 13495
Denton, TX 76203

Telephone: (817) 565-2324

FAX: (817) 565-4060

Telecommunications Contact: Tom Newell

Title: Manager, Telecommunications

Address: P.O. Box 13527
Denton, TX 76203

Telephone: (817) 565-2654

FAX: (817) 565-4919

Notes of interest to readers:

Expect to register all students by telephone in Fall 1993; PIN number is birthdate or 6 random digits.

UNIVERSITY OF RHODE ISLAND

Address: Kingston, Rhode Island 02881-0806

Author(s) Represented: JACK DEMITROFF

Enrollment: 15,590

Funding Source: State

Institution Type: Four-year with master's, doctoral, and professional programs

Academic Calendar: Semester

Voice Response Applications: Registration, Admissions Inquiry, Meal Plan Update

Future Goals: Bursar/Financial Inquiry, Dormitory Assignment, Grade Inquiry

Current # of Telephone Lines: 32

Host Computer: IMB ES9000

Operating System: MUS/XA

Memory Size: 32MB

Disk Size: 30GB

Database Used: Software AG (ADABAS)

Persons Supporting Student Information System: 2.5

Student Information System Software:

Developed in-house; Programming in natural and COBOL/CIES

Voice Response Software: Periphonics V/OS, Version 3.2.b

Voice Response Hardware: Periphonics, VPS7500

Interface: Bisynchronous

First Application (Term/Year/Name): Registration, April 1991

Weeks TT/VR Is Available Each Term: VR availble throughout year; registration through end of drop period each semester.

Implementation Time: 11 months

Student Security Control(s): PIN

Gender of Voice Used: Male

Name of TT/VR System: Telephone Registration

Primary Contact: Jack Demitroff

Title: Registrar

Address: 11 Carlotti Admin Building
University of Rhode Island
Kingston, RI 02881-0806

Telephone: (401) 792-4468

FAX: (401) 792-2910

E-Mail: RFJ101@URIACC.URI.EDU

Student Information System Contact: Gary Boden

Title: Senior Programmer Analyst

Address: Lippitt Hall
University of Rhode Island
Kingston, RI 02881

Telephone: (401) 792-2611

FAX: (401) 792-5479

E-Mail: GBODEN@URIACC.URI.EDU

Voice Response Contact: Gary Boden

Telecommunications Contact: Gary Boden

UNIVERSITY OF SOUTH CAROLINA

Address: Columbia, South Carolina 29208

Author(s) Represented: ROBERT F. ASKINS,
T. LUTHER GUNTER,
WILLIAM L. SALTER

Enrollment: 26,000 at Columbia campus; 43,000
in system

Funding Source: State

Institution Type: Four-year with master's and
doctoral programs

Academic Calendar: Semester

Voice Response Applications: Registration, Grade
Inquiry, Bulletin Board, Credit Card Payment,
Financial Aid

Future Goals: Expanded fee payment, open class
search capability, admissions functions

Current # of Telephone Lines: 96 to 76 lines for
registration 16 for financial aid, 4 for bulletin
board

Host Computer: IBM 3090-400E Mainframe; 4
Wells American 386 (VRS mini-computer) +
Texas Micro-System

Operating System: IMS Mainframe, MVS/XA for
IMS, DOS (VRS minicomputer)

Memory Size: File server 1.2 Gigabytes

Disk Size: 120 Megabyte hard drive per mini

Student Information System Software: IMS

Voice Response Software: EPOS Corporation -
CCS Firstline

Interface: IBM 3270

First Application: Summer 1989, Grades and
ASKUS Bulletin Board

Weeks TT/VR Is Available Each Term: All

Implementation: 6 months

Student Security Control(s): Social Security # and PIN

Gender of Voice Used: Male

Name of TT/VR System: Telephone Information
Processing System

Acronym: TIPS

Unique Features: ASKUS Bulletin Board,
Registration Appointment Time Inquiry

Primary Contact: T. Luther Gunter

Title: University Registrar

Address: University of South Carolina
Columbia, SC 29208

Telephone: (803) 777-4840

FAX: (803) 777-6349

E-Mail:
IRECO11@UNIVSCVM.CSD.SCAROLINA.EDU

Student Information System Contact:
Steve Graham

Title: Senior Systems Analyst

Address: University of South Carolina
Columbia, SC 29208

Telephone: (803) 777-5211

FAX: (803) 777-4760

E-Mail:
C0244@UNIVSCVM.CSD.SCAROLINA.EDU

Voice Response Contact: Steve Graham
(see Student Information System Contact)

Telecommunications Contact: Mark Bradley

Title: Communications Manager

Address: University of South Carolina
Columbia, SC 29208

Telephone: (803) 777-7474

FAX: (803) 777-4760

UNIVERSITY OF SOUTHERN CALIFORNIA

Address: Los Angeles, California 90089-0911

Author(s) Represented: FRED M. DEAR

Enrollment: 27,620

Funding Source: Independent

Institution Type: Four-year with master's, and doctoral programs

Academic Calendar: Semester

Voice Response Applications: Registration, Verification of Enrollment

Future Goals: Payment of Fees

Current # of Telephone Lines: 32

Host Computer: PRIME

Operating System: PRIMOS

Memory Size: 256 Megabytes

Disk Size: 17 Gigabytes

Database Used: Prime Information

Persons Supporting Student Information System: 25

Student Information System Software: Developed in-house

Voice Response Software: PerceptionTechnology

Voice Response Hardware: Perception Technology

Interface: Developed in-house

First Application (Term/Year/Name): Spring 1988

Weeks TT/VR Is Available Each Term: 16 weeks

Implementation Time: 2 years

Student Security Control(s): Social Security # and Birthdate

Gender of Voice Used: Female

Name of TT/VR System: DIVA

Primary Contact: Fred Dear

Title: Associate Registrar

Address: Registration 104
Los Angeles, CA 90089-0912

Telephone: (213) 740-5306

FAX: (213) 740-8710

Student Information System Contact:
Melvin M. Soriano

Title: Database Administrator

Address: STO-102C UPC
Los Angeles, CA 90089-1144
Telephone: (213) 740-5342

FAX: (213) 740-8431

E-Mail: M.SORIANO@USC.EDU

Voice Response Contact: Massis Isagholliam

Title: Project Manager, Registration

Address: STO-105 UPC
Los Angeles, CA 90089-1144

Telephone: (213) 740-5346

FAX: (213) 740-8431

E-Mail: I.MASSIS@AIS0.USC.EDU

Telecommunications Contact: Mike O'Rear

Title: Director, Operations

Address: STO-105 UPC
Los Angeles, CA 90089-1144

Telephone: (213) 740-5346

FAX: (213) 740-8431

E-Mail: MSO@EEYORE

UNIVERSITY OF WASHINGTON

Address: Seattle, Washington 98195

Author(s) Represented: MELANIE MOORE
BELL (now at Gonzaga University),
EARL W. HAWKEY (now at the University of
Nebraska), W. W. (Tim) Washburn

Enrollment: 34,598 on the main campus; 896 at
two branch campuses

Funding Source: State

Institution Type: Four-year with master's, doctoral,
and professional programs

Academic Calendar: Quarter

Voice Response Applications: Registration, Billing
Inquiry, Grade Inquiry, Student Loan Status,
Financial Aid Status, Current Optional Charge
Selections

Future Goals: Enrollment Verifications, Student
Elections

Current # of Telephone Lines: 64

Host Computer: UNISYS A-16

Operating System: MCP/AS

Memory Size: Real-96 Megabytes, Virtual-192
Megabytes

Disk Size: 70 Gigabytes

Database Used: DMSII

Persons Supporting Student Information System: 9

Student Information System Software: Developed
in-house

Voice Response Software: Perception Technology

Voice Response Hardware: Perception Technology

Interface: Screen-based

Application: Registration Autumn 1988 with regitration
for new students and continuing students who did
not preregister

Weeks TT/VR Is Available Each Term: Continuous

Time It Took to Implement: 6 months from
signing of contract

Student Security Control(s): Institution assigned
student # and date of birth; students then
choose a private access code (PAC) number.

Gender of Voice Used: Male

Name of TT/VR System: Student Telephone
Assisted Registration

Acronym: STAR

Unique Features: Speaks current schedule to
students, checks open/closed status of sections,
gives up to 8 alternate sections when initial
course is not available, gives class location,
allows any format of dateof birth entry (e.g.,
M/D/Y, Y/M/D), collects decisions on student
insurance and optional contributions to student
lobbies, collects where various mailings are to
be sent, checks for math prerequisites before
registration in math courses.

Primary Contact: Van Johnson

Title: Associate Registrar

Address: 209 Schmitz Hall, PD-10
University of Washington
Seattle, WA 981915

Telephone: (206) 685-2553

FAX: (206) 685-3660

E-Mail:
  VJOHNSON@UWAVM.U.Washington.EDU

Student Information System Contact:
  William (Bill) Shirey

Title: Manager, Student Systems

Address: 4545 15th Avenue NE, JE-41
  University of Washington
  Seattle, WA 98195

Telephone: (206) 543-6324

FAX: (206) 543-0831

E-Mail: BSHIREY@CAC.WASHINGTON.EDU

Voice Response Contact: Van Johnson

Telecommunications Contact: Scott Mah

Title: Manager, Telecom Network Services

Address: 3732 University Way NE, HA-60
  University of Washington
  Seattle, WA 98195

Telephone: (206) 543-5411

FAX: (206) 685-3732

E-Mail: SCOTTM@CAC.WASHINGTON.EDU

Notes of interest to readers:

Permission, overload authorization, and exceptions to course priorities/restrictions are accommodated through the use of entry codes (random 5 digit # used once)

UNIVERSITY OF WISCONSIN-MADISON

Address: 750 University Avenue
  Madison, Wisconsin 53706

Author(s) Represented: DONALD J. WERMERS

Enrollment: 43,196

Funding Source: State

Institution Type: Four-year with master's, doctoral, and professional programs

Academic Calendar: Semester

Voice Response Applications: Registration, Collect Degree Expected, Course List including Grades, Financial Aid Application Status and Check Availability, Reservation for Summer Orientation Program

Future Goals: Admission Application Status and Tracking, Expansion of Financial Aid Applications, Housing Application Status and Tracking, ID Card Validation, Student Certifications

Current # of Telephone Lines: 144

Host Computer: IBM 3090 200J

Operating System: MVS ESA

Memory Size: Real-192 Megabytes

Disk Size: 130 Gigabytes

Database Used: IMS, DB2

Persons Supporting Student Information System: Up to 20

Student Information System Software: Developed in-house

Voice Response Software: Perception Technology

Voice Response Hardware: Perception Technology

Interface: Conversational

First Application (Term/Year/Name): Registration piloted in Fall 1988 with graduates and seniors. All registration usage in Fall 1989.

Weeks TT/VR Is Available Each Term: Early registration begins in 11th week of classes. Information and access for that semester is available for 1 year. Students can add and drop courses through the established deadlines and then can access course lists and grades (when available) for the remainder of the year.

Implementation Time: March 1988 to August 1988

Student Security Control(s): Social Security # and PIN

Gender of Voice Used: Female

Name of TT/VR System: Extended Access to Student Information-applies to all student direct access methods via terminals and touch tone telephones.

Acronym: EASI

Unique Features: Checks prerequisites in Math, English, Chemistry and placement scores; speaks current schedule; gives available sections one time through all open sections; collects indication if student plans to graduate; allows special authorizations; has ability to block current registration in specific courses and control registration for major/minor, classification, class level, college of enrollment.

Primary Contact: Donald J. Wermers

Title: Registrar

Address: Room 130 Peterson Building
        750 University Avenue
        Madison, WI 53706

Telephone: (608) 262-3964

FAX: (608) 262-6002

E-Mail:
        DON.WERMERS@MAIL.ADMIN.WISC.EDU

Student Information System Contact:
        Elizabeth Conklin

Title: Management Information Supervisor

Address: 2283 Computer Science and Statistics
        1210 W. Dayton Street
        Madison, WI 53706

Telephone: (608) 263-4866

FAX: (608) 262-4679

E-Mail: elizabeth.conklin@mail.admin.wisc.edu

Voice Response Contact: Ronald C. Niendorf

Title: Special Assistant to the Registrar

Address: 66 Peterson Building
        750 University Avenue
        Madison, WI 53706

Telephone: (608) 262-0130

FAX: (608) 262-6002

E-Mail:
        RON.NIENDORF@MAIL.ADMIN.WISC.EDU

Telecommunications Contact: Dale Beske

Title: Management Information Specialist

Address: 2219 Computer Science and Statistics
        1210 W. Dayton Street
        Madison, WI 53706

Telephone: (608) 263-4006

FAX: (608) 262-4679

E-Mail: dale.beske@mail.admin.wisc.edu

Directory of Vendors

VOICE RESPONSE VENDORS

Applied Voice Technology
11410 NE 122nd Way
P.O. Box 97025
Kirkland, Washington 98083
(206) 820-6000, Ext. 3321
FAX (206) 820-4040
Dave Egan, National Sales Manager

AT&T CONVERSANT
Voice Information Systems
AT&T Suite 150
300 W. Wilson Bridge Rd.
Worthington, OH 43085
(614) 431-7718, FAX (614) 431-7705
Dennis Mahley, Conversant Sales Specialist

EPOS Corporation
391 Industry Drive
P.O. Box 3140
Auburn, AL 36830
(205) 826-7056, FAX (205) 826-7285
Mark P. Lindsey, Sales Manager

IBM
Voice Reponse Contact:
The Robinson Group (TRG)
2411 W. 14th Street
4th Floor
Tempe, AZ 85281-6942
(602) 731-8900, FAX (602)   731-8850
John Robinson, President

InterVoice, Inc.
17811 Waterview Parkway
Dallas, TX 75252
(214) 669-3988, FAX (214) 907-1079

Perception Technology Corporation
40 Shawmut Road
Canton, MA 02021-1490
(617) 821-0320, FAX (617) 828-7886
Wendy Ziner, Director of Marketing

Periphonics Corporation
4000 Veterans Memorial Highway
Bohemia, NY 11716-1024
(516) 467-0500, FAX (516) 737-8520
Karen L. Ferraro, Marketing Manager

Syntellect, Inc.
15810 North 28th Avenue
Phoenix, AZ 85023
(602) 789-2800, FAX (602) 789-2899
Craig Sparkes, Director, Marketing Programs

Systems & Computer Technology Corporation
(SCT)
4 Country View Road
Malvern, PA 19355
(215) 647-5930, in PA (800) 223-7036
Gayle Steinberg, Manager of Communications

SERVICE BUREAU VENDORS

Touch-Talk, Inc.
722 W. 66th Street, #205
Minneapolis, MN 55423
(612) 823-0993, FAX (612) 825-2422
Rick Purifoy, Application Specialist

Voice FX Corporation
Lee Park Office Complex
1100 E. Hector Street
4th Floor
Conshohocken, PA 19428
(215) 941-1000, FAX (215) 941-9844
Charles L. Dowburd, Director,
    Telephone Registration Network

Sponsor Profiles

EPOS Corporation

EPOS is a leading supplier of voice response systems for telephone registration and other applications. Over 100 colleges and universities nationwide and in Canada are currently using FirstLine for all their voice response needs. A few FirstLine institutions are listed below:

Auburn University
Boston University
Clackamas Comm. College
College of DuPage
Comm. Coll. of Philadelphia
Del Mar College
George Washington University
Indiana State University
Middle Tenn. State University
Mississippi State University
Montgomery College
Mount Royal College
Mt. San Antonio Comm. College
Pacific Lutheran University
Seminole Community College
University of Arkansas
University of British Columbia
Univ. of Colorado-Boulder
Univ. of Hartford
Univ. of Houston
Univ. of North Carolina
Univ. of South Carolina
Univ. of Texas-Austin
Univ. of Texas-San Antonio
Univ. of Virginia
Univ. of Wisconsin
Valencia Comm. College
Vancouver Comm. College
Waukesha Tech. College
West Texas State University

and many more...

Perception Technology Corporation

Perception Technology designs, manufactures, markets and supports a family of interactive voice processing and audiotext systems that provides users with direct access to central computer data bases through touch-tone telephones. Perception Technology's voice processing systems typically serve as front-end peripherals to a wide variety of computer systems, providing a cost-effective and highly reliable alternative to traditional methods of data base access such as computer terminals and human operators.

Perception Technology is the leading vendor of voice processing systems in the Higher Education Industry. Each year, over one million students at more than 100 colleges and universities across the nation and in Canada utilize our voice processing systems to register for classes, add to an existing course list, drop previously selected courses, verify their schedules, and much more. Perception systems are also used for grade reporting, financial aid status, loan information, and scheduling of interviews and tours. In fact, voice processing technology can be utilized in virtually every office on campus: admissions, bursars, business, financial aid and housing offices' operations.

The Perception Technology Higher Education User Group was established in 1990 and meets annually in conjunction with the American Association of Collegiate Registrars and Admissions Officers convention. The purpose of the User Group is twofold: to share information and experiences among users and provide Perception with input regarding marketplace requirements. The User Group also publishes a complete directory that is utilized by members as a reference source.

The combination of experience in the marketplace, a unique approach to system design and a continued emphasis on support position Perception Technology as the premier vendor in the marketplace.

Corporate contact:
Wendy Ziner
Director of Marketing
Perception Technology
40 Shawmut Road
Canton, Massachusetts 02021-1490
(617) 821-0320; FAX (617) 828-7886

Periphonics Corporation*

For over twenty years, Periphonics Corporation has been a leading supplier of voice processing systems for interactive voice response and audiotext applications. Today, more than 80 universities in the United States, Canada, and Europe have implemented Periphonics systems to process student registrations using the touch-tone telephone.

Students can now register for classes using the touch-tone telephone when TeleRegistrar is in place at the university. TeleRegistrar, the touchtone student registration system, prompts the student in a digitized human voice to input course selections or deletions on the touch-tone keypad. The system responds by verifying course selections and notifying the student of cancelled courses, schedule conflicts, tuition amounts, and the payment due date. The benefit to students — no more standing in line on registration day.

The same system can accept credit card payments, and report test scores and class grades. If students need additional information or special assistance, the system can refer them to the administrative staff.

Beyond touch-tone registration, the system an handle "voice bulletin board" applications which provide students and faculty access to information 24 hours a day. Such information may include announcements of special events, course schedule changes, job openings, library and club information, instructions for registration, admissions and applications procedures, financial aid or directions for ordering transcripts.

These applications are designed to run on Periphonics' Voice Processing System Series, the VPS. Applications can be developed with natural and effective phrasing of speech. With the VPS, applications and messages can be created by Periphonics' staff, or the school's own data processing group with the easy to use application development tools that are available.

Periphonics has specialized in voice processing systems and stands behind every system installed. The staff of Periphonics provides nationwide service ranging from routine maintenance to 24 hour support on site. Support and service complete the Periphonics product line.

Corporate contact:
Karen L. Ferraro, Marketing Manager
Periphonics Corporation
4000 Veterans Memorial Highway
Bohemia, New York 11716-1024
(516) 467-0500; FAX (516) 737-8520

AACRAO Corporate Member

*N*o more line ups. No more sign ups. Just a simple call up on a touch tone phone. That's all it takes for your students to select and confirm all of their scheduled courses on registration day. And what does it take to offer this time saving convenience? TeleRegistrar. The touch-tone registration system that's working to improve student services and save money on campuses across the country. And as enrollment increases, the system can be easily expanded to include grade reporting, admissions status, tuition payments and more. Give Periphonics a call today. It's a sure way to save your faculty and students from registration frustration.

NO FRUSTRATION REGISTRATION

The First Word in Voice Response.

Periphonics

CORPORATION
4000 Veterans Memorial Highway
Bohemia, New York 11716 • (516) 467-0500
FAX: (516) 737-8520

Syntellect, Inc.*

Syntellect, Inc. provider of the INFOBOT Family of Interactive Voice Response Systems (IVR) was founded in 1984 and is currently the largest vendor of interactive voice response systems in the United States. Syntellect has shipped over 5,000 INFOBOT systems worldwide to 800 customers in the United States and 27 foreign countries.

Colleges are finding out that they must reduce current workload and lines at on-line registration sites, increase enrollment, and decrease overall costs. Syntellect's INFOBOT Interactive Voice Response Systems can help by providing students convenient and efficient touch-tone access to on-line registration and general information 7 days a week, 365 days a year.

Because of the ease of implementation associated with INFOBOT systems, colleges utilize this technology to serve their students better and to reduce the expenses associated with these services.

Colleges that have implemented INFOBOT say the system provides students with a convenient and efficient method of registration, reduces the registration period, decreases the cost of the registration process, ensures the privacy and security of students' records, and improves student services.

INFOBOT easily expands to handle services such as grade reporting, admissions status, voice bulletin boards, housing locator information, pre and co-requisite information, course changes and modifications as well as tuition payments.

To ensure successful installation of the Syntellect INFOBOT Family of Interactive Voice Response Systems, Syntellect offers on-site installation support from our application specialists who train customers to work with the system. The Syntellect Training System makes INFOBOT the easiest in the industry to use. At its headquarters Syntellect runs an ongoing program of training known as INFOBOT U.

Syntellect provides a 24-hour, seven-day-a-week Help Line to respond to customer needs. To create a forum for user recommendations about product and service strategies, Syntellect was the first voice response vendor to support an independent users group. The groups meets annually to discuss industry issues and product applications.

As the needs of the academic community continue to expand, Syntellect will respond by developing applications tailored specifically to the academic market.

Corporate contact:
Craig Sparkes
Director, Marketing Programs
Syntellect, Inc.
15810 North 28th Avenue
Phoenix, AZ 85023
(602) 789-2800; FAX (602) 789-2899

AACRAO Corporate Member

No Lines ... Guaranteed

Few things are as frustrating for students as standing in lines
waiting to register for classes. Automate your registration with
Syntellect's INFOBOT® Interactive Voice Response System.
TouchTone Registration allows students to register for classes over
the telephone, anywhere, anytime.

TouchTone Registration shortens the registration period and
reduces costs for you.

INFOBOT also lets students inquire about grades, obtain financial
aid information, and request transcripts.

Let Syntellect demonstrate to you that our voice response solution
is the easiest to install and to maintain.

The longest line your students should have to wait for is this long...

And that's NO LINE.

To learn more about TouchTone Registration and to hear a
demonstration, call 602-789-2800.

SYNTELLECT INC.®

15810 North 28th Avenue
Phoenix, Arizona 85023
(602) 789-2800
(602) 789-2899 FAX

Systems & Computer Technology Corp.*

Systems & Computer Technology Corp. (SCT) is one of the nation's leading providers of application software, services and information resource management to higher education. With its subsidiaries, SCT has licensed administrative software systems to more than 800 higher education clients worldwide. SCT employs a large talent pool of industry experts. Of its 1,300 employees, 500 are dedicated to the development, implementation, and maintenance of software products.

The bulk of the product development and maintenance activity takes place in SCT's Software & Technology Services (STS) Division. STS maintains a long-term commitment to its products and its clients and takes an aggressive approach in systems development and administrative software systems.

In June 1992, SCT acquired Information Associates (IA) of Rochester, New York, and since then has integrated IA into the STS Division. IA had been a leading supplier of administrative software since 1968, with a full range of administrative software systems.

At the time of the acquisition, SCT also purchased the IA-Plus Series of software products. Through the combined operation of a single division, STS now supports both the IA-Plus product line and the BANNER Series. With these offerings, SCT becomes the supplier of choice in technology, software solutions, and service. Clients may choose among hardware platforms —mainframes, minis, or client/servicer; operating systems and data base management systems. Also innovative client support and maintenance services are available for any and all product choices.

Founded in 1968, SCT is headquartered in Malvern, Pennsylvania, and maintains offices in California, Georgia, Illinois, Indiana, Kentucky, Louisiana, New York, Ohio, South Carolina, Texas, Virginia, and Puerto Rico.

Corporate contact:
Gayle Steinberg
Manager of Communications
Systems & Computer Technology Corporation
4 Country View Road
Malvern, PA 19355
(215) 647-5930 in PA; (800) 223-7036

*AACRAO Corporate Member

Exhibits

The following representative exhibits have been shared by various institutions. Other exhibits appear as figures or tables in the body of the text. Please request more complete documentation or samples developed by other institutions from the authors, or other institutional contacts listed in the author or institution profiles.

A. **Newsletters**
1. Keeping in Touch with Automated Registration, University of Wisconsin - Madison
2. Our Line, The Ohio State University

B. **Request for Proposal**
"Voice Response Bid Document," The Ohio State University

C. **Scenarios**
"STAR Scenario," University of Washington

D. **Final Specifications**
Excerpts from "Telephone Registration System Final Specifications," University of Washington

E. **Scripts**
"Touchtone Registration Dialogue," University of Wisconsin - Madison

F. **Worksheets and Registration Instructions**
1. "Registration Worksheet," The Ohio State University
2. Excerpts (Registration/Academic Calendar, Financial Aid Voice Response System - FAVORS, Registration Procedures, Teleregistration) from Schedule of Classes, University of North Texas

G. **Communication Strategies**
1. Question and Answer Script, University of Southern California
2. U-Dial Video Script, Boston College
3. BRUTUS Video Script, The Ohio State University
4. Skit, University of Washington

Exhibit A.1

Keeping In Touch
With Automated Registration

Office of the Registrar
Instructional Space Office
Administrative Data Processing

University of Wisconsin-Madison   Memo # 1   October 7, 1987

To: Deans, Directors, and Department Chairs
        Designated *Timetable* and Registration Liaisons

From: Rose Barroilhet, Director, Space Management Office
        Jack Duwe, Director, Administrative Data Processing
        Don Wermers, Registrar

This is the first of a series of memos that will help you plan for the implementation of the new Automated Registration System in your school, college, division, or department.

Automated Registration has been considered for years at UW-Madison. As a result of specific consideration of this project in the 1987-89 State Budget Bill, the campus has decided that implementation will proceed on a strict schedule described later in this memo. The schedule permits initial implementation of the most essential features of Automated Registration, with additional features added in future semesters or years. The system involves changes to many current practices for colleges and departments and for the campus-wide support offices.

Our intentions for this series of memos are to communicate important information to all the involved offices and staff as soon as it is available and to respond to questions and concerns of general interest. More detailed information will be referenced here as it becomes available. Issues affecting individual offices will be addressed directly with those offices.

We would like to hear your comments and questions. Representatives of the Study Team on Automated Registration are eager to attend faculty and department meetings, informal brown bag luncheons, and other gatherings to discuss this important project. To arrange a meeting or to learn more about Automated Registration, contact Ron Niendorf at 262-2467.

Automated Registration:
An overview
by Ron Niendorf
Chair, Automated Registration Study Team

The University of Wisconsin-Madison has committed to developing an automated system for student registration. A pilot registration, in which continuing graduate students and seniors will register using the new system, will be run for the fall semester of 1988. That's less than a year away, and there is much to be done between now and then.

Advantages of an online system
The new Automated Registration System will be online, which offers several advantages over the existing system:

- It will be able to check for validity as the student is registering. This eliminates, for example, the possibility of a student registering for an invalid course or section.

- Eventually, departments will be able to monitor the registration process, using up-to-the-minute information, and make adjustments as required.

- Students will be able to directly enter their course requests using touchtone telephones. The new system will allow students to call a phone number and connect to the ADP computer. Students will enter course requests using the touchtone keypad, and the computer will respond with a recorded human voice informing the student of the result of the request.

Some features of the new system
- System Controls The Automated Registration System will provide limited controls for allowing students into courses or sections. Class size will be controlled for all sections, and departments will be able to limit registration based on college, major, classification, and year in school. Controls may be changed during the registration period. For example, departments may choose to set class sizes lower than the·

maximum and then increase them as registration proceeds.

- Authorizations Some courses will require that students be specially authorized to register. The department will be able to enter these authorizations on the Authorization File before or during the registration period. For example, if a student does not meet the controls set for a course but has the consent of the instructor, an entry on the Authorization File will allow the student into the course.

- Call numbers To facilitate the registration process, students will use a five-digit call number to register for a course/section. A single five-digit number will register the student for all sections of a multi-range course, reducing the number of digits the student must enter.

Some effects of the new system

- Expanded registration period The registration period will be expanded to three weeks for the 1988 pilot. The first two weeks will be used for the automated pilot for continuing grads and seniors. During the third week, the remaining students will register using the current manual system. We do not know how many weeks will be needed for registration when the entire student body uses the automated system in 1989.

- Earlier Timetable The fall 1988 pilot will mean an accelerated schedule for *Timetable* production. See Rose Barroilhet's article on the next page for details.

- Advising Since students will not be on campus while they are registering, general advising should be available to students before they leave campus the previous semester. Departments may wish to consider developing procedures to provide registration advising and respond to other student inquiries during the two-week Automated Registration period before regular Registration Week.

Implementation schedule

The new system will be implemented in several stages. The first stage will be a pilot for the fall semester of 1988 including all continuing graduate students and seniors. The pilot is scheduled to begin August 15, 1988 through August 24.

Each succeeding implementation stage will depend on the success of the previous one. The current plan is to allow additional students to use the Automated Registration system until all students are eligible for the fall semester of 1989.

New features and capabilities will be added to the system on an ongoing basis. The 1988 pilot system will have features required to register grads and seniors. More features will be added to accommodate the groups that become eligible to use the system. We anticipate that this tuning process will continue well beyond the scheduled full registration in 1989, as experience reveals new needs.

Teleprocessing access will be important

To take advantage of the features of the system, departments will need teleprocessing access to the ADP mainframe computer. Twice during the semester, teleprocessing access to the ADP mainframe computer will be particularly important. The first period will be when course information is being prepared for the *Timetable*. The second will be during the actual registration process.

Some colleges have terminal or PC networks that enable departments to gain access to the ADP mainframe computer. These networks will be able to use the new transactions for *Timetable* and Registration management, although additional terminals or PCs may be required. Schools and colleges that do not now have such networks in place will need to determine how access will be provided for departments.

In addition to ensuring the availability of hardware for departments, schools and colleges will have to authorize specific individuals in each department for the different terminal transactions. The usual ADP Teleprocessing Network Authorization Form (ADP Form # 172) will be used, with authorization approved by the school or college, the Instructional Space Office (ISO), and the Registrar. A department concerned about terminal access should contact the appropriate dean's office. Schools and colleges may call on their usual ADP contact or Ron Niendorf (2-2467) for necessary advice and assistance.

Progress so far

In October 1985, the Chancellor established two ad hoc committees to assist with the development of an automated student registration system. One committee, chaired by Associate Vice-Chancellor Joe Corry, was concerned with policy issues; the other, chaired by Office of Information Technology Director Tad Pinkerton, focused on technical issues. Later, a steering committee, chaired by Registrar Don Wermers, was set up to coordinate the efforts of the two ad hoc committees and the Study Team on Automated Registration.

In May of 1986, the committees recommended to the Chancellor that UW-Madison establish a process of automated registration based on a touch-tone telephone voice response system. The Chancellor accepted these recommendations in June 1986. The committees remain actively involved in setting the direction of the Automated Registration Project.

2

ADP, the Registrar's Office, and the Space Management Office are now working to acquire the needed voice response equipment, develop the necessary computer programs to handle student requests, and make any needed changes to existing procedures. This work is based largely on a Project Definition paper written last April by the Study Team on Automated Registration and distributed to schools, colleges, and departments.

The paper describes in general terms what the new system will eventually look like. A version of this system, without some of the functions mentioned in the paper, will be used in the August 1988 pilot.

Our schedule has been accelerated since the release of the Project Definition paper, so the features of the Automated Registration System will be implemented in a different sequence than originally planned. If you would like a copy of the Project Definition paper, contact Ron Niendorf, Chair of the Study Team, at 262-2467.

New Timetable schedules and procedures
by Rose Barroilhet
Director, Space Management Office

The fall 1988 pilot of the Automated Registration System will require an earlier *Timetable*, some new procedures to accommodate this compressed schedule, and the collection of additional information necessary to support the registration process.

New Timetable schedule for fall 1988
Since additional information will be requested in support of the fall 1988 pilot, the time allowed to academic departments for initial *Timetable* updates will be extended. According to the preliminary schedule, the Timetable Call will be sent to departments on Monday, April 11, 1988, two weeks earlier than in the past. Initial updates will be due in ISO as follows: (1) Monday, May 9, one week earlier than in the past, for those departments that do not enter their timetable updates online; or (2) Wednesday, May 18, three days later than in the past, for those departments that use online transactions to make their updates. Briefly then, departments will have from one to slightly more than two additional weeks to complete the initial Timetable update process.

In order to meet the earlier *Timetable* publication schedule, final Timetable updates will be due in ISO by Wednesday, July 6 (a week earlier than in the past). The printed *Timetable* will be available no later than Monday, August 8, 1988.

New TP transactions for registration
During the fall 1988 pilot registration period, most departments will want to take advantage of new, automated ways of controlling and monitoring the registration process and making course/section adjustments as appropriate. A combination of ISO/Registrar teleprocessing transactions will provide this inquiry and update capability. Specific transactions and their uses will be described in future memos.

Training is available
Academic departments with current access to the ADP mainframe computer are encouraged to become acquainted with the ISO update transactions recently made available. ISO has begun training sessions for departments that have elected to update online their next *Timetable* and other course/section information. Training sessions have been scheduled for this October. Additional training sessions will be available as needed.

If you did not receive the September 8 memo which described the online update capability now available to academic departments, please contact either Sharon Pero (2-4415) or Nori Roden (2-6956).

Student registration procedures
by Don Wermers
Registrar

Current plans for the procedures needed for the fall 1988 pilot of the Automated Registration System, using touchtone telephones, are outlined below. Because the system must be developed so quickly, development efforts are being limited to those system functions needed to register the pilot group in the fall of 1988. After that, work will begin on features needed to register all students in 1989-90.

Before the registration period
Approximately 12,000 to 15,000 continuing graduate students and continuing seniors are expected to participate in the pilot automated registration in August 1988 for the fall semester. During the preceding spring semester, the pilot students will be notified of their eligibility to register and will be given the option of receiving the necessary materials by mail during the summer. These students will be encouraged to begin preparing for fall registration (by removing holds, obtaining general advising, etc.) before they leave campus for the summer.

Registration materials and a *Timetable* will be distributed to eligible students in early August 1988. The telephone registration period will start two weeks before the standard registration week and will last for nine days. The Automated Registration System will be available up to sixteen hours each day.

3

The registration process

Using a touchtone telephone, students may register at any time between their registration appointment time and the close of the touchtone phase prior to the regular registration week. The system will prevent the registration of students who have academic, financial, or disciplinary holds or those who lack required adviser permission. The system will also be able to control for maximum credit limits to prevent students from registering for more than the allowable number of credits.

The system also will be able to control for course/section size, major, class level, college, and classification. In addition, some courses will require auditions or some other permission before the student is permitted to register. For these courses, departments will use a computer terminal to enter on a file an authorization for students who have received permission. When the student requests the course, the system will verify that the student is authorized before permitting the course registration.

Batch, automated systems in tandem

As the Automated Registration System is gradually implemented, two registration systems will be in operation. For several semesters, students who do not participate in the automated system will register using the existing batch registration system. Also, procedures and forms will be developed to permit students who have participated in automated registration to adjust their schedules during the standard registration week if needed.

Starter class rosters for each course/section will list those students who registered via touchtone. "Blank" class roster forms for courses/sections for which no touchtone registrations were entered will also be provided. Departments will receive these rosters on the Friday before regular registration begins, and assignment committees will be able to use them to complete the regular registration.

Keeping In Touch
With Automated Registration

This series of memos is published by the Study Team on Automated Registration at the University of Wisconsin-Madison. The Study Team includes staff from Administrative Data Processing, the Office of the Registrar, and the Space Management Office.

Keeping In Touch is sent to the following at UW-Madison: members of the Automated Registration Liaison group, academic deans and directors, UW-Madison administration, directors of support units, academic department chairpersons, school/college administrators, heads of academic programs and support units, directors and heads of administrative support units, and department secretaries.

To join the mailing list or to obtain more information about the Automated Registration Project, contact Ron Niendorf, Chair of the Study Team, by phone at 262-2467 or by electronic mail (ron.niendorf@mail.admin.wisc.edu).

A glossary of terms

Some important terms are defined below. If you need more definitions, let us know.

ADP — Administrative Data Processing

Batch processing — process whereby information is submitted to the computer and stored for processing at a later time. Usually used for running lengthy programs and jobs and producing output.

Hardware — the physical equipment that makes up the computer. Includes peripheral equipment such as printers, terminals, and data storage devices.

Input — information given to the computer for processing; the raw material with which the computer does its work. Input may be entered in many forms; for example, through a terminal keyboard, as data from a tape, cartridge, or communications line, or through an optical scanner that reads entries from a paper form.

ISO — Instructional Space Office

Mainframe — a large computer, like ADP's IBM 3081. The term refers in particular to a computer to which other computers can be connected to share the facilities that the mainframe provides (e.g., PCs attach to a mainframe so they can upload and download data and programs).

Online — equipment or process that sends information directly to a computer for immediate processing and immediate results.

Output — information that results from the computer's processing and is delivered to users of the computer in various forms such as paper reports or documents, screen displays, and tapes.

Program — a sequence of instructions that a computer follows to complete a task.

Software — a computer program or set of programs.

SMO — Space Management Office

Teleprocessing (or "TP") — the use of a computer from a terminal connected to it directly or connected through other computers. You can send a "question" and get back an answer, or send new information to be filed or used in the computer.

3270 — thirty-two seventy, or IBM's name for the communication protocol or type of terminal that is used to communicate with the University's administrative computer. Many brands of terminals and PCs can be used to emulate a 3270 terminal.

Transaction — a computer program (usually with a cryptic, four-letter name) that selects and organizes information stored in the computer for a particular user function from a terminal.

4

Exhibit A.2

OUR LINE

Office of the University Registrar
The Ohio State University

Vol. 1   No. 4   Special Issue

B.R.U.T.U.S. PREMIERES

HALF OF OSU STUDENTS TO USE THE NEW METHOD

AGRICULTURE
EDUCATION
GRADUATE SCHOOL
NATURAL RESOURCES
NURSING
UNIVERSITY COLLEGE
AND
AGRICULTURAL TECHNICAL INSTITUTE

Join Arts, Business and Home Economics in using BRUTUS for WI88 Registration!

Ten colleges will be using the new touch-tone/voice response registration during Winter Quarter advanced registration. Students in these units will enter Winter Quarter course selections by using Better Registration Using Touch-tone phones for University Students.

The Students in each of these enrollment units will receive a "new look" registration form called a Registration Work Sheet (see the example inside). Following advisement and completion of the boxes on this Registration Work Sheet, students are ready to enter their WI88 primary course requests and secondary or alternate course requests. For many this is the first time they will be able to give alternate instructions to the Computer Assisted Scheduling routine.

Some students will receive their Work Sheets in the mail, others will pick them up in their college or departmental offices and still others will find them in their student mailboxes. Regardless of the manner of delivery, the Work Sheet should arrive by October 20th.

Each Work Sheet will contain the student's "window" or the time period during which the student is permitted to use a touch-tone phone to call BRUTUS. The opening and closing times are clearly noted next to the phone number. Students who miss their window will find registration unchanged and will suffer from decreased priority for scheduling. Some may continue to have procrastinators sore feet also!

Most students will receive a four digit Personal Access Code either printed on their Work Sheet or directly from their advisors following advisement. This PAC, like a bank automated teller system password, is required to access BRUTUS and prevents unauthorized persons from a student's record.

Complete step-by-step instructions for using BRUTUS can be found in the WI88 Master Schedule of Classes if those on the reverse of the Work Sheet aren't enough.

Students enrolled in colleges not listed above, or attending a Regional Campus, will begin using the new registration system for Spring Quarter 1988 as advanced registration begins in February 1988. For Winter Quarter they will use the traditional registration forms and process.

All students will use the traditional methods of add/drop (Change Tickets) and registration (Walk-thru) after the Winter Quarter '88 advance registration concludes.

Questions or problems related to using BRUTUS should be directed to the Office of the University Registrar at 292-8500.

——— QUESTION BOX ———

Q. Can a secondary (alternate) request be a different section of the same course?

A. No. The Scheduler tries to place the student in other sections that are available. The student must use another course as a secondary request.

Q. Who can we call if we want training sessions on BRUTUS?

A. We will be happy to help you organize training sessions. Call the systems area of the University Registrar at 292-3947.

Q. What time is BRUTUS open?

A. BRUTUS is at work from 8:00 am - 8:00 pm on Monday through Saturday and from 1:00 pm - 8:00 pm on Sundays (except University Holidays).

Q. Are you anticipating a problem with students being unable to get through to BRUTUS (getting a busy signal)?

A. No. One of the ways we are avoiding busy signals is by staggering the appointment times so that not all the students are calling the 64 phone lines at the same time.

Q. How does a student make a change to their mailing address with BRUTUS?

A. When a student accesses their first call, the system will repeat the address we will use to mail their fee statement and schedule. If this is incorrect, the student is switched to the answering machine where they can give the correct address. The following morning, Registrar's personnel take the addresses off the answering machines tapes and correct the system.

REGISTRATION WORK SHEET

SCREEN SCENES

by Carolyn Glover
Systems Training Specialist
Student Systems

The Advisor Review Subsystem, part of the on-line/telephone Advanced Registration System, provides easy access for the advisors to review his/her advisees' course registration. Two screens which are utilized and bridged together to formulate the advisor review procedure are the Advisor Assignment by Major Screen (RAST) (Exhibit A) and the Student Course Request Screen (Exhibit B).

The RAST (from the Advisor Tracking System) organizes and displays advisors by campus. Under each advisor, his/her advisees are listed by the student's major. For each advisee under the column of "RVW" (Review Status), the code "R" indicates that the advisee's course registration is ready for review.

The adviser can scan his/her list of advisees and determine which advisee's schedule to begin the review process with, by entering the line number of the advisee's record being displayed. This initiates the advisor review procedure and brings up the selected advisees' Course Request Screen.

Adjustments to the course requests are permitted by the advisor. It is expected that the advisor will notify the advisees of any adjustments made. Upon completion of each student's schedule review, the next schedule eligible for review will automatically be retrieved and displayed. Once the student's schedule has been reviewed, it will not remain eligible for review during subsequent advisor review process unless the student has made adjustments to his schedule in the meantime.

Detailed documentation on this screen will be available soon to colleges that will be participating in BRUTUS for Winter Quarter 1988.

```
RAST COL/AGR/BAILEY/AU87                    16:09 08/20/87 JLB
                     ADVISER ASSIGNMENT BY MAJOR
BEGIN REVIEW       CAMPUS: COL   COLLEGE: AGR    QT-YR: AU87

ADVISER NAME: BAILEY    M   MAJOR: 020  FTE: 000   LEVEL:    COUNT: 00005

LN RVW    STUDENT NAME          SSN      MAJ  CL STS RK RES EXPECT DEG
01   -  BUCKLEY JANET         288-88-6571  020  C  0   2  R   SP 90 45
02   R  DOE JOHN SCOTT JR     999-99-7756  020  C  0   2  R   SP 88 45
03      FROST ALICIA LOUISE   269-66-6611  020  M  0   1  M   ?? ?? ??
04   Y  JOHNS JILL            777-77-6552  020  O  0   3  R   SU 88 45
05   R  ZOLLINGER ROY         001-02-3333  020  C  0   2  R   AU 90 45




ACTION:    LN NO:    TO    SSN:         TO ADVISER:         INIT:
27                                      DISPLAY COMPLETE - ENTER CHANGES

                         EXHIBIT A
```

```
RAST 999997756/AU87                           14:53 08/19/87 JLB
999 99 7756 DOE JOHN SCOTT JR     DOB 01/16/65   SEX M  HOLD F-- RLSE Y
QTR AU87  STATUS O  RK 2  CMP COL CL C(O)  FEE N  COLL AGR6  MAJ1 020 AGR ECON
SCHEDULE REVIEWED Y      *** STUDENT COURSE REQUESTS ***
           CR HOURS 17   PAC 3186   PRIORITY C   APPOINTMENT TIME 02:45 PM 05/28/87
           MAX HOURS 20   CAS M                  FIRST ACTIVITY 11:30 AM 06/01/87
                                  O    T                                    O
A  DEPARTMT COURSE  CALL   CRP D SECR DAYS   TIME     BLD ROOM   SECOND CRP D
   AGR ECON  489   001815 03    I         ARR
   LAGR ECON 694.04 001980 04   O    T R  0300-0430P AA  032B   003895 01
   ANIML SC  430   007403 05    L    MTWR 0900     A AS  0202
   ANIML SC  430   007424 05    B    F    0800-1000A VM  0126
   COMMUNIC  315   039875 O5P   L    T R  1200     A EL  100B   155900 04
                               RB   M W  0900     A 0B  0229
              *** SECONDARY REQUESTS ***                       PRIMAR
  +AG M&SYS  293   003895 01    I         ARR                  001980 04
   STAT      133   155900 04    L    M W F 0800     A IH  0100  039875 05P
                               R    T    0800     A OL  0713


MLTH INS: EXEMPT N STO Y      SPOUSE N     CHILD N      OFF-QUARTER N
VEHICLE REG: AUTO N   CYCLE N     CONTRIB: SCHOLAR/LOAN Y   STD GOVT Y

27B                                       DISPLAY COMPLETE - ONLY PAGE

                         EXHIBIT B
```

PERMISSION REQUIRED

When a course is listed with a restrictor in the Master Schedule of Classes the new registration system is ready to assist us by enforcing it. All the restrictors, except 10, Permission of Instructor, will require compliance in advance. That is, students cannot enter course requests if they do not meet the requirement(s) without permission entered into the system in advance of their request.

Permission of the Instructor, restrictor code 10, is handled slightly differently. During advanced registration students who request the course and have not yet had permission posted to their record are notified that their request is being accepted subject to receiving permission. If permission is not noted on their request they will not be scheduled for the course.

Administrative units with terminal access and the proper authorization can enter the permissions through online screens by using the class roster or the student course request screen. Which to use will depend on the choice of the operator. Generally, if you were trying to enter several for the same class the roster would serve best as it is the easiest to use.

If terminal access is not available or is inconvenient, a Course Enrollment Permission Form must be completed. This form has been revised slightly to clarify the intent of the authorization. If one is in doubt if the form is needed, we recommend it be completed and the type of permission noted by checking the box or simply writing a note on the form. It should be forwarded to the course's instructional college or the student's enrollment unit for entry. All permission must be entered by November 15th for the Winter Quarter 1988 advanced registration period or students will not be scheduled for permission courses. Forms are available in all departmental offices.

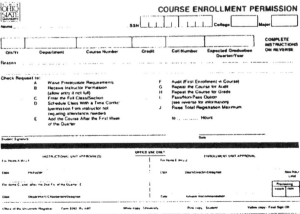

Back to Campus Crossword   By Joe Cool

ACROSS

1 New registration system
6 Type of telephone
11 Course option
12 Pass/ _____
16 _____ Hall
17 Popular UVC Cap Code
19 Affirmative
20 So so grade
21 Student's use this to
   pay fees
22 Place or evaluation
24 Type of annual reg.
25 Bad grade
26 Colts mom
27 to be
29 2nd state to use touch
   tone registration
31 LSU mascot
32 The British princess who
   could use BRUTUS
34 Woman in white (from college
   using BRUTUS Winter Quarter)
36 No old system, but _____
38 Black _____
39 Grade option
40 "R" (requires permission)
42 Play division
45 OSU Marching Band
47 A student's curse, a
   _____ course
49 Physical Facilities
   funds (var.)
50 Game of change (like drop/
   add at time)
52 The Golden _____
53 Campus "sweat shop"
56 Test
57 Type of credit
59 Home of the Reg.
61 Honey _____
62 Clubhouse
63 Advisor's responsibility

DOWN

1 "Dapper Dan" in hat and suit
2 Freshman
3 Matt Frantz's asset
4 _____ Sam
5 Worm
6 See 6 across
7 Campus bldg.
8 Greek hero (he'd love BRUTUS)
9 See 20 across

10 Rds
13 Inflexible
14 University governing body
15 Type of pre-enrollment
   report or state
18 Prof's org.
22 Red _____
23 Big or hand
28 Former president
30 Second string
33 The have and have _____
34 BRUTUS or football
35 Time div.
37 Former Journalism professor
   or Marine general

41 Big Ten school or sick
43 Your author
44 Dir.
46 Spring _____
47 Drop/add slip (no longer
   needed after Spring Quarter)
48 Peers
51 Great state
52 Type of degree
54 Over (abbr)
55 Plural of Reus
57 Chem bldg.
58 Who benefits most from
   BRUTUS?
60 Prof's asst.

Office of the University Registrar
320 Lincoln Tower
1800 Cannon Dr.
Columbus, Ohio 43210-1230

Return Requested

If you would like to add, update or
delete your name and address from our
mailing list, or add the name of someone
you think should be receiving OUR LINE,
indicate below and return this page to
the above address.

_____ Please add name and address at right to your
            mailing list.

_____ Please remove my name from your mailing list.

_____ Please update my name/address as shown at right.

Editor .... Chris Richte

Associate Editors .... Jack Damron
                    ....Jim Noe
                    ....Gene Schuster
                    ....Paul Simmons

Circulation .... Kathy Pond

Exhibit B

OHIO STATE UNIVERSITY
VOICE RESPONSE BID DOCUMENT
JANUARY 1986

General Bid Instructions

Respond to each section of the Request for Purchase (RFP) document in specific and detailed language. In referencing your system documentation or the RFP document, give specific page or section references.

Submit three (3) copies of the proposal and associated material. The Ohio State University (OSU) will not be liable for any costs associated with the preparation or transmittal of any proposal or materials submitted in response to this RFP. All responses and documentation become the property of OSU.

Summarize the detailed purchase costs into a separate section in the proposal. The response must include prices for the software, hardware, manuals, maintenance, installation, training and consultation. All quoted purchase prices for the software and hardware are to be on a furnish and install basis at Kinnear Road Center, 1121 Kinnear Road, Columbus, Ohio 43212-1153. Quotations included in your proposal must be valid for at least 120 days.

Include copies of all contracts, agreements, etc. as may apply under the terms of your proposal. Complete warranty information of the software and hardware must be included with your proposal.

Include as a part of the response a complete list of deliverables. This list should include: (i) all software and hardware to operate the system as described in Section II; (ii) a complete set of documentation; (iii) a description of the amount of consultation or assistance you will provide; (iv) a description of the type and amount of training you will provide to The Ohio State University personnel to operate the software and hardware.

If a proposal is accepted, the award will be made by the Purchasing Department in accordance with the laws of the State of Ohio.

OSU reserves the right to reject any or all bids. OSU reserves the right to exercise sole judgement in any decisions resulting from this RFP.

Questions regarding the data processing content of this RFP should be directed to Charlie Rice, Project Manager, University Systems (614-422-3687); questions regarding the bid and response protocol should be made to Sandi Algeo, Purchasing Department (614-422-7592).

OHIO STATE UNIVERSITY
VOICE RESPONSE BID DOCUMENT
JANUARY 1986

I   Objectives

The Ohio State University is interested in acquiring a computing system to assist student registration by using Touch-Tone (Registered Trade mark of AT&T) telephones, for tone input and/or voice recognition. The student would enter a new transaction by tone input and/or voice recognition in order to register and process adds or drops for classes. The student's requests would be processed against the Student Data Base, Course Data Base and the Class Roster Data Base, which resides on our Amdahl computer, then the necessary information would be returned to your System which would emulate as a terminal for input and display.

The anticipated connection mode would be for the device to emulate a remote IBM 3274 controller operating in Bisync mode. Connection to the mainframe would be via a bisync port on the communicating controllers. The device must operate with both Memorex 1270 and Amdahl 4705 controllers. An alternate configuration would allow the device to be connected to an actual IBM 3274 controller via a Type A coaxial cable connection. Other configurations such as emulating a channel attached (local) 3274 controller are acceptable but must be demonstrated as being operational as these pose a larger potential risk to our system's stability.

The system must support The Ohio State University's registration of up to 80,000 students per quarter (which occurs 4 times each year), with a daily transaction rate of 62,920 (based on 5,720 students per day with each student entering 11 transactions, where a transaction is defined as an entry followed by a # sign.

The system must be capable of:

a) Operating several telephone lines simultaneously over a minimum number of host interfaces.

b) If speech generation techniques are used, the device must store a total vocabulary of 5000 words and 500 phases. We estimate this to represent about 5-15 hours of total recording time.

c) Providing the voice response with no degradation in voice response, throughput, or response time.

d) Having a direct attachment for the telephone line to a standard USOC single line (RJ11C) or multi-line telephone jack.

e) Controlling call referral without sacrificing functionality on any phone line attached to the system.

f) Unlimited phrase length (i.e., a single item reference from the host can cause a phrase as long as the system limits on voice memory to be played out on a line).

g) Establishing and maintaining consistent communication with The Ohio State University's Amdahl V7 and V8, operating with a MVS/SP Operating System.

OHIO STATE UNIVERSITY
VOICE RESPONSE BID DOCUMENT
JANUARY 1986

h) Interfacing on the mainframe computer must emulate a IBM 3270 (as noted above) to the Customer Information Control System (CICS version 1.6.1) (BTAM and VTAM).

i) Being delivered, installed and accepted within 90 days after the acceptance of the Agreement.

j) The device must be capable of speaking simultaneously to all phone lines. We estimate this will require that the device must store 500-1000 seconds of speech in memory.

k) The device must accept a command from CICS that will lock-out further entries until an unlock command is sent. This would work similar to the keyboard lock of the IBM 3278.

The evaluation of the system will be based on our determination of how well your proposed system meets the needs described above. Your response to the following questions will help us evaluate the applicability of your proposal. Therefore, you should specifically address these questions in the order and format indicated in your bid document as well as provide other information you believe is appropriate.

II   Questions

GENERAL:

1. What is the software base and the expansion capabilities?

2. What is the hardware base and the expansion capabilities?

3. Does your computer system have the capability to store the students request offline when the host computer is not available?

   If YES, how many student request records can be recorded offline, and how does the subsequent processing work?

4. Describe what statistical information is provided (transaction count, transaction count per line, line activity, etc.), and it can it be accessed during the operation of the system?

5. Describe the Systems that you have successfully installed, give contact person and telephone number.

6. Do you have a demonstratable system that can actually register students for courses. If your system has been successfully installed, tested, and implemented in an on-line college registration system supply references from at least two colleges or universities (and more if you have them). Also, describe these installations as to size of data bases and number of students. References to installations which interface with CICS on the mainframe computer will be helpful.

OHIO STATE UNIVERSITY
VOICE RESPONSE BID DOCUMENT
JANUARY 1986

7. How many copies of this product have been installed? Of those installed, how many run under CICS?

TELEPHONE:

1. Over how many telephone lines will the system be capable of speaking the same or different text simultaneously without degradation of voice quality on any line?

2. Can phone lines be added, and what is the incremental unit?

3. What is the maximum number of phone lines the system can support?

4. Does your system have the capability of controlling call referral without sacrificing functionality on any phone line attached to the system?

5. What are the telephone line requirements?

6. Can your system identify faulty telephone lines and will it inform us which telephone lines are causing problems?

DOCUMENTATION

1. What documentation comes with the package?

2. Are documentation updates available, and are they sent out on a regular basis or upon request?

3. Will we be given access to the software source code?

VOCABULARY

1. Can the vocabulary be expanded and on an incremental cost basis?

2. What are the system's capabilities in regard to vocabulary storage?

3. Can we record, digitize, and install our own speech? Describe the process as to how this is done.

4. What is the turn-around time for recording and speech digitizing services?

5. Is the vocabulary memory-based? If YES, how many seconds can be stored in memory?

6. Describe the process of how the vocabulary is updated. How is the new vocabulary installed? Describe the software changes required on the host computer when there are changes made to the vocabulary on your system.

OHIO STATE UNIVERSITY
VOICE RESPONSE BID DOCUMENT
JANUARY 1986

PRODUCT

1. What are the environmental requirements?

2. What are the power supply requirements?

3. Is the system capable of automatic recovery after its own crash, and how is it perceived by the callers?

4. Is your system capable of detecting that the host computer is down, and how is it perceived by the callers? How does your system recognize when the host is back up again?

5. How long does a recovery take for your system? What process and manual intervention is required?

6. What, if any, host computer software do you provide?

7. What is the minimum amount of host memory required to run your system?

8. Is memory incrementing necessary when adding additional users or phone lines to the system?

9. Describe the timeout capability of your system.

10. Give a description of the communications interface with the host computer.

11. What Baud rates are supported by your system?

12. Give a description of the data format transmitted from the host computer in order to generate speech.

CICS

1. Describe how the software on your system interfaces with CICS.

2. What features must the CICS system have to run your system?

3. What type of CICS system table modifications are necessary to support your system with respect to:
    1) PCT
    2) FCT
    3) PPT
    4) PDIR
    5) DDIR
    6) DCT
    7) other system tables

4. Can your system run in an Multiple Region Operation (MRO) environment?

OHIO STATE UNIVERSITY
VOICE RESPONSE BID DOCUMENT
JANUARY 1986

5. Does your system have its own on-line recovery and backout processing capability?

6. What versions of CICS are compatible with your system?

7. Do you maintain upward compatibility with respect to new versions of CICS once these versions are made available by IBM?

8. What programming language/level are required to support your system?

9. Are there any specific features which your system requires or utilizes in a CICS environment?

10. Describe how your system initiates CICS transactions.

FILES

1. What kind of files does this system use/support (i.e. IMS, VSAM, ISAM, BDAM, other) on the mainframe?

2. Is any disk space required on the host computer?

3. Do you require any special maintenance for the files required to support your system with respect to:
    1) tuning
    2) recovery
    3) backup & restoration

4. If speech is stored on disk, how is it backed up and how often?

SOFTWARE AND HARDWARE RELEASES

1. What enhancements are coming for your software and hardware?

2. What is the date of the last release and the projected date of the next release for your software and hardware?

3. What ongoing help is available for problem determination and resolving problems with the software and hardware? State name and telephone number of the nearest qualified support vendor.

4. How are the fixes distributed?

5. Are fixes released on a regular basis, upon request, or both?

6. If fixes are released on a regular basis, how often?

7. For what period of time do you support back releases of your software and hardware once new versions/releases are available?

OHIO STATE UNIVERSITY
VOICE RESPONSE BID DOCUMENT
JANUARY 1986

8. How is notice given when you suspend support of back releases for your software and hardware?

9. Is support available 24 hours a day, and if not what are the hours for support/consultation? State name and telephone number of the nearest qualified support vendor.

10. How do you handle minor and serious failures under a maintenance contract?

11. How do you handle minor and serious failures under a time and materials contract?

12. What is the average turnaround time for problem resolution with or without a maintenance contract?

13. How are the software files backed up and how often?

14. Will it be necessary for us to do programming on the voice response computer. If YES, describe the languages and procedures.

INSTALLATION

1. What assistance will be given to installing this system?

2. How long does it normally take to install your system?

3. Will you provide CICS programs for testing the system and the CICS inferface in order to demonstrate that it meets the specifications, and performs the functions as defined in the Agreement.

TRAINING

1. What type of training is provided and at what price?

2. Are self-teaching materials available and at what price?

3. What training do you recommend that customers acquire?

III   Financial Information

As part of the proposal, supply financial information sufficient to show that your company is financially sound and able to supply on-going maintenance and other services which will be agreed upon in contractual agreements.

Summarize detailed purchase costs into a separate section in the proposal. Specify the optional payment terms, e.g., cash, lease, lease with option to buy, etc. Your response must include prices for the software, hardware, manuals, maintenance, training and consultation. All quoted prices are to be on a furnish and installed basis at The Ohio State University Kinnear Road Center, 1121 Kinnear Road, Columbus, Ohio 43212-1153.

OHIO STATE UNIVERSITY
VOICE RESPONSE BID DOCUMENT
JANUARY 1986

The Ohio State University is an agency of the State of Ohio and is, therefore, tax exempt and will not pay for any taxes associated with this contract, software, or hardware.

All billings and payments for the use of the software, hardware, and any miscellaneous charges will be made based on the contract to be created between The Ohio State University and the successful bidder. No subcontractor billings are to be received by The Ohio State University; nor will they be paid by The Ohio State University.

You may reduce the charges proposed in your response to this RFP at any time.

COST INFORMATION

1. What is the cost of recording and speech digitizing services and the cost of making changes?

2. What is the cost of storing digitized vocabulary in both volatile and non-volatile high speed memory?

3. Specify the purchase price of the system.

4. What educational discounts apply?

5. What maintenance fees apply?

6. Itemize the prices so we may choose feature by feature.

7. Is there a short term agreement available (i.e., rental), so that we may determine the functionality of the system in our environment without substantial investment?

OHIO STATE UNIVERSITY
VOICE RESPONSE BID DOCUMENT
JANUARY 1986

IV   Legal and Contractual

Instructions

All of the questions in this section (IV) must be answered in full for the proposal to be considered by The Ohio State University. General answers such as "Yes, see form agreement," are unacceptable.

All technical and operation specifications, equipment descriptions, and marketing materials submitted or made in connection with this RFP may be incorporated into, and made a part of the Agreement. This situation should be considered when formulating responses to this section and in preparing a proposal and any marketing presentation.

If you believe that any question in this section is unclear or is reasonably susceptible to more than one interpretation, indicate the ambiguity or uncertainty, in the applicable response. If your response is conditioned in any way, the response must include a full explanation of the condition(s).

Questions - Legal and Contractual

Software/Hardware and Software/Hardware Schedule

1. a.   The hardware, software, source code and documentation are warranted to be original works, free of any third party claims whether based on proprietary rights, tort, patent, copyright, contract or trade secret law.

   b.   The software and hardware package is warranted to be free of any lien, encumbrance, or security interest of any third parties.

   c.   The software and hardware shall be fit for the purposes as stated in the objectives and shall be delivered in a condition conforming to the reliability standards stipulated in Exhibit A. THE VENDOR shall cure all programming and hardware defects free of charge for a period of twelve (12) months after final acceptance.

   d.   THE VENDOR shall use its best efforts to cure defects in a timely fashion during the warranty period. If a material system failure lasts longer than seven (7) days, during the warranty period, THE UNIVERSITY may, at its discretion, employ alternative means to conduct its business, and THE VENDOR shall pay the cost of such alternative means.

   e.   The software shall contain no pre-programmed termination routines, and hardware "locks" or "turnkey" devices shall not be used.

   f.   THE VENDOR shall not subcontract its obligations without the prior written consent of THE UNIVERSITY, which consent THE UNIVERSITY shall be under no obligation to provide.

2. Can the software or hardware configuration be changed after the Agreement is executed but before the system is (i) shipped; (ii) installed; or (iii) accepted? Explain, including any penalties.

OHIO STATE UNIVERSITY
VOICE RESPONSE BID DOCUMENT
JANUARY 1986

Transfer of Title

1. Will you warrant that you have good title to the software and hardware, free and clear of all liens, and that you have the legal authority to transfer all unencumbered title to the software and hardware to The Ohio State University pursuant to the Agreement? Explain.

2. When will title to each item of software and hardware pass to The Ohio State University? Explain the relationship between contractual provisions relating to passage of title to provisions relating to insurance, risk of loss, payment dates, and acceptance. (NOTE: The Ohio State University generally requires that all of these provisions be consistent and that all relate to the passage of title at acceptance.)

3. Will you require that The Ohio State University grant you a security interest in the software or hardware? Explain. (NOTE: The Ohio State University generally requires that the expenses of any such interest be borne by the Vendor and that the Vendor promptly file a timely release at Vendor's expense.)

Terms of Payment

1. Payments schedule is as follows:
   25% due after order is placed.
   25% due upon delivery.
   25% due thirty (30) days after system acceptance.
   25% due thirty (30) days after system is operational.

2. Will you include a "most favored nation" provision in the Agreement, warranting that the total price being paid by The Ohio State University is at least as favorable to The Ohio State University as the price paid by any other user during a specified period of time? Explain, indicating the acceptable time period.

3. How will disputed billings be handled? Explain. (NOTE: The Ohio State University does not agree to pay any late charges or interest penalties.)

4. If the price of any item of software, hardware, or services decreases between the date the Agreement is executed and the date the software is accepted, will the price paid by The Ohio State University be decreased? Explain.

Delivery

1. Will the Agreement include a binding delivery schedule consistent with The Ohio State University's delivery requirements? Explain, including any conditions. (NOTE: The Ohio State University usually does not contract for the purchase of services of software or hardware unless a binding delivery schedule is included in the Agreement.)

OHIO STATE UNIVERSITY
VOICE RESPONSE BID DOCUMENT
JANUARY 1986

2. Specify the method of shipment, delivery, and installation. Explain, indicating the party or parties responsible for performing and/or paying for each step involved. If The Ohio State University is required to pay for any portion of the shipment, delivery, packing, unpacking, installation or similar expenses, will the Agreement place any dollar limit on these costs or The Ohio State University's possible exposure in connection with such costs? Explain.

3. Will the Agreement specify that no item of software, hardware, or service will be deemed to be delivered (or installed) unless and until all items listed in the Agreement have been delivered (or installed)? Explain.

4. Will the Agreement permit The Ohio State University to alter the shipment, delivery, or installation dates? Explain, including any related consequences.

5. The software and hardware is to be delivered, installed and accepted by 1 June 1986.

Installation

1. a. The Bidder shall provide a PERT or suitable chart giving a calendar listing of the proposed software and hardware installation events beginning with receipt of order through installation (when the system is ready for the University's acceptance evaluation to begin).

   b. The Bidder shall explicitly list all of the items that will have to be done by the University in order for successful completion of the project. Any overtime and/or holiday work for installation shall be minimized.

   c. A Bidder "Hotline" shall be available during installation hours. The Bidder shall assure it is staffed with personnel of expertise in the fields involved with the software and hardware installation.

   d. The Bidder will show the University that all software and hardware has been installed and is fully operational. Installation testing is not synonymous with acceptance testing.

2. Will you verify that the software and hardware has been successfully installed by performing an installation test? The results of any installation test should be provided to The Ohio State University. These results must show to The Ohio State University's satisfaction that all software and hardware has been successfully installed and is fully operational. Installation testing is not synonymous with Acceptance testing (see below).

3. If you agree to provide an installation test, specify in detail the installation criteria and tests to be used for: (i) each major software module, (ii) all hardware equipment, and (iii) the system as a whole including all items of software and hardware. Indicate the duration of all tests, the criteria to be applied (including any applicable performance percentage), and the provisions to be made for re-running the tests and correcting deficient performance. Explain.

OHIO STATE UNIVERSITY
VOICE RESPONSE BID DOCUMENT
JANUARY 1986

4. Will the Agreement specify that no item of software and hardware will be deemed to be installed unless and until all items of software and hardware listed in the Agreement have been installed? Explain.

Acceptance

1. The Bidder shall provide all features of the RFP and expand upon the Bidder's features of Installation, item 1. The Bidder shall provide a listing of items constituting a working software and hardware package. This listing along with items considered in the best interests of the Product Manager will be evaluated for acceptance after the acceptance performed within sixty (60) days after Bidder's notification of the software and hardware being installed and operating correctly. After the University's Project Manager contacts all University entities involved in the software and hardware output and they agree the installed software and hardware is performing as desired, the written acceptance will proceed as in the agreement to (i) software and hardware meets the specifications and performs the functions as defined in the Agreement; (ii) facilities usage and run times are reasonable as defined by University Systems; (iii) the documentation supplied is acceptable; (iv) a test of each individual program by Bidder and the University to determine that each program meets the user requirements; (v) a test is to be conducted by Bidder and the University to determine that each program links to the total system; (vi) live data is used at the final stage to insure that the system can handle basic activity.

2. Will the Agreement specify that no item of software or hardware will be deemed to be accepted unless and until all items of software and hardware listed in the Agreement have been accepted?

3. Will the Agreement specify that the terms of the Agreement shall not commence until formal acceptance is made by The Ohio State University?

4. Specify the provisions to be made in the Agreement for correcting deficient performance.

Insurance and Risk of Loss

1. Indicate which parties will be responsible for obtaining and/or payment for each item of software and hardware between the date of the Agreement and the date or dates accepted and paid for in full by The Ohio State University. Explain, (i) the coverage required or to be provided; (ii) any restrictions or limitations on required or available coverage; and (iii) whether the insurance companies providing coverage must be approved by The Ohio State University or by you.

OHIO STATE UNIVERSITY
VOICE RESPONSE BID DOCUMENT
JANUARY 1986

2. Specify how the Agreement will cover a casualty or other loss or damage to the software and hardware. Explain, including (i) the allocation of insurance proceeds; (ii) the party or parties responsible for any deficiencies or gaps in coverage; (iii) how and to what extent the Agreement (including applicable delivery and acceptance schedules) will be or can be modified, terminated, extended, or continued after loss, damage or other casualty.

3. Provide The Ohio State University with (i) "business termination" insurance; (ii) a performance bond; or (iii) a guarantee of performance by a parent, subsidiary, affiliated or other company or individual in connection with your obligation pursuant to the Agreement.

Default and Damages

1. Specify the conditions or events that will be deemed to be a "default" under the Agreement (i) by you; and (ii) by The Ohio State University.

2. Notice of a "default;" and an opportunity to remedy the "default" must be provided for in the Agreement.

3. Specify all remedies and damages to be provided in the Agreement: (i) in the event of a default by you; and (ii) in the event of a default by The Ohio State University. Explain, including any applicable references to specific performance and actual, consequential, punitive, and liquidated damages.

4. Specify the extent to which the Agreement will limit any remedies or damages: (i) in the event of a default by you; and (ii) in the event of a default by The Ohio State University. Explain, including any applicable references to force majeure or "act of God" provisions, limitations on warranties, and limitations of liability. (NOTE: The Ohio State University generally expects to have appropriate legal recourse in the event of non-performance or inadequate performance by a Vendor.)

Patents

1. Specify the extent to which you will warrant that the software and hardware does not infringe any patent or other ownership right binding in the United States. Explain, including (i) whether you will defend any and all infringement claims and suits at your expense; (ii) The Ohio State University's recourse and damages in the event you or The Ohio State University loses any such suits or contest; (iii) any restrictions of limitations.

Warranties

1. To the extent not otherwise explained above, indicate all warranties to be provided directly or indirectly to The Ohio State University in the Agreement. Explain, including any exceptions and conditions.

OHIO STATE UNIVERSITY
VOICE RESPONSE BID DOCUMENT
JANUARY 1986

2. To the extent not otherwise explained above, indicate all limitations and restrictions imposed by the Agreement on warranties that might otherwise be provided to The Ohio State University in connection with the proposed transaction.

3. Explain the interrelationship between the coverages provided by (i) warranties to be provided you; and (ii) maintenance to be provided by a maintenance agreement. Explain, including whether and why a maintenance agreement is required during all or any part of a warranty period.

Assignment, Use, and Resale

1. Will the Agreement or any related maintenance agreement include any restrictions or assignment of the Agreement (i) by The Ohio State University, and (ii) by you? Explain.

2. Will the Agreement or any related maintenance agreement include any restrictions on the unconditional use by The Ohio State University of the software, hardware and service? Explain, including any applicable reference to restrictions on use, lease and resale.

3. Will the Agreement or any related maintenance agreement include any restrictions upon moving all or part of the software or hardware; or upon using the software at more than one location or computing system? Explain.

4. Will the Agreement or any related maintenance agreement include any restrictions on who can use or operate the software or hardware? Explain.

5. Will the Agreement or any applicable maintenance agreement specify that The Ohio State University may make copies of any and all documentation to the extent required for The Ohio State University's internal use of the software or hardware?

6. Indicate all provisions related to The Ohio State University's right to modify the software programs especially such provisions pertaining to warranties and continuing support.

7. Will the Agreement or any related agreement impose any continuing, additional, or subsequent charge, expense, or liability to (i) a software license or similar permit, (ii) software and hardware maintenance or support, (iii) assignment of software and hardware? Explain.

Termination

1. Under what circumstances, if any, can the Agreement be terminated by The Ohio State University or by you? Explain, including any penalties.

OHIO STATE UNIVERSITY
VOICE RESPONSE BID DOCUMENT
JANUARY 1986

Agreement Coverage

1. Will the Agreement include any provision limiting or excluding any oral or written representations you make in response to or in connection with this RFP? Explain.

2. Explain the extent to which the Agreement will specifically incorporate by reference oral or written representations, technical and operating specifications, descriptions, and marketing materials submitted or made in response to or in connection with this RFP.

3. Do you propose to cover any portion or aspect of the proposed transaction outside of the formal Agreement or any related maintenance agreement, letter of understanding, branch-level commitment or oral promise? Explain. (NOTE: The Ohio State University generally refuses to contract for equipment or services unless all aspects of the transaction are embodied in a binding written agreement).

4. Specify the language proposed to be used in the Agreement to cover your commitments to provide conversion, programming, and systems support services. (NOTE: The Ohio State University generally expects the Agreement to include firm, binding obligations rather than nebulous "best efforts" and "advice and assistance" provisions.)

Execution Authority and Legal Assistance

1. Specify by name and title the individual or individuals within your organization that presently have legal corporate authority to execute the Agreement and any related agreements (including any amendments) on your behalf.

OHIO STATE UNIVERSITY
VOICE RESPONSE BID DOCUMENT
JANUARY 1986

Indemnification

The Vendor shall indemnify and save and hold harmless The Ohio State University, its Board of Trustees, and its officers, agents and employees from and against any and all loss, liability, damage, cost and expenses, including but not limited to reasonable attorney fees, for injury, death, loss or damage of whatever nature to any person, property, or any other claim, by the Vendor, or its officers, employees, agents, customers, licensees, invitees, or any other person, firm or corporation resulting from the performance of the terms and conditions of this Agreement. In the event that any action or proceeding is instituted against The Ohio State University by reason of any such claim or event, the Vendor shall resist and defend such action or proceeding at their sole cost and expense or cause it to be resisted or defended by an insurer.

Security and Confidentiality

Personnel, working to complete the successful implementation of your system, must agree to and sign the "Code of Responsibility for Security and Confidentiality of Data Files" see Exhibit B.

The Ohio State University may bring legal action against the vendor and/or the individual(s) who violate this agreement, and the individual(s) will be prohibited from the premises of The Ohio State University.

OHIO STATE UNIVERSITY
VOICE RESPONSE BID DOCUMENT
JANUARY 1986

EXHIBIT "A"
DETAIL OF PERFORMANCE TESTS

I. The performance test(s) shall be conducted upon THE UNIVERSITY'S hardware stipulated in the RFP.

II. The performance test(s) shall be conducted using THE UNIVERSITY database stipulated in the RFP.

III. The program shall successfully complete the following criteria:

The Bidder shall state a detailed description of the proposed software and hardware tests, including procedures to be used, functions to be tested and most importantly objectively measurable criteria to determine whether the test succeeded or failed. Use additional sheets if required.

_____

_____

_____

_____

EXHIBIT B

OSU Communication

Subject   Code of Responsibility for Security and
Confidentiality of Data Files

University Systems (2-3687)

Date   May 17, 1984

From   J. Carroll Notestine

To   University Systems Staff

Our business at University Systems is to help other departments utilize EDP technology in their course of business affairs. Because we must necessarily have the user's documents, files, and reports to perform the EDP function we have an extraordinary responsibility to act in their best interest. Additionally, it behooves us to help our users understand what measures are appropriate for the safety, security, and integrity of their data.

Please read the attached statement and sign the bottom portion of this page.

Ohio Revised Code, section 102.03(B):

"No present or former public official or employee shall disclose or use, without appropriate authorization, any information acquired by him in the course of his official duties which is confidential because of statutory provisions, or which has been clearly designated to him as confidential when such confidential designation is warranted because of the status of the proceedings or the circumstances under which the information was received and preserving its confidentiality is necessary to the proper conduct of government business."

Violation of this statute is punishable by up to six months in jail, up to a $1000 fine, or both.

- -

I have read, understand, and will comply with the University Systems Code of Responsibility for Security and Confidentiality of Data Files and the Ohio Revised Code, section 102.03(B).

_____   _____
(Signature)   (Date)

See reverse side for addressing
The Ohio State University

The Ohio State University

University Systems

1121 Kinnear Road
Columbus, Ohio 43212-9998

Phone 614-422-3687

CODE OF RESPONSIBILITY FOR SECURITY AND CONFIDENTIALITY OF DATA FILES

Security and confidentiality is a matter for concern of all University Systems employees and of all other persons who have access to our facilities whether they be vendors, users, or others. University Systems is a repository of information in computerized data files for The Ohio State University. Each person working at University Systems holds a position of trust relative to this information and must recognize the responsibilities entrusted to them and to University Systems in preserving the security and confidentiality of this information. Their conduct either on or off the job may threaten the security and confidentiality of this information. Therefore, a University Systems employee or a person authorized access to University Systems:

is not to make or permit unauthorized use of any information in files maintained, stored, or processed by University Systems,

is not to seek personal benefit or permit others to benefit personally by any confidential information which has come to them by virtue of their work assignment,

is not to exhibit or divulge the contents of any record or report to any person except in the conduct of their work assignment and in accordance with University Systems policies,

is not to knowingly include or cause to be included in any record or report a false, inaccurate, or misleading entry,

is not to remove any office record (or copy) or report from the office where it is kept except in the performance of their duties,

is not to operate or request others to operate any University equipment for purely personal business,

is to immediately report any violation of this code to their supervisor,

is not to aid, abet, or act in conspiracy with another to violate any part of this code.

For University Systems employees, violation of this code may lead to a reprimand, suspension, or dismissal, consistent with the general personnel policies of the University.

For others, violation of this code will result in denial of access to University Systems facilities and reporting the violation to the offender's office.

Exhibit C. Excerpts from STAR SCENARIOS, University of Washington (Revised June 8, 1988)

The scenarios describe how STAR will inform and/or prompt students in various situations.

COMPUTER MAINFRAME VERIFICATION

SCENARIO 1: A STUDENT IS REGISTERING, AND THE COMPUTER GOES DOWN WHILE HE/SHE IS ON THE TELEPHONE LINE -
  STAR: "The system has become inoperable. Please call back later to complete your registration."

SCENARIO 2: STUDENTS CALLING INTO THE SYSTEM WHEN THE COMPUTER IS DOWN -
  STAR: "The telephone registration system is temporarily unavailable. Please call back later to complete your registration."

INTRODUCTION/AVAILABILITY VERIFICATION

SCENARIO 3: IF SYSTEM IS AVAILABLE AND REGISTRATION IS TAKING PLACE -
  STAR: "Welcome to the University of Washington Telephone Registration System. Enter the registration quarter now."

SCENARIO 4: IF TELEPHONE REGISTRATION IS NOT TAKING PLACE -
  STAR: "Telephone registration has ended. To register or make course changes, you must go to Sections Office, Schmitz Hall, Room 264.

SCENARIO 5: STUDENT ENTERS THE QUARTER CODE (1-WINTER, 2-SPRING, 3-SUMMER-, 4-AUTUMN)
  STAR: "The quarter code entered is invalid. Review the instructions on the worksheet and re-enter a quarter code now."

SCENARIO 6: STUDENT ENTERS AN INVALID QUARTER CODE FOR THE SECOND TIME -
  STAR: "The quarter code entered is invalid. For assistance, please call the Registration Office at 543-6970, 543-6970. Thank you for calling the University of Washington." (Telephone is disconnected.)

SCENARIO 7: TELEPHONE REGISTRATION FOR THAT QUARTER HAS NOT STARTED -
  STAR: "Please review the dates for registration in the Time Schedule and call back on the appropriate date. Thank you for calling the University of Washington." (Telephone is disconnected.)

ELIGIBILITY VERIFICATION

SCENARIO 8: STUDENT IS PROMPTED TO ENTER STUDENT ID NUMBER -
  STAR: "Enter your 7 digit student number now."

SCENARIO 9: STUDENT ENTERS LESS THAN 7 DIGITS -
  STAR: "You have not entered a 7 digit student number. Enter your 7 digit student number now."

SCENARIO 10: STUDENT ENTERS LESS THAN 7 DIGITS FOR SECOND TIME -
  STAR: "You have not entered a 7 digit student number. For assistance, please call the Registration Office at 543-6970, 543-6970." (Telephone is disconnected.)

SCENARIO 11: STUDENT IS PROMPTED TO ENTER BIRTH DATE -
  STAR: "Enter the month, day, and year of your birth as 6 digits, followed by the number sign key."

SCENARIO 12: STUDENT ENTERS INVALID BIRTH DATE -
  STAR: "Your birth date is invalid. Please make sure you are entering it in the correct format. Enter the month, day, and year of your birth as 6 digits, followed by the number sign key."
SCENARIO 13: STUDENT ENTERS INVALID BIRTH DATE FOR A SECOND TIME -

STAR: "Your birth date is invalid. For assistance, please call the Registration Office at 543-6970, 543-6870." Thank your for calling the University of Washington." (Telephone is disconnected.)

SCENARIO 14: STUDENT ENTERS VALID BIRTH DATE -
STAR: "Please wait while your transaction is processed."

SCENARIO 15: IF STUDENT HAS REGISTRATION HOLDS -
STAR: "You have a hold on your record which prevents you from registering. To remove the hold you must go to Suzzalo Library, Cashier's Office, Plaza Level (or other appropriate location where holds are placed). Thank you for calling the University of Washington." (Telephone is disconnected.)

SCENARIO 16: IF STUDENT IS ADMITTED FOR A FUTURE QUARTER -
STAR: "You are not eligible to register for this quarter. For assistance, please call the Registration Office at 543-6970, 543-6870. Thank you for calling the University of Washington." (Telephone is disconnected.)

SCENARIO 17: IF STUDENT NEEDS TO REAPPLY FOR READMISSION
STAR: "You must apply for readmission before you register for this quarter. For assistance, please call the Registration Office at 543-6970, 543-6970. Thank you for calling the University of Washington." (Telephone is disconnected.)

SCENARIO 18: IF A NEW STUDENT CALLS BEFORE THEIR ADVISING APPOINTMENT -
STAR: "You cannot register before your advising and appointment day. If you need assistance, please call the Registration Office at 543-6970, 543-6970. Thank you for calling the University of Washington." (Telephone is disconnected.)

SCENARIO 19: IF THE STUDENT CALLS IN BEFORE HIS OR HER REGISTRATION PERIOD -
STAR: "Your registration period has not started. Please review the dates for registration in the Time Schedule and call back on the appropriate date. Thank you for calling the University of Washington." (Telephone is disconnected.)

INFORMATION REQUIRED ONLY WITH INITIAL REGISTRATION EACH QUARTER

SCENARIO 20: STUDENT ENTERS INVALID TYPE OF INSURANCE -
STAR: "Your entry is not valid. Please enter the appropriate Student Health Insurance option now."

SCENARIO 21: INTERNATIONAL STUDENT SELECTED OPTION 0 (no insurance) -
STAR: "International students are required to carry insurance. If you have questions or believe you have other qualifying insurance, go to the International Services Office, Schmitz Hall, Room 459."

SCENARIO 22: STUDENT RECEIVES TYPE OF INSURANCE SELECTED -
STAR: "You have selected student annual insurance." (one of 9 options)

SCENARIO 23: STUDENT IS ASKED TO MAKE ASUW SELECTION -
STAR: "Do you want to be a member of the Associated Students of the University of Washington? This will not affect your tuition bill. Press Y if you want to be a member or N if you don't want to be a member."

SCENARIO 24: STUDENT INDICATES WHETHER TO SEND THE REGISTRATION CONFIRMATION/ID TO THE LOCAL OR PERMANENT ADDRESS -
STAR: "Do you want your registration confirmation/ID card sent to your local address or your permanent address? Press L for local or P for permanent."

SCENARIO 25: STUDENT INDICATES WHETHER TO SEND BILLING STATEMENT TO THE LOCAL OR PERMANENT ADDRESS -
STAR: "Do you want your billing statement sent to your local address, or your permanent address?

Press L for local or P for permanent."

SCENARIO 26: STUDENT INDICATES WHETHER TO SEND QUARTERLY GRADE REPORT TO THE LOCAL OR PERMANENT ADDRESS -
STAR: "Do you want your quarterly grade report sent to your local address, or your permanent address? Press L for local, or P for permanent."

SCENARIO 27: STUDENT IS READY TO REGISTER -
STAR: "Enter your transaction followed by the number sign key."

SCENARIO 28: IF REGISTRATION TRANSACTION IS INVALID -
STAR: "Your entry is not valid. Please review the instructions and enter your transaction followed by the pound key."

SCENARIO 29: IF REGISTRATION TRANSACTION IS INVALID FOR THE SECOND TIME -
STAR: "Your entry is not valid. For assistance, please call the Sections Office, 543-5927, 543-5927. Thank you for calling the University of Washington." (Telephone is disconnected.)

SCENARIO 30: IF ADD TRANSACTION IS VALID -
STAR: SLN....<department> <course number> <section> added for <# of credits> credits, meeting on <days> at <times> in <building> <room>. Your total credits are <# of total credits registered for>.

SCENARIO 31: REMINDER TO ADD LAB, QUIZ, OR CONFERENCE SECTION WHEN REGISTERING FOR A LECTURE -
STAR: "Remember to add the lab, quiz, or conference section for this course or this lecture will be dropped from your schedule."

SCENARIO 32: COURSE IS CLOSED AND NO ALTERNATES ARE AVAILABLE -
STAR: "The section you requested is closed, and no alternate sections of the course are open."

SCENARIO 33: COURSE IS CLOSED AND ALTERNATES ARE AVAILABLE -
STAR: "The section you requested is closed; however, the following sections are open: SLN<>, Section <>, meeting on <day> and <day>, from <time> to <time>. SLN<>, Section <>, meeting on <day> and <day>, from <time> to <time>. Enter your transaction followed by the number sign key."

SCENARIO 34: COURSE HAS BEEN WITHDRAWN BY THE UNIVERSITY AND NO OTHER SECTIONS ARE OPEN -
STAR: "The section you requested has been cancelled, and no alternate sections of the course are open."

SCENARIO 35: COURSE HAS BEEN WITHDRAWN BY THE UNIVERSITY AND ALTERNATES ARE AVAILABLE -
STAR: "The section you requested has been cancelled; however, the following sections are open: (followed by SLN, section, meeting days and times)."

SCENARIO 36: IF STUDENT DOES NOT MEET COURSE PRIORITY REQUIREMENTS -
STAR: "You are not presently eligible to register for that course. Refer to the Time Schedule for course restrictions."

SCENARIO 37: IF STUDENT HAS NOT MET THE MATH PLACEMENT REQUIREMENT -
STAR: "You are not eligible to take that course because you do not have the placement requirement. For information on what you can do, go in person, to Central Advising, B-10 Padelford Hall. Again, go in person to Central Advising, in B-10 Padelford Hall."

SCENARIO 38: IF THE STUDENT WILL GO OVER THE MAXIMUM CREDITS IF COURSE WERE ADDED -
STAR: "The course you requested will take you over the maximum credits allowed for registration

at this time."

SCENARIO 39: IF THE STUDENT NEEDS TO ADD A LINKED LECTURE BEFORE THIS LAB/QUIZ -
STAR: "You must add the lecture section of this course before you can add this section."

SCENARIO 40: IF THE MEETING TIME OF THIS COURSE CONFLICTS WITH ANOTHER COURSE ON THE STUDENT'S SCHEDULE -
STAR: "The section you requested cannot be added because it meets at the same time as another course on your schedule. To add a time conflict section, you must go to Sections, Schmitz Hall, Room 264."

SCENARIO 41: IF THE STUDENT IS ALREADY REGISTERED FOR THIS COURSE AND IT IS NOT A DUPLICATABLE COURSE -
STAR: "The section you requested cannot be added because you are already registered for that course."

SCENARIO 42: IF THE STUDENT SUPPLIES A VALID ENTRY CODE BUT THE COURSE HAS BEEN OVERENROLLED BY THE DEPARTMENT -
STAR: "The section you requested is closed. For assistance, contact the academic department that issued the entry code."

SCENARIO 43: IF THE STUDENT DOES NOT INDICATE VARIABLE CREDIT -
STAR: "The course you requested has variable credit (of <minimum>or<maximum>) between (<minimum> and <maximum>). Enter the credits now followed by the number sign key; otherwise press the number sign key to cancel this request."

SCENARIO 44: IF STUDENT INDICATES INVALID NUMBER OF VARIABLE CREDITS -
STAR: "You have requested an incorrect number of credits. Enter the credits now followed by the number sign key. Otherwise press the number sign key to cancel this request."

SCENARIO 45: IF STUDENT INDICATES INVALID NUMBER OF VARIABLE CREDITS FOR A SECOND TIME -
STAR: "You have requested an incorrect number of credits. For assistance, please call the Sections Office at 543-5927, 543-5927."

SCENARIO 46: IF COURSE REQUIRES ENTRY CODE -
STAR: "This class requires departmental permission to add. If you have permission,, enter the entry code now; otherwise, press the number sign key to cancel this request."

SCENARIO 47: IF ENTRY CODE IS INVALID -
STAR: "Your entry is not valid. If you have permission, enter the entry code now. Otherwise press the number sign key to cancel this request."

SCENARIO 48: IF STUDENT DROPS A COURSE -
STAR: "SLN <nnnn>, <department>, <course number>, <section>, has been dropped from your schedule. Your total credits are <total number of credits>."

SCENARIO 49: IF STUDENT ISN'T REGISTERED FOR THE COURSE -
STAR: "SLN <nnnn> is not on your schedule."

SCENARIO 50: IF COURSE DROPPED IS STUDENT'S ONLY ACTIVE COURSE -
STAR: "If you want to drop all of your courses you must enter the university withdrawal transaction code. However, if your are correcting your schedule, you should add another course, and then drop this section."

SCENARIO 51: IF STUDENT MUST FIRST DROP LAB, QUIZ, OR CONFERENCE SECTION -
STAR: "You must drop the lab, quiz, and conference sections before you can drop this lecture section."

SCENARIO 52: IF THE COURSE CANNOT BE DROPPED BY TELEPHONE BECAUSE THE STUDENT IS TAKING IT MULTIPLE TIMES -
 STAR: "To drop this course in which you are enrolled multiple times, you must go to Sections Office, Schmitz Hall, Room 264."

SCENARIO 53: SECTION STATUS INQUIRY -
 STAR: "SLN <nnnn>, <dept>, <course>, <section> is open." or "Check the Time Schedule for course restrictions." or "SLN <nnnn>, <dept>, <course>, <section> is closed. However, the following sections are open...." or "Requires departmental permission to add." or "Has been cancelled." or "SLN <nnnn> does not exist."

SCENARIO 54: LIST CURRENT SCHEDULE -
 STAR: "Your current schedule for <quarter> is SLN <nnnn>, <dept>, <course>, <section>, for <credits>, meeting on <days> at <times> in <building> and <room>. Your total credits are <total number of credits>."

SCENARIO 55: WITHDRAWAL FROM THE UNIVERSITY IF QUARTER HAS NOT STARTED -
 STAR: "You have requested to withdraw completely from the University of Washington for <quarter>. All of your courses will be dropped. You must apply for readmission as a returning student before you register for a future quarter. If you still want to withdraw, press Y and your withdrawal will be processed, otherwise, press N to cancel your withdrawal."

SCENARIO 568:WITHDRAWAL FROM THE UNIVERSITY IF QUARTER HAS STARTED -
 STAR: "You have requested to withdraw completely from the University of Washington for <quarter>. All of your courses will be dropped. For continuing registration eligibility information, call the Registration Office, 543-6970, 543-6970. If you still want to withdraw, press Y. Press N to cancel your withdrawal."

SCENARIO 57: IF STUDENT TRIES TO COMPLETELY WITHDRAW BUT IS NOT REGISTERED -
 STAR: "You are not enrolled as a student this quarter so your withdrawal cannot be processed.

SCENARIO 58: TO TERMINATE CALL AND EXIT STAR PRIOR TO MAILING OF REGISTRATION CONFIRMATION/ID CARD -
 STAR: "Your Registration Confirmation Schedule and ID Card will be mailed to your <local or permanent> address. Thank you for calling the University of Washington."

SCENARIO 59: TO TERMINATE CALL AND EXIT STAR AFTER INITIAL MAILING OF REGISTRATION CONFIRMATION/ID CARD -
 STAR: "You may pick up your ID card and registration confirmation after 10 a.m. on the next working day at the Registration Office, second floor Schmitz Hall."
 or
 STAR: "You may pick up your ID card and registration confirmation after 10 a.m. in two working days at the Registration Office, second floor Schmitz Hall."

SCENARIO 60: ON UPDATED REGISTRATION ACTIVITY -
 STAR: "An updated registration confirmation schedule will be mailed to your <address>."

Exhibit D. Excerpts from Final Specifications, University of Washington

Editor's Note: Four sections — Scenario, Flowchart, Script, and Screens — comprise the final specifications for the University of Washington (February 26, 1988). The Scenario includes general specifications, user parameter table, mainframe verification, introduction/availability verification, eligibility verification, initial registration, enter transaction, add course, drop course, section status inquiry, list current schedule, withdrawal, and terminate call sections. Screens include processor to mainframe screen, and mainframe to processor screen.

The following excerpts are reproduced in this guide: general specifications, user parameter table, mainframe verification, introduction/availability verification, eligibility verification, and initial registration. The first two pages of the flowchart covering the transactions *up to* initial registration are included.

GENERAL SPECIFICATIONS

The scenario described on the following pages and diagrammed in the flowchart is to be performed simultaneously for all active telephone lines. The paragraph numbers in the scenario refer to page and box numbers on the flowchart. Paragraph numbers beginning with "P" refer to functions of the telephone registration system software; paragraphs beginning with "T" refer to actions of the person at a telephone; paragraphs beginning with "M" refer to functions of ADP's mainframe system.

Each telephone processor will have 32 logical stations connected to ADP. Logical stations will be dynamically assigned to telephone lines when transactions are sent to ADP.

ADP will use Group Polling to determine if any of the logical stations have anything to send ADP.

Entry of * # by the student should result in the telephone processor discarding any partial touchtone input and repeating the entire previous message.

Telephone entry syntax description: In the [University of Washington] scenario the following conventions are used in the definition of the syntax of the telephone entries:

- Capital letters and * and # keys define the exact key to be pressed.

- Small letters refer to a variable field being entered. The text will state whether the field is a fixed length or variable length.

- Items surrounded by [brackets] are optional.

For example, if the syntax is defined as

A s s s s [* v v] [* p p p p p] #

and "v v" is defined as one or two digits and "p p p p p" is defined as fixed five digits, the following are all valid entries:

        2 1 2 3 4 * 1 #
        2 1 2 3 4 #
        2 1 2 3 4 * 2 3 4 5 6 #
        2 1 2 3 4 * 0 4 * 2 3 4 5 6 #

USER PARAMETER TABLE

A parameter table or file can be easily updated by the Registrar's Office as needs dictate to control the system.

Contents: Winter quarter registration status
              Spring quarter registration status
              Summer quarter registration status
              Autumn quarter registration status

      Each field can have one of the following values:
          0 = registration not yet started for this quarter
          1 = telephone registration available for this quarter
          2 = registration in Schmitz Hall available but not by telephone
          3 = registration completed for this quarter

Initial student-entry timeout periods (0 to 999) (a period is 5 seconds)
Final student-entry timeout periods (0 to 999)

Mainframe response timeout periods (0 to 999)
Mainframe verification interval periods (0 to 99)

Maximum length of phone call (Periods) (0 to 999)

Withdrawal transaction allowed indicator (Y or N)

MAINFRAME VERIFICATION

If any transaction has been sent to the mainframe and no response has been received within a table-specified period *(mainframe response timeout periods)*, the system should tell all active phone lines that the transaction cannot be completed and should hang up all telephone lines.

    Message M89:
        The Star system has become inoperable.

        followed by message M96:
        Please call back later to complete your registration.

    Processor hangs up all telephone lines.

Any subsequent callers should be given a message that the system is temporarily unavailable.

    Message M92:
        The telephone registration system is temporarily unavailable.

        followed by message M96:
        Please call back later to complete your registration.

    Processor hangs up the telephone.

The system should send a mainframe verification transaction (action code 00) to the mainframe at system startup and then at a table-specified interval *(mainframe verification interval periods)* to verify that the mainframe and the registration application are operating. If a correctly formatted response screen is returned, the mainframe is operating and student calls should be processed normally. If no response is received or the response does not match the specifications, the mainframe is not available.

INTRODUCTION/AVAILABILITY VERIFICATION

P1.1   Welcome message

Processor answers telephone line and gives initial greeting. However, if the user parameter table indicates that no telephone registration is taking place, or if the system has determined that the mainframe is not operating, different messages will be spoken.

If the system is available and registration is taking place, message M1:
Welcome to the University of Washington Telephone Registration System. Enter the registration quarter code now.

Processing continues with T1.1.

If telephone registration is not taking place, message M6:
Telephone Registration has ended. To register or make course changes, you must go to the Sections Office, Schmitz Hall, Room 264.

Processor hangs up telephone.

If the mainframe is not operating, message M92:
The telephone registration system is temporarily unavailable.

followed by message M96:
Please call back later to complete your registration.

Processor hangs up telephone.

T1.1   Student response

Student enters quarter code.

Entry format: q

where q is the quarter desired: 1 = Winter
2 = Spring
3 = Summer
4 = Autumn

P1.2   Edit quarter code

Student's entry is edited against the rules above.

If the entry is correct, processing continues with P1.5.
If incorrect or missing (time out error) and this is the first try, processing continues with P1.3.
If incorrect or missing (time out error) and this is the second try, processing continues with P1.4.

P1.3   Initial quarter error response

Message M2:
The quarter code entered is invalid.

followed by message M3:
Review the instructions on the worksheet and re-enter a quarter code now.

Processing continues with T1.1.

P1.4   Second quarter error response

Message M2:
The quarter code entered is invalid.

followed by message M4:
For assistance, please call the Registration Office at 543-6970, 543-6970.

followed by message M5:
Thank you for calling the University of Washington.

Processor hangs up telephone.

P1.5   Validate registration availability

Parameter table of registration quarters is checked to see if registration is available now for the requested quarter.

If registration is available, processing continues with P1.7.
If registration is not available, processing continues with P1.6.

P1.6   Tell student that registration is not available

Message to speak depends on the reason registration is not available.

If registration now in Schmitz Hall only, message M6:
Telephone Registration has ended. To register or make course changes, you must go to the Sections Office, Schmitz Hall, Room 264.

followed by Message M5:
Thank you for calling the University of Washington.

Processor hangs up telephone.

If before registration has started, message M7:
Telephone registration for that quarter has not started.

followed by message M8:
Please review the dates for registration in the Time Schedule and call back on the appropriate date.

followed by message M5:
Thank you for calling the University of Washington.

Processor hangs up telephone.

ELIGIBILITY VERIFICATION

P1.7   Ask student to enter Student ID

Message M9:
Enter your 7-digit Student Number now.

T1.2   Student enters Student ID

Entry format: 9 9 9 9 9 9 9

where 9 9 9 9 9 9 9 is the student's 7-digit ID; no leading zeros

P1.8   Edit Student ID

Student's entry is edited against the rules above.

If correct, processing continues with P2.1.
If incorrect or missing/partial (timeout error) and this is the first try, continues with P1.9.
If incorrect or missing/partial (timeout error) and this is the second try, continues with P1.10.

P1.9   Initial Student ID error response

Message M10:
You have not entered a 7-digit Student Number.

followed by message M9:
Enter your 7-digit Student Number now.

Processing continues with T1.2.

P1.10   Second Student ID error response

Message M10:
You have not entered a 7-digit Student Number.

followed by message M4:
For assistance, please call the Registration office at 543-6970 543-6970.

followed by message M5:
Thank you for calling the University of Washington.

Processor hangs up telephone.

P2.1   Ask student to enter birth date

Message M11:
Enter the month, day, and year of your birth as four digits, followed by the pound key.

T2.1   Student Response: birth date

Entry format: n n n n n n #

where   n n n n n n   is the student's birth date; ideally in MMDDYY format, but the only
                        edit requirement is that at least four digits must be entered.
        #   signals end of entry.

P2.2   Edit birthdate

Student's entry is edited against the rule above. If a timeout error occurs and the entry was
four, five, or six characters long, treat it as a valid entry. Other timeouts should be treated
as errors.

If correct, processing continues with P2.5.
If incorrect the first time, processing continues with P2.3.
If incorrect the second time, processing continues with P2.4.

P2.3   Initial birthdate error response

Message M14:
        Your birth date is invalid.

        followed by message M15:
        Please make sure you are entering it in the correct format and

        followed by message M11:
        Enter the month, day, and year of your birth as six digits, followed by the pound
        key.

        Processing continues with T2.1.

P2.4   Second birthdate error response

Message M14:
        Your birth date is invalid.

        followed by message M4:
        For assistance, please call the Registration Office at 543-6970.

        followed by message M5:
        Thank you for calling the University of Washington.

        Processor hangs up telephone.

P2.5   Ship eligibility transaction to mainframe

Message M19:
        Please wait while your transaction is processed.

        Assemble Quarter, Student ID, and Birthdate into a logical screen and send it to the
        mainframe. (*Transaction type 01.*)

M2.1   Validate eligibility
Mainframe verifies that Student ID and birthdate are valid, and that the student is eligible to register at this time. Mainframe's response includes indicator showing if this is the initial registration for this student and also includes current value of insurance selection.

P2.6   Determine response and branch accordingly

Telephone processor checks response code and branches to appropriate routine to continue or speak error message.

Mainframe error responses:

(1) Not eligible to register: processing continues with P2.7.
(2) Invalid ID: processing continues with P2.8 if first time or P2.9 if second time.
(3) Invalid birth date: processing continues with P2.10 if first time or P2.11 if second time.

If no error occurs, processing continues with P3.1.

P2.7   Not eligible to register

Telephone processor will speak back message text string provided by mainframe explaining reason for ineligibility. Examples of possible responses:

If the student has registration holds, message M17:
        You have a hold on your record which prevents you from registering. To remove the hold you must go to

        followed by one or more of messages M201 through M212:
        Suzzallo Library cashier's office, plaza level.
        the Student Accounts Office, Schmitz Hall, Room 129.
        etc.

        followed by message M5:
        Thank you for calling the University of Washington.

        Processor hangs up the telephone.

If the student is admitted for a future quarter, message M16:
        You are not eligible to register for this quarter.

        followed by message M4:
        For assistance please call the Registration Office at 543-6970, 543-6970.

        followed by message M5:
        Thank you for calling the University of Washington.

        Processor hangs up the telephone.

If the student needs to apply for readmission, message M25:
        You must apply for readmission before you register for this quarter.

        followed by message M4:
        For assistance, please call the Registration Office at 543-6970, 543-6970.

followed by message M5:
Thank you for calling the University of Washington.

Processor hangs up the telephone.

If a new student calls before his/her advising appointment, message M18:
You cannot register before your advising and registration appointment day.

followed by message M4:
For assistance, please call the Registration Office at 543-6970, 543-6970.

followed by message M5:
Thank you for calling the University of Washington.

Processor hangs up the telephone.

If the student calls in before his/her registration period, message M26:
Your registration period has not started.

followed by message M8:
Please review the dates for registration in the Time Schedule and call back on the appropriate date.

followed by message M5:
Thank you for calling the University of Washington.

Processor hangs up the telephone.

P2.8   Initial invalid ID error response

Message M12:
Your Student Number is invalid.

followed by message M13:
Please recheck the number and

followed by message M9:
Enter your 7-digit Student Number now.

Processing continues with T1.2.

P2.9   Second invalid ID error response

Message M12:
Your Student Number is invalid.

followed by message M4:
For assistance, please call the Registration Office at 543-6970, 543-6970.

followed by message M5:
Thank you for calling the University of Washington.

Processor hangs up the telephone.

P2.10 Initial invalid birth date error response

> Message M14:
>> Your birth date is invalid.
>
>> followed by message M15:
>> Please make sure you are entering it in the correct format and
>
>> followed by message M11:
>> Enter the month, day, and year of your birth as six digits, followed by the pound key.
>
> ***Processing continues with T2.1.***

P2.11 Second invalid birth date error response

> Message M14:
>> Your birth date is invalid.
>
>> followed by message M4:
>> For assistance, please call the Registration Office at 543-6970, 543-6970.
>
>> followed by message M5:
>> Thank you for calling the University of Washington.
>
> ***Processor hangs up the telephone.***

INITIAL REGISTRATION

P3.1   Determine if this is initial registration

Response screen from mainframe will include indication that this is student's first registration session. In that case an extended script must be executed.

If this is the first session, processing continues with P3.2.
If this is not the first session, processing continues with P6.1.

P3.2   Determine if student should make insurance selection

Response screen from mainframe will include current insurance selection. If one is present, do not need to ask student to make selection.

If insurance is present, processing continues with P3.7.
If insurance is not present, processing continues with P3.3.

P3.3   Ask student to make insurance selection

> Message M27:
>> Please enter the appropriate Student Health Insurance option code.

T3.1   Student response: insurance selection

Student enters type of insurance desired.

Entry format:　n

where　　n　is the type of insurance desired:
0 = no insurance
1 = student quarterly
2 = student/spouse quarterly
3 = student/spouse/child quarterly
4 = student/child quarterly
5 = student annual
6 = student/spouse annual
7 = student/spouse/child annual
8 = student/child annual

P3.4　Edit insurance selection

Student's entry is edited against rules above. If student makes no entry (timeout error) 1 should be assumed. If mainframe screen shows that student is foreign, 0 response is not permitted.

If the entry is correct, processing continues with P3.7.
If the entry is incorrect the first time, processing continues with P3.5.
If the entry is incorrect the second time, processing continues with P3.6.

P3.5　Initial insurance error response

Error message depends on edit which has failed.

If bad selection made (key 9), message M38:
Your entry is not valid.

followed by message M27:
Please enter the appropriate Student Health Insurance option code.

Processing continues with T3.1.

If foreign student selected key 0, message M39:
Foreign students are required to carry insurance. If you have questions or believe you have other qualifying insurance, go to the International Services Office, Schmitz Hall, Room 459.

followed by message M27:
Please enter the appropriate Student Health Insurance option code.

Processing continues with T3.1.

P3.6　Second insurance error response

Assign the student insurance type 1.

Processing continues with P3.7.

P3.7　Confirm Insurance/See if ASUW selection required

Confirm type of insurance selection made. Message M28:
> You have selected

followed by the message that corresponds to the type of insurance selected:

Selection	Message	Text
0	M37	No insurance
1	M29	Student quarterly insurance
2	M30	Student and spouse quarterly insurance
3	M31	Student, spouse, children quarterly insurance
4	M32	Student and children quarterly insurance
5	M33	Student annual insurance
6	M34	Student and spouse annual insurance
7	M35	Student, spouse, and children annual insurance
8	M36	Student and children annual insurance

If mainframe indicates ASUW is true, processing continues with P4.2.
Otherwise processing continues with P4.1.

P4.1   Ask student to make ASUW selection

Message M40:
> Do you want to be a member of the Associated Students of the University of Washington? This will not affect your tuition bill. Press Y if you want to be a member or N if you don't want to be a member.

T4.1   Student response: ASUW selection

Student indicates whether or not ASUW membership is desired.

Entry format: Y or N

where   Y   indicates that they want to join ASUW.
         N   indicates that they do not want to join ASUW.

P4.2   Process ASUW

If student presses Y, set ASUW indicator in mainframe update transaction to Y. If the student does not enter anything (timeout error) or presses something other than Y, set the indicator to N.

P4.3   Ask student to make WSL selection

Message M45:
> Do you want to support the Washington Student Lobby by contributing one dollar which will be added to your tuition bill? Press Y if you want to contribute, or N if you do not want to contribute.

T4.2   Student Response: WSL

Student indicates whether or not he/she wants to be billed for WSL.

Entry format: Y or N

where   Y   indicates he/she wants to be billed for WSL.

N indicates he/she does not want to be billed.

P4.4   Process WSL: ask student to make WashPIRG selection

If student presses Y, set WSL indicator in mainframe update transaction to Y. If student makes no entry (timeout error) or enters something other than Y, set the indicator to N.

Message M43:
> Do you want to support the Washington Public Interest Research Group by contributing two dollars which will be added to your tuition bill? Press Y if you want to contribute, or N if you do not want to contribute.

T4.3   Student Response: WashPIRG

Student indicates whether or not he/she wants to be billed for WashPIRG.

Entry format: Y or N

where Y indicates he/she wants to be billed for WashPIRG.
       N indicates he/she does not want to be billed.

P5.1   Process WashPIRG: ask student to make schedule address selection

If student presses Y, set WashPIRG indicator in mainframe update transaction to Y. If student enters nothing (timeout error) or enters something other than Y, set the indicator to N.

Message M47:
> Do you want your registration confirmation and ID card sent to your local address or your permanent address?

> followed by message M48:
> Press L for local or P for permanent.

T5.1   Student Response: Schedule address usage

Student indicates whether to send the schedule confirmation to the local or permanent address.

Entry format: L or P

where L selects local address
       P selects permanent address

P5.2   Process schedule address: solicit bills address selection

If student presses L, set schedule address to L. If student presses P, set schedule address to P. If student does not select anything (timeout error) or enters something other than L or P, set schedule address to space.

Message M51:
> Do you want your billing statement sent to your local address, or your permanent address?

followed by message M48:
Press L for local or P for permanent.

T5.2   Student Response: Billing address usage

Student indicates whether to send the billing statement to the local or permanent address.

Entry format: L   or   P

where   L   selects local address
        P   selects permanent address

P5.3   Process billing address: solicit grade report address selection

If student presses L, set billing address to L. If student presses P, set billing address to P.
If student does not select anything (timeout error) or enters something other than L or P,
set billing address to space.

Message M50:
        Do you want your quarterly grade report sent to your local address, or your
        permanent address?

        followed by M48:
        Press L for local or P for permanent.

T5.3   Student Response: Grade report address usage

Student indicates whether to send the grade report to the local or permanent address.

Entry format: L   or   P

where   L   selects local address
        P   selects permanent address

P5.4   Process grades address: ship initial registration transaction to mainframe

If student presses L, set grades address to L. If student presses P, set grades address to P.
If student does not select anything (timeout error) or enters something other than L or P,
set grades address to space.

Message M19:
        Please wait while your transaction is processed.

*Assemble quarter, Student ID, birthdate, insurance selection, ASUW, address usage
selections, WASHPIRG, and Student Lobby selection into a logical screen and send it to
the mainframe. (Transaction type 06.)*

M5.1   Process initial registration update

Mainframe will update insurance, ASUW, address usage, WashPIRG, and Student Lobby.

Processing continues with P6.1.

SCENARIO FLOWCHART

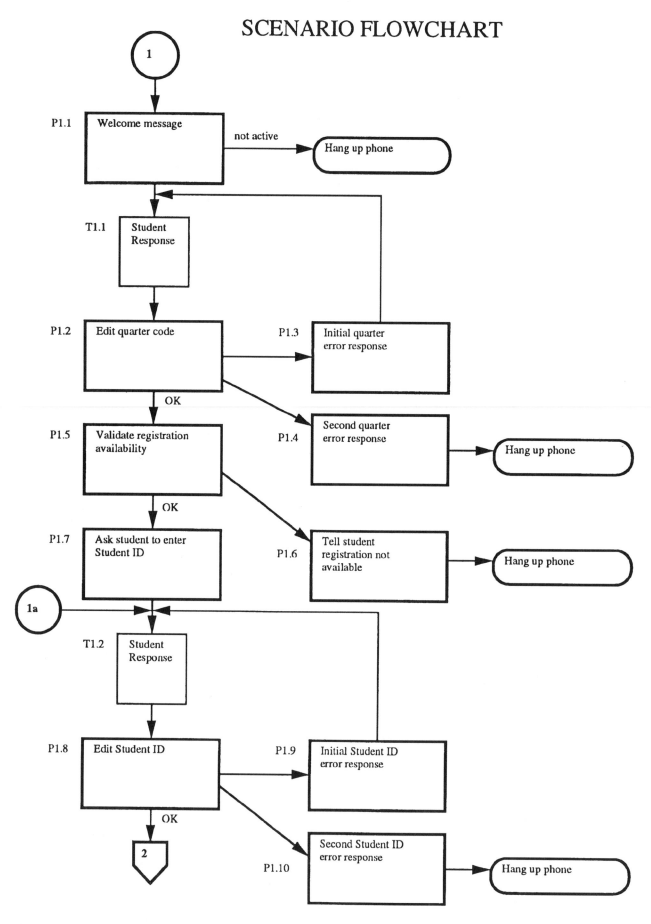

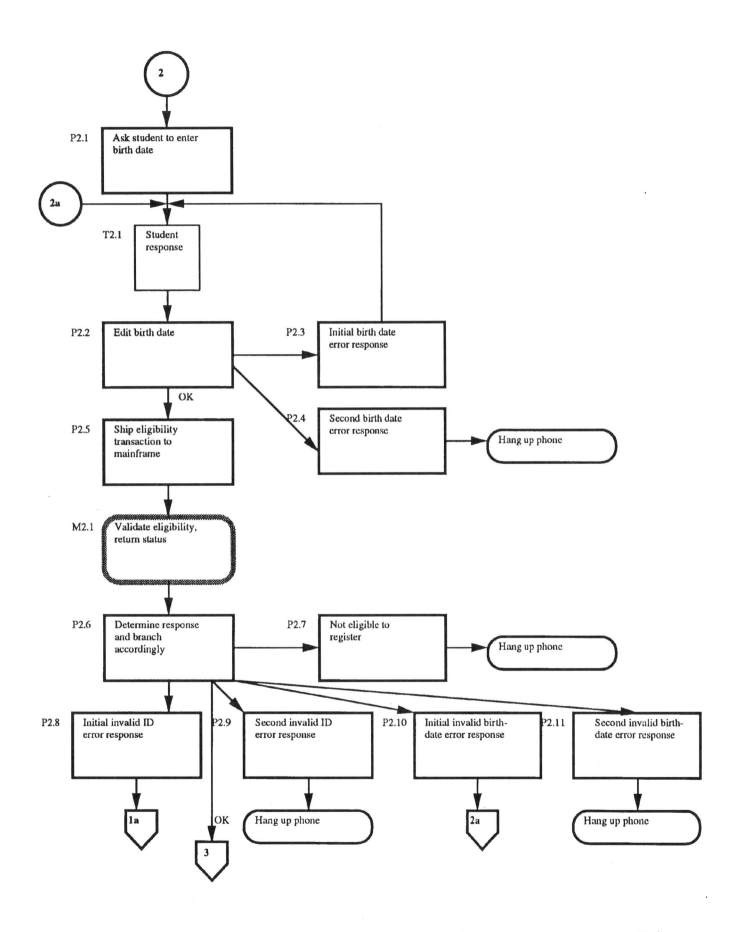

Exhibit E. Touchtone Registration Dialogue, University of Wisconsin - Madison

CALLER: [dials the registration voice response system]

SYSTEM: [production system]

WELCOME TO THE UNIVERSITY OF WISCONSIN-MADISON'S TOUCHTONE
SYSTEM. PLEASE ENTER YOUR STUDENT I-D NUMBER FOLLOWED BY THE
POUND KEY.

CALLER: [enters ID number and #]

SYSTEM: NOW ENTER YOUR FOUR DIGIT PIN NUMBER FOLLOWED BY THE POUND
KEY.

CALLER: [enters PIN and #]

SYSTEM: DON'T MISS IMPORTANT MAIL FROM THE UNIVERSITY. CHECK YOUR
ADDRESS INFORMATION AT THE E A S I STATIONS OR CONTACT THE
REGISTRAR'S INFORMATION BOOTH AT 608 262 3811. FOR FALL, PRESS ONE,
FOLLOWED BY THE POUND KEY. FOR SPRING, PRESS TWO, FOLLOWED BY
THE POUND KEY. FOR SUMMER, PRESS THREE, FOLLOWED BY THE POUND
KEY.

Dialog for probable graduating students - first call only.

SYSTEM: IF YOU EXPECT TO GRADUATE IN [MAY], PRESS [1], FOLLOWED BY THE #
KEY. IF YOU DO NOT EXPECT TO GRADUATE IN [MAY], PRESS [9],
FOLLOWED BY THE # KEY.

CALLER: [enters something followed by the # key]

If the response is a 1
SYSTEM: YOU HAVE INDICATED THAT YOU EXPECT TO GRADUATE IN [MAY]. PLEASE
ENTER YOUR FIRST REQUEST.

If the response is a 9
SYSTEM: YOU HAVE INDICATED THAT YOU DO NOT EXPECT TO GRADUATE IN [MAY].
IF YOU EXPECT TO GRADUATE IN [AUGUST] AND WISH TO ATTEND THE
[MAY] COMMENCEMENT CEREMONY, PRESS [5] FOLLOWED BY THE # KEY,
OTHERWISE PRESS [9] FOLLOWED BY THE # KEY.

If the response is a 5
SYSTEM: YOU HAVE INDICATED THAT YOU WISH TO ATTEND THE [MAY]
COMMENCEMENT CEREMONY. PLEASE ENTER YOUR FIRST REQUEST.

If the response is a 9
SYSTEM: YOU HAVE INDICATED THAT YOU DO NOT WISH TO ATTEND THE [MAY]
COMMENCEMENT CEREMONY. PLEASE ENTER YOUR FIRST REQUEST.

If invalid responses are given to the first dialogue
SYSTEM: THE RESPONSE GIVEN WAS INVALID. IF YOU EXPECT TO GRADUATE IN
[MAY], PRESS [1], FOLLOWED BY THE # KEY. IF YOU DO NOT EXPECT TO
GRADUATE IN [MAY], PRESS [9], FOLLOWED BY THE # KEY.

If invalid responses are given to the second dialogue
SYSTEM: THE RESPONSE GIVEN WAS INVALID. IF YOU EXPECT TO GRADUATE IN
[AUGUST] AND WISH TO ATTEND THE [MAY] COMMENCEMENT CEREMONY,

PRESS [5] FOLLOWED BY THE # KEY, OTHERWISE PRESS [9] FOLLOWED BY THE # KEY.

System allows 3 invalid responses to the graduation information and then proceeds into the normal registration dialogue

SYSTEM: **THE RESPONSE GIVEN WAS INVALID. FOR ASSISTANCE, PLEASE CONSULT YOUR REGISTRATION INSTRUCTIONS.**

Note: The commencement ceremony question is used only for a second semester's registration. It is not used for a fall or summer registration.

Normal registration process.

SYSTEM: **PLEASE ENTER YOUR FIRST REQUEST.**

CALLER: [enters '2' OR '4' followed by the 5-digit call number and #]
        [add fixed credit course]

SYSTEM: **(department) (course number), (number/type of credits) CREDITS, (type of instruction) (section number), (continue with types of instruction and section numbers) HAS BEEN ADDED. PLEASE ENTER YOUR NEXT REQUEST.**

    e.g.,   1.   MATH 99, 3 CREDITS, LECTURE 1 HAS BEEN ADDED. PLEASE ENTER YOUR NEXT REQUEST.
                2.   MATH 221, 5 HONORS CREDITS, LECTURE 2, DISCUSSION 312 HAS BEEN ADDED. PLEASE ...
                3.   MATH 112, AUDIT CREDITS, LECTURE 3, DISCUSSION 301, LAB 601 HAS BEEN ADDED. PLEASE ...

or

[request for identical course]

YOU ARE ALREADY REGISTERED FOR (department) (course number), (number/type of credits) CREDITS, (type of instruction) (section number), (continue with types of instruction and section numbers). PLEASE ENTER YOUR NEXT REQUEST.

    e.g.,   1.   YOU ARE ALREADY REGISTERED FOR MATH 112, 5 HONORS CREDITS, LECTURE 2, DISCUSSION 312, LAB 601. PLEASE..

or

[section or credit change]

(department) (course number), (number/type of credits) CREDITS, (type of instruction) (section number), (continue with types of instruction and section numbers) HAS BEEN DROPPED. (department) (course number), (number/type of credits) CREDITS, (type of instruction) (section number), (continue with types of instruction and section numbers) HAS BEEN ADDED. PLEASE ENTER YOUR NEXT REQUEST.

    e.g.,   MATH 221, 5 CREDITS, LECTURE 2, DISCUSSION 312 HAS BEEN DROPPED. MATH 221, 5 CREDITS, LECTURE 1, DISCUSSION 304 HAS BEEN ADDED. PLEASE ENTER YOUR NEXT REQUEST.

CALLER: [enters '2' or '4' followed by the 5-digit call number and #]
        [add variable credit course]

SYSTEM: **(department) (course number) IS A VARIABLE CREDIT COURSE. ENTER THE NUMBER OF CREDITS BETWEEN (X) AND (Z), AND PRESS THE POUND KEY.**

CALLER: [enters Y AND #]

SYSTEM: **(department) (course number), (Y) CREDITS, (type of instruction) (section number), (continue with types of instruction and section numbers) HAS BEEN ADDED. PLEASE ENTER YOUR NEXT REQUEST.**

       e.g.,   ART 103, 3 CREDITS, LECTURE 1, LAB 302 HAS BEEN ADDED. PLEASE ENTER YOUR NEXT REQUEST.

       (Note: section change message type can occur with a variable credit course and has the same format as the section change message for a fixed credit course.)

OPEN SECTION PROCESSING DIALOGUE

CALLER: [section requested is closed and an available call number is found]

SYSTEM: **(type of instruction) (section number) OF (department) (course number) IS CLOSED. [A NEW] CALL NUMBER (call number) (department) (course number) (type of instruction) (section number), (continue with types of instruction and section numbers), IS AVAILABLE (AT THE SAME TIME/AT ANOTHER TIME). [PLEASE CALL THE DEPARTMENT FOR MORE INFORMATION.] IF YOU WANT TO REGISTER FOR THIS CALL NUMBER, PRESS 2 FOLLOWED BY THE POUND KEY. IF YOU WANT TO HEAR THE NEXT OPEN CALL NUMBER, PRESS 6 FOLLOWED BY THE POUND KEY, OR PLEASE ENTER YOUR NEXT REQUEST.**

CALLER: [caller presses 6# above and a new choice is offered]

       [A NEW] CALL NUMBER (call number) (department) (course number) (type of instruction) (section number), (continue with types of instruction and section numbers), IS AVAILABLE (AT THE SAME TIME/AT ANOTHER TIME). [PLEASE CALL THE DEPARTMENT FOR MORE INFORMATION.] IF YOU WANT TO REGISTER FOR THIS CALL NUMBER, PRESS 2 FOLLOWED BY THE POUND KEY. IF YOU WANT TO HEAR THE NEXT OPEN CALL NUMBER, PRESS 6 FOLLOWED BY THE POUND KEY, OR PLEASE ENTER YOUR NEXT REQUEST.

CALLER: [caller presses 6# above and no more call numbers remain]
       Single-range course

       THERE ARE NO OTHER OPEN CALL NUMBERS FOR (department) (course number). PLEASE ENTER YOUR NEXT REQUEST.

       Multi-range course

       THERE ARE NO OTHER OPEN CALL NUMBERS FOR (instruction type-1) (section number-1) [WITH DISCUSSION] [AND LAB]] FOR (department) (course number). PLEASE ENTER YOUR NEXT REQUEST.

CALLER: [section requested is closed and there are no open call numbers to offer]

       Single-range course

SYSTEM: **THERE ARE NO OPEN CALL NUMBERS FOR (department) (course number) [FOR WHICH YOU ARE ELIGIBLE]. PLEASE ENTER YOUR NEXT REQUEST.**

SYSTEM: **THERE ARE NO OPEN CALL NUMBERS FOR (type of instruction) (section number), (continue with types of instruction and section numbers), OF (department) (course number) [FOR WHICH YOU ARE ELIGIBLE]. PLEASE ENTER YOUR NEXT REQUEST.**

CALLER: [enters '3' and 5-digit call number and #]
           [drop course]

SYSTEM: **YOU HAVE DROPPED (department) (course number) FOR (number/type of credits) CREDITS. PLEASE ENTER YOUR NEXT REQUEST.**

        e.g.,   1.   YOU HAVE DROPPED BOTANY 415 FOR 4 CREDITS. PLEASE ENTER YOUR NEXT REQUEST.
              2.   YOU HAVE DROPPED BOTANY 415 FOR 4 HONORS CREDITS. PLEASE ...
              3.   YOU HAVE DROPPED BOTANY 415 FOR AUDIT CREDITS. PLEASE ...

CALLER: [enters '*5' and #]
           [list courses]

SYSTEM: **YOU ARE NOT REGISTERED FOR ANY COURSES. PLEASE ENTER YOUR NEXT REQUEST.**

OR

YOUR CLASS SCHEDULE (is/continues):

    for each course, there are three possible formats:
        standard course add format, including grade if available
        cancelled course
        course with cancelled sections

[standard course add format, including grade if available]
    (department) (course number), (number/type of credits) CREDITS, (type of instruction) (section number), (continue with types of instruction and section numbers), (grade of [grade]).

    e.g.,   ART 442, 3 HONORS CREDITS, LECTURE 1, DISCUSSION 301, LAB 601, GRADE OF A.

    Note - System speaks letter grades A, AB, B, BC, C, and D and uses the following words for other grades:

'I' or 'IN'	-	Incomplete
'F'	-	Failure
'S'	-	Satisfactory
'U'	-	Unsatisfactory
'CR'	-	Credit
'N'	-	No Credit
'P'	-	Progress
'M'	-	Unreported
'EI'	-	Extended Incomplete
'PI'	-	Permanent Incomplete
'Q'	-	Question on Credits
'NR'	-	No Report

or

[cancelled course still on student's schedule]
    Note - this message is used only if the last call number of the course has been cancelled.

(department) (course number) HAS BEEN CANCELLED.

e.g., ART 919 HAS BEEN CANCELLED.

or

[course with cancelled sections]

> Note - when any section of a multi-range course is cancelled, the entire call number is cancelled.

> (department) (course number), (number/type of credits), CREDITS, (type of instruction) (section number), (continue with types of instruction and section numbers). (Type of Instruction) (section number) (continue with types of instruction and section numbers) (has/have) BEEN CANCELLED.

> > e.g.,   ART 920, 3 CREDITS, LECTURE 1, DISCUSSION 301. DISCUSSION 301 HAS BEEN CANCELLED.

FOLLOWED BY

[all course data and total credits/courses can be spoken in one message]

> YOU ARE REGISTERED FOR (number of credits) CREDITS AND (number of courses) (COURSE/COURSES). PLEASE ENTER YOUR NEXT REQUEST.

or

[not all data can be spoken in message]

> TO LIST MORE COURSES, ENTER THE STAR KEY FOLLOWED BY THE NUMBER FIVE; THEN PRESS THE POUND KEY.

CALLER: [enters '*' and #]
> [ignore entry]

SYSTEM: **PLEASE ENTER YOUR NEXT REQUEST.**

CALLER: [enters '*7' and #]
> [repeat last message]

SYSTEM: **repeats last message**

CALLER: [enters '*9' and #]
> [exit system]

SYSTEM: **THANK YOU FOR CALLING THE UNIVERSITY OF WISCONSIN-MADISON'S TOUCHTONE REGISTRATION SYSTEM. GOODBYE.** [call terminated]

NOTE: The following sentence is also being recorded as a more generic thank you and may be used at a later time:

> **THANK YOU FOR CALLING THE UNIVERSITY OF WISCONSIN-MADISON'S TOUCHTONE SYSTEM.**

ERROR MESSAGES

TYPE	MESSAGE TO CALLER

Timeout
> **PLEASE COMPLETE YOUR ENTRY AND PRESS THE POUND KEY.**

Maximum timeouts
> **GOODBYE.** [call terminated]

Invalid ID number

> THE STUDENT I-D NUMBER ENTERED IS NOT VALID. PLEASE VERIFY AND THEN REENTER YOUR STUDENT I-D NUMBER FOLLOWED BY THE POUND KEY.

Invalid PIN

> THE PIN NUMBER ENTERED IS NOT VALID. PLEASE VERIFY AND THEN REENTER YOUR FOUR DIGIT PIN NUMBER FOLLOWED BY THE POUND KEY.

Student not eligible to register

> YOU ARE NOT ELIGIBLE TO REGISTER FOR THE (term)(year) SEMESTER. GOODBYE. [call terminated]

Student not eligible for touchtone

> YOU ARE NOT ELIGIBLE FOR TELEPHONE REGISTRATION. FOR ASSISTANCE, CONSULT YOUR REGISTRATION INSTRUCTIONS. GOODBYE. [call terminated]

Call is too early

> YOUR TELEPHONE REGISTRATION TIME BEGINS (month) (day) (year) AT (hours) (minutes) (AM/PM) MADISON TIME. PLEASE CALL AFTER THAT TIME. GOODBYE. [call terminated]
>
> e.g., YOUR TELEPHONE REGISTRATION TIME BEGINS AUGUST 16 1992 AT 11:23 A.M. MADISON TIME. PLEASE ...

Hold(s) exist

> YOU HAVE ONE OR MORE HOLDS ON YOUR REGISTRATION. YOU MUST CLEAR ALL HOLDS BEFORE YOU CAN REGISTER. FOR ASSISTANCE, CONSULT YOUR REGISTRATION INSTRUCTIONS. GOODBYE. [call terminated]

4-digit Call number entry

> THE REQUEST ENTERED IS NOT VALID. PLEASE REENTER YOUR REQUEST BY PRESSING AN ADD OR DROP CODE; THEN THE FIVE DIGIT CALL NUMBER FOLLOWED BY THE POUND KEY.

Invalid request

> THE REQUEST ENTERED IS NOT VALID. PLEASE ENTER YOUR NEXT REQUEST.

Invalid Call number

> NO COURSE OR SECTION HAS THE CALL NUMBER (5-digit call #). PLEASE ENTER YOUR NEXT REQUEST.
>
> e.g., NO COURSE OR SECTION HAS THE CALL NUMBER 23553. PLEASE...

Call number unavailable

> CALL NUMBER (5-digit call #) IS NOT AVAILABLE AT THIS TIME. PLEASE ENTER YOUR NEXT REQUEST.

Course not on Touchtone [course add]

> (department) (course number) IS NOT AVAILABLE FOR TELEPHONE REGISTRATION. PLEASE ENTER YOUR NEXT REQUEST.
>
> e.g., LAW 990 IS NOT AVAILABLE FOR TELEPHONE...

Course cancelled

> (department) (course number) HAS BEEN CANCELLED. PLEASE ENTER YOUR NEXT REQUEST.
>
> e.g., ART 103 HAS BEEN CANCELLED. PLEASE...

Conference course authorization not found

> YOU HAVE NOT BEEN AUTHORIZED TO REGISTER FOR CONFERENCE

COURSE (department) (course number). PLEASE ENTER YOUR NEXT REQUEST.

e.g.,   YOU HAVE NOT BEEN AUTHORIZED TO REGISTER FOR CONFERENCE COURSE BOTANY 990. PLEASE...

Section not found

SECTION (section number) OF (department) (course number) IS NOT AVAILABLE AT THIS TIME. PLEASE ENTER YOUR NEXT REQUEST.

e.g.,   SECTION 602 OF ART 224 IS NOT...

Section(s) cancelled

(type of instruction) (section number) (continue with other sections) OF (department) (course number) (is/are) CANCELLED. PLEASE ENTER YOUR NEXT REQUEST.

e.g.,   DISCUSSION 301, LAB 601 OF CHEMISTRY 108 ARE CANCELLED. PLEASE ...

Sections(s) closed

(registration limit greater than zero)

(type of instruction) (section number) (continue with other sections) OF (department) (course number) (is/are) CLOSED. PLEASE ENTER YOUR NEXT REQUEST.

e.g.,   DISCUSSION 301, LAB 601 OF CHEMISTRY 108 ARE CLOSED. PLEASE ...

or

(registration limit equal zero)

(type of instruction) (section number) (continue with other sections) OF (department) (course number) (is/are) NOT AVAILABLE FOR REGISTRATION AT THIS TIME. PLEASE ENTER YOUR NEXT REQUEST.

e.g.,   DISCUSSION 301, LAB 601 OF CHEMISTRY 108 ARE NOT AVAILABLE FOR REGISTRATION AT THIS TIME. PLEASE ...

Ineligible for course

YOU ARE NOT ELIGIBLE TO REGISTER FOR (department) (course number). PLEASE ENTER YOUR NEXT REQUEST.

e.g.,   YOU ARE NOT ELIGIBLE TO REGISTER FOR BUSINESS 234. PLEASE...

Ineligible for section

YOU ARE NOT ELIGIBLE TO REGISTER FOR (type of instruction) (section number) OF (department) (course number). PLEASE ENTER YOUR NEXT REQUEST.

e.g.,   YOU ARE NOT ELIGIBLE TO REGISTER FOR SEMINAR 123 OF MUSIC 206. PLEASE...

Invalid credit entry

THE NUMBER OF CREDITS ENTERED IS NOT VALID. PLEASE VERIFY AND REENTER THE NUMBER OF CREDITS BETWEEN (number of credits) AND (number of credits); THEN PRESS THE POUND KEY.

Maximum credit load

YOUR REQUEST WOULD EXCEED THE COLLEGE LIMIT OF (number of credits) CREDITS. FOR ASSISTANCE, CONSULT YOUR REGISTRATION INSTRUCTIONS. PLEASE ENTER YOUR NEXT REQUEST.

Data base limit exceeded

CALL NUMBER (5-digit call #). WE CANNOT PROCESS YOUR REQUEST. PLEASE ENTER YOUR NEXT REQUEST.

Course not on Touchtone [course drop]

YOU CANNOT DROP (department) (course number), BY TELEPHONE. PLEASE

ENTER YOUR NEXT REQUEST.

Call # to be dropped is not on student record

WE CANNOT PROCESS YOUR REQUEST. YOU ARE NOT REGISTERED FOR CALL NUMBER (5-digit call number). PLEASE ENTER YOUR NEXT REQUEST.
e.g., WE CANNOT PROCESS YOUR REQUEST. YOU ARE NOT REGISTERED FOR CALL NUMBER 60551. PLEASE...

Multiple registration drop problem

YOU CANNOT DROP CALL NUMBER (5-digit call#), (department) (course number), BY TELEPHONE. FOR ASSISTANCE, CONSULT YOUR REGISTRATION INSTRUCTIONS. PLEASE ENTER YOUR NEXT REQUEST.
e.g., YOUR CANNOT DROP CALL NUMBER 14220, LAW 990, BY TELEPHONE. FOR ...

Maximum List requests

WE CANNOT PROCESS FURTHER REQUESTS FOR COURSE LISTS. FOR ASSISTANCE, CONSULT YOUR REGISTRATION INSTRUCTIONS. GOODBYE.
[call terminated]

Security counters maxima exceeded

YOU APPEAR TO BE HAVING DIFFICULTY. WE CANNOT PROCESS YOUR REQUEST. FOR ASSISTANCE, CONSULT YOUR INSTRUCTIONS OR CALL OUR REGISTRATION HELPLINE DURING OFFICE HOURS. GOODBYE. [call terminated]

PTC waiting for host response

PLEASE WAIT. YOUR REQUEST IS BEING PROCESSED.

Communication problems from host to PTC

WE ARE HAVING TECHNICAL DIFFICULTIES. PLEASE CALL BACK AT A LATER TIME. [call termimated]

Call is too late

YOUR TOUCHTONE REGISTRATION TIME HAS ENDED. FOR ASSISTANCE, CONSULT YOUR REGISTRATION INSTRUCTIONS. GOODBYE. [call terminated]

Disaster message

WELCOME TO THE UNIVERSITY OF WISCONSIN-MADISON'S TOUCHTONE REGISTRATION SYSTEM. WE ARE HAVING TECHNICAL DIFFICULTIES. THE SYSTEM IS UNAVAILABLE FOR TOUCHTONE REGISTRATION. TO REGISTER FOR THE (term) (year) SEMESTER, PLEASE FOLLOW THE PROCEDURES FOR IN-PERSON REGISTRATION OUTLINED IN THE TIMETABLE. WE ARE SORRY FOR ANY INCONVENIENCE THIS MAY CAUSE. GOODBYE. [call terminated]

REPLY WORDS

Fall	January	credit
Spring	February	credits
Summer	March	audit
Session	April	honor
first	May	honors
second	June	course
third	July	courses
fourth	August	
fifth	September	lecture
sixth	October	lab
seventh	November	discussion
eighth	December	conference

ninth	-oh	seminar
tenth	zero	field
eleventh	one	section
twelfth	two	
thirtheenth	three	is
fourteenth	four	are
fifteenth	five	continues
sixteenth	six	semester
seventeenth	seven	at
eighteenth	eight	of
nineteenth	nine	cancelled
twentieth	ten	closed
for	eleven	thirtieth
1988	twelve	and
1989	thirteen	has
1990	fourteen	have
A.M.	fifteen	or
P.M	sixteen	goodbye
Monday	seventeen	
Tuesday	eighteen	grade of
Wednesday	nineteen	point
Thursday	twenty	
Friday	thirty	
Saturday	forty	Sunday
fifty	sixty	seventy
eighty	ninety	hundred
A	J	S
B	K	T
C	L	U
D	M	V
E	N	W
F	O	X
G	P	Y
H	Q	Z
I	R	

REPLY WORDS - DEPARTMENT NAMES and PRONUNCIATION

DEPARTMENT NAME	PRONUNCIATION GUIDE
AFRICAN	
AFRO-AMERICAN	
AMERICAN INSTITUTIONS	
ANTHROPOLOGY	
ART HISTORY	
ASTRONOMY	
BOTANY	
BULGARIAN	
CHEMISTRY	
CLASSICS	
COMM ARTS	COMM as in MOM
COMMUNICATIVE DISORDERS	
COMP LIT	COMP as in COMPare
COMPUTER SCIENCE	
CONTEMPORARY TRENDS	
CZECH	CHECK
EAST ASIAN	
ECON	EE'-CON
ENGLISH	

FOLKLORE
FRESHMAN FORUM   FRENCH
GEOGRAPHY
GEOLOGY
GERMAN
GREEK
HEBREW
HISTORY OF SCIENCE
HISTORY
I L S   EYE-EL-ESS
INDUSTRIAL RELATIONS
L&S INTERDIS   L AND S INTERDIS
ITALIAN
JOURNALISM
L I S   EL-EYE-ESS
LATIN
LINGUISTICS
LIT TRAN AFRICAN
LIT TRAN EAST ASIAN
LIT TRAN CLASSICS
LIT TRAN FRENCH, LIT TRAN ITALIAN
LIT TRAN GERMAN
LIT TRAN HEBREW
LIT TRAN SOUTH ASIAN
LIT TRAN SCANDINAVIAN
LIT TRAN SLAVIC   as in SLAH'-VICK
LIT TRAN SPANISH
MATH
MEDIEVAL   MID-EE'-VUHL
METEOROLOGY
MOLECULAR BIO   MOH-LECK-YOU-LER BUY-OH
M S A E   EM-ESS-AY-EE
MUSIC PERFORMANCE
MUSIC
PHILOSOPHY
PHYSICS
POLITICAL SCIENCE
POLISH   POH'-LISH
PORTUGUESE
PSYCHOLOGY
PUBLIC AFFAIRS
RELIGIOUS STUDIES
RUSSIAN
SOUTH ASIAN
SCANDINAVIAN
SERBO-CROATIAN   SERBO CROH-AY'-SHUN
SLAVIC   SLAH-VICK
SOCIOLOGY   SOH-CEE-AH'-LOH-GEE
SOCIAL WORK
SPANISH
STATISTICS
THEATRE   THEE'-AH-TUHR
URBAN PLANNING
WOMENS STUDIES
ZOOLOGY   ZOH-OL'-OH-GEE
AG ECON   AG as in AGriculture
                           EE'-CON

AG ENGINEERING
AG JOURNALISM

AG LIBRARY
AGRONOMY   AH-GRON'-AH-MEE
BACTERIOLOGY
BIOCHEM   BUY-OH KEM
DAIRY SCIENCE
ENTOMOLOGY
FOOD SCIENCE
FORESTRY
GENETICS
HORTICULTURE   HORE'-TI-CULTURE
CALS INTERDIS   CALS as in PALS
                                                  INTERDIS as in INTER-DIS

LANDSCAPE ARCHITECTURE
M A S   EM-AY-ESS
NUTRITION
PLANT PATHOLOGY
POULTRY SCIENCE
RURAL SOSH   SOSH as in SOHSH
SOIL SCIENCE
VETERINARY SCIENCE   VEH-TRIN-ERRY SCIENCE
WILDLIFE
ART
ART ED
COUNSELING PSYCH AND COUNSELOR ED   PSYCH=SIKE
C & I   CEE AND EYE
ED ADMIN   ED AD-MIN'
ED POLICY
ED PSYCH   PSYCH=SIKE
P E DANCE   PEE-EE DANCE
P E ELECT   PEE-EE EE-LECT
P E PRO   PEE-EE PRO
REHAB PSYCH AND SPECIAL ED   REE-HAB SIKE AND SPECIAL ED
CHILD AND FAMILY
CONSUMER SCIENCE
E T D   EE-TEE-DEE
FAMILY COMMUNCATIONS
FAMILY RESOURCES INTERDIS
CHEM ENGINEERING   KEM ENGINEERING
CIVIL ENGINEERING
E C E   EE-CEE-EE
ENGINEERING MECHANICS
GENERAL ENGINEERING
I E   EYE-EEM & M EEM AND EM-EE
M E   EM-EE
NUCLEAR ENGINEERING
PROFESSIONAL ORIENTATION
BUSINESS
NURSING
MED TECH   MED TECK
O T   OH-TEE
PHYSICIAN ASSISTANT
P T   PEE-TEE
ALLIED HEALTH INTERDIS
MED CHEM   MED KEM
PHARMACEUTICAL BIO   FARM-A-SOO'-TICAL BUY-OH
PHARMACY PRACTICE
PHARMACEUTICS
PHARMACOLOGY
S & A PHARMACY   ESS AND AY PHARMACY

AIR FORCE
MILITARY SCIENCE
NAVAL SCIENCE
BIOCORE   BUY-OH-CORE
C A V E   CEE-AY-VEE-EE
CONSERVATION
ENVIRONMENTAL TOXICOLOGY
ENVIRONMENTAL STUDIES
NEUROSCIENCE
UNDERGRAD ED
UNIVERSITY FORUM
LAW
PRE LAW   PREE LAW
COMPARATIVE BIO   BIO as in BUY-OH
MEDICAL SCIENCE
PATH BIO   PATH BUY-OH
SURGICAL SCIENCE
ANATOMY
ANESTHESIA   AN-US-THEE'-ZHA
FAMILY MED
HUMAN ONCOLOGY   HUMAN ON-COLL'-OH-GEE
HISTORY OF MED
MED GENETICS
MED MICRO   MED MY-CROW
MED PHYSICS
MEDICINE
NEUROLOGY
NEUROPHYSIOLOGY
O B G Y N   OH-BEE-GEE-WHY-EN
ONCOLOGY
OPTHAMOLOGY
PATHOLOGY
PEDIATRICS   P CHEMPEE CHEM
PHYSIOLOGY
PREVENTIVE MED
PSYCHIATRY
RADIOLOGY
REHAB MED   REE-HAB MED
SENIOR MED
SURGERY
GEOLOGICAL ENGINEERING
E P D   EE-PEE-DEE

ADDITIONAL PRONUNCIATION

U-W   YOU DOUBLE-YOU
I-D   EYE-DEE

revised 7/24/92

Exhibit F.1. Registration Work Sheet

Office of the University Registrar

REGISTRATION WORK SHEET
AUTUMN 1992

MAIL TO:

COL   06/11/92   **FEE STATUS**
RESIDENT

HOLD   SPECIAL MESSAGES

ACADEMIC ADVISOR
? ????????????

COLLEGE   RANK   MAJOR   SPECIALIZATION/MINOR   EXPECTED DEGREE
ASC   2   365 PHILOS

VERIFY ALL THE ABOVE DEGREE PROGRAM INFORMATION.   REPORT DISCREPANCIES TO YOUR ENROLLMENT UNIT PRIOR TO REGISTERING.

BEFORE PROCEEDING PLEASE READ INSTRUCTIONS ON BACK OF THIS FORM, AND, IF REQUIRED, CONSULT WITH YOUR ACADEMIC ADVISOR

STEP 1.   TO REGISTER. CALL THIS NUMBER   STEP 2.   ENTER QUARTER AND YEAR FOR REGISTRATION
(614) [2] [9] [3] - [9] [9] [9] [9] AFTER 08:00 AM JUNE 24, 1992 AND   OR [A] [U] YR [9] [2] (Quarter: AU=Autumn, WI=Winter,
                                  BEFORE 08:00 PM JUNE 29, 1992   SP=Spring, SU=Summer)
STEP 3.   ENTER SSN AND PERSONAL ACCESS CODE TOGETHER
[ ] [ ] [ ] [ ] [ ] [ ] [ ] [ ] [ ] - [ ] [ ] [ ] [ ]
SOCIAL SECURITY NUMBER   PERSONAL ACCESS CODE (IF A PERSONAL ACCESS CODE IS NOT LISTED, YOU MUST SEE YOUR
                                                 ENROLLMENT UNIT/ADVISOR TO COMPLETE REGISTRATION)

STEP 4.   ENTER COURSE REQUEST WITH A SECONDARY REQUEST IF DESIRED.   PLAN REQUESTS IN THE SPACE PROVIDED ON THE REVERSE SIDE BEFORE CALLING

STEP 5.   CONFIRM THE FEES MARKED BELOW. IF SET AS DESIRED, SKIP TO STEP 6. IF NOT, CIRCLE THE CHANGES AND ENTER [*] [0] TO AMEND THE SELECTIONS.
HEALTH INSURANCE: (YOU ARE AUTOMATICALLY BILLED FOR YOURSELF UNLESS YOU REQUEST EXEMPTION AND ACCEPT RESPONSIBILITY FOR ANY MEDICAL EXPENSE)

ADDITIONAL COVERAGE: [ ] Spouse   [ ] Children
[ ] I REQUEST EXEMPTION FROM STUDENT HEALTH INSURANCE
[ ] OFF-QUARTER INSURANCE FOR WINTER QUARTER 1993
ANNUAL VEHICLE REGISTRATION: [ ] Auto   [ ] Motorcycle

OPTIONAL CONTRIBUTIONS: [X] $2 FOR SCHOLARSHIPS AND LOANS
                        [X] $1 FOR STUDENT GOVERNMENT PROJECTS

STEP 6.   ENTER [*] [#] TO END SESSION —— CONFIRM YOUR ADDRESS

AUTUMN APPROVED SCHEDULE AND FEE STATEMENT WILL BE SENT 08/92 TO:
HOME ADDRESS: 112 E 4TH AVE
              COLUMBUS   OH   43201
              (614) 294-4354

——— 00110

REVIEW CURRENT SUMMER 1992 CLASS SCHEDULE (AS OF 06/11/92). VERIFY ACCURACY, REPORT ANY DISCREPANCIES IMMEDIATELY TO YOUR COLLEGE OFFICE.

DEPT	COURSE	CALL NO	O CR D	DAYS	TIME	INSTRUCTOR	DEPT	COURSE	CALL NO	O CR D	DAYS	TIME	INSTRUCTOR
GEOL SCI	121	08418-2	05	M WRF	10	TETTENHORST							
				T	12 -02	CANCELLED							

REGISTRATION WORK SHEET INSTRUCTIONS
GENERAL INSTRUCTIONS

- **CHECK ALL THE INFORMATION LISTED ON THE FRONT OF THIS WORK SHEET CAREFULLY, ESPECIALLY THE COLLEGE OF ENROLLMENT.** Permission to register has been cleared only for this unit. If it is not current, contact the correct enrollment unit before proceeding with registration.

- If you select a course which requires PERMISSION, you should obtain this permission prior to attempting registration. Enrollment units (or the Registrar) must enter this permission on your record before a PERMISSION course can be scheduled. IF PERMISSION is not posted prior to the end of the Registration period, a course request requiring permission will not be scheduled.

- All HOLDS on your record at the time your Work Sheet was printed have been listed in the HOLD section on the front. If a HOLD is placed after the printing of the Work Sheet, BRUTUS will inform you when you call. Although you can still enter course requests during Registration or process a drop with a HOLD on your record, ALL POSTED HOLDS MUST BE CLEARED BY THE DATE BRUTUS INDICATES OR YOUR COURSE REQUESTS WILL NOT BE SCHEDULED. During Late Registration, you will not be permitted to add a course with a HOLD on your record. You must clear all HOLDS prior to registration.

- **CHECK THE ADDRESS LISTED ON THE FRONT OF THE WORK SHEET CAREFULLY AND CORRECT IT AS INSTRUCTED (STEP 6).** This is where your STATEMENT OF ACCOUNT and APPROVED SCHEDULE will be mailed. If you do not receive a STATEMENT OF ACCOUNT with an APPROVED SCHEDULE printed on the reverse side by the date published in the Master Schedule of Classes for the Registration Period, or a STATEMENT OF ACCOUNT within a week during Late Registration, contact the Office of the University Registrar at 292-8500. You are not considered enrolled for the quarter until you have paid fees, or confirmed your enrollment if you do not have any balance due.

- During Registration, you are entering course requests only, except for Summer Quarter when you are actually being scheduled into each course you request. Your APPROVED SCHEDULE will be printed on the reverse side of your STATEMENT OF ACCOUNT listing the courses for which you have been scheduled.

- During Late Registration, you are actually being scheduled into each course you request.

- If you are currently enrolled, check your current quarter schedule listed on the front of the Work Sheet. If there appears to be an error, contact your enrollment unit immediately.

EVERY EFFORT WILL BE MADE TO HAVE BRUTUS AVAILABLE:
8:00am to 8:00pm Monday through Saturday
1:00pm to 8:00pm on Sunday

ADDITIONAL HOURS DURING BUSY PERIODS ARE:
7:15am to 9:45pm Monday through Saturday
10:15am to 9:45pm on Sunday

TIPS FOR USING BRUTUS

1. Use only a touch-tone phone. BRUTUS cannot understand phones which make an undifferentiated tone, or no tone at all!

2. Listen for a voice response to guide you after each entry. Press an entire sequence of numbers when told to do so. For example, to make a request to add a course, call number 394215, you would enter:

   [A] [3] [9] [4] [2] [1] [5]

3. LISTEN CAREFULLY to the response after each of your entries. After each course has been entered, BRUTUS will confirm which course you have selected or ask for additional information about your request (VARIABLE CREDIT COURSES will require entry of the number of credit hours requested, and some courses will require entry of 2 call numbers). BRUTUS will prompt you for this additional information. After you have entered each request, BRUTUS will confirm the Department/Course and Days/Time the course meets. IF YOU HAVE SELECTED AN INCORRECT SECTION, you can cancel the request by entering [*] [X]. After cancelling your previous request, try entering the call number again. If the response still indicates an incorrect section, you probably copied the wrong call number. You might want to complete the rest of your requests and re-enter the system at a later date to enter the course when you have the correct call number.

4. You are encouraged to select SECONDARY REQUESTS for all of your courses before you call. BRUTUS will only schedule a secondary course if it is unable to schedule your primary course. Using this option during Registration will save you the time and inconvenience of adding a course after you receive your schedule if you are closed out of a primary request.

5. Each student will receive an appointment window during which he or she will be permitted to call BRUTUS (step 1). The timing of your appointment window has no bearing on your chances of receiving the courses you requested; scheduling priority is determined by the elapsed time between when your window opens and when you first call BRUTUS.

6. If BRUTUS is busy, call back at a later time (see schedule above). If your line is accidentally cut off before you have completed your course requests, call back and complete your session by re-entering the system. Enter [*] [L] after completing steps 1-3 to list the course requests recorded by the system before your line was cut off.

7. Protect your Personal Access Code (PAC). It has been issued exclusively for your use and is not transferable. If you misplace or lose it, please contact your enrollment unit.

8. If you have any questions or problems when using BRUTUS, call the Office of the University Registrar (292-8500) between 9:30am and 5:00pm (4:30pm during the summer months), or your enrollment unit during normal business hours.

Additional information can be obtained in the BRUTUS section of the Master Schedule of Classes Bulletin.

STEP 4. PLAN YOUR COURSE REQUESTS BEFORE CALLING BRUTUS.

FUNCTIONS

COURSE REQUESTS–(STEP 4)

[A] [1] [2] [3] [4] [5] [6]   Add primary 12345-6

[S] [4] [5] [6] [7] [8] [9]   Add Secondary 45678-9

[D] [1] [2] [3] [4] [5] [6]   Drop primary 12345-6
secondary 45678-9
will be automatically
dropped

TO CANCEL
[*] [X]   Cancel previous entry

TO LIST (PLAYBACK) COURSE REQUESTS
[*] [L]

FEE OPTIONS–(STEP 5)
[*] [O]   LIST/CHANGE FEE OPTIONS

Rev.—12/91

Financial Aid Voice Response System - Favors

Financial Aid Voice Response Information

You can access the latest financial aid information by telephone using the convenient FAVORS program. FAVORS allows you to get general information or check your financial status report from any touch-tone phone without commuting or standing in line.

This summary of the services you can access with FAVORS is intended to help you begin using the program. Within each of the categories below, there are many options you'll discover after you dial up.

Know Before You Call

When you dial the financial aid office, your call is answered electronically by a voice response computer. The voice prompts you to choose among various services by punching the appropriate keys on your telephone keypad. You can get information about financial aid programs, general requirements to receive financial aid, or how to have a financial aid form (FAF) application packet sent. You may also check on your financial aid status if you have already filed your FAF.

If incorrect or invalid information is entered at any time, the system will request that you re-enter information.

Hanging up at any time automatically disconnects you from the system. But it's preferable to exit the system by pressing * *, so that you will hear any final announcements the system makes to you regarding your information requests. After listening to the final announcements, you simply hang up.

Preparing to Call

Have a pen and paper at hand. Fill out the blanks below, and refer to this material as you use FAVORS--these numbers will help you as you go through the FAVORS system.

Social Security Number

__ __ __ - __ __ - __ __ __ __

Personal Identification Number (birthdate)

__ __ / __ __ / __ __

Semester Code (see page 9 for this semester's code)

__ __ __ __

Here are several helpful codes to have at hand.

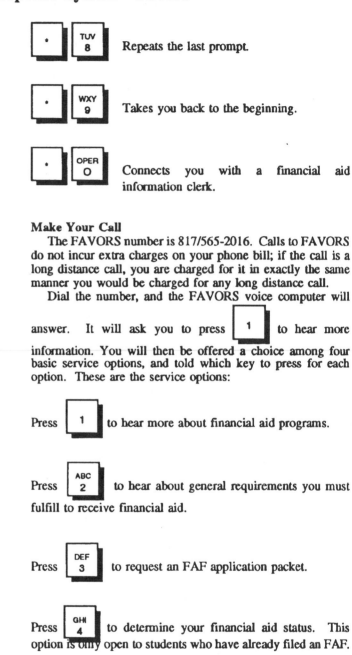

Disconnects you from FAVORS and gives you any final announcements.

Moves you backward one step within the system.

Repeats the last prompt.

Takes you back to the beginning.

Connects you with a financial aid information clerk.

Make Your Call

The FAVORS number is 817/565-2016. Calls to FAVORS do not incur extra charges on your phone bill; if the call is a long distance call, you are charged for it in exactly the same manner you would be charged for any long distance call.

Dial the number, and the FAVORS voice computer will answer. It will ask you to press [1] to hear more information. You will then be offered a choice among four basic service options, and told which key to press for each option. These are the service options:

Press [1] to hear more about financial aid programs.

Press [2] to hear about general requirements you must fulfill to receive financial aid.

Press [3] to request an FAF application packet.

Press [4] to determine your financial aid status. This option is only open to students who have already filed an FAF.

SPRING 1993

REGISTRATION PROCEDURES

UNT has two kinds of registration: teleregistration, which is available to any currently enrolled student and Coliseum registration, which is open to new students and students who do not teleregister.

Teleregistration offers several advantages. You may register from any place with a touchtone phone. Teleregistration is UNT's only early registration option, and more class sections are available to those who teleregister.

Like Coliseum registration, teleregistration follows a schedule. You are assigned a date when you should call. Find the date by looking up your last name's first letter in the chart.

Teleregistered students who complete fee payment arrangements by the payment deadline can take advantage of the schedule revision period, January 4 - January 11. Schedules are mailed out on or about November 19; you can revise your schedule if necessary during the schedule revision period if you teleregistered. Otherwise, revision has to wait until the add/drop period, January 18 to January 20.

Students are encouraged to take advantage of teleregistration. A guide to the process follows.

Instructions for students who must participate in Coliseum registration begin on page 16.

Teleregistration
October 19 - November 11

Students who were enrolled spring 1992 and/or summer 1992 and /or fall 1992 may teleregister according to the following schedule based on their current classification and the first letter of their last name and/or anytime on open days, November 9 - 11. Teleregistration is busiest from 7 to 9 a.m. Call later if you can. Teleregistration is scheduled from 7 a.m. to 10 p.m.

Graduate Students

A	Tues. Oct. 20	Oct. 27	Nov. 3
B-C	Wed. Oct. 21	Oct. 28	Nov. 4
D-G	Thurs. Oct. 22	Oct. 29	Nov. 5
H-L	Fri. Oct. 23	Oct. 30	Nov. 6
M-P	Sat. Oct. 24	Oct. 31	Nov. 7
Q-S	Mon. Oct. 19	Oct. 26	Nov. 2
T-Z	Tues. Oct. 20	Oct. 27	Nov. 3

Freshmen

A	Wed.	Nov. 4
B-D	Thur.	Nov. 5
E-I	Fri.	Nov. 6
J-M	Mon.	Nov. 2
N-S	Tues.	Nov. 3
T-Z	Wed.	Nov. 4
Open	Sat.	Nov. 7 (Freshmen only)

Seniors

A-G	Tues.	Oct. 20
H-O	Wed.	Oct. 21
P-Z	Mon.	Oct. 19
Open	Thur.	Oct. 22 (Seniors only)

All Students
Mon. Nov. 9

A-K	7:00 a.m. - 12:00 noon
L-Z	12:00 noon - 5:00 p.m.
Open	5:00 p.m. - 10:00 p.m.

Juniors

A-G	Sat.	Oct. 24
H-O	Mon.	Oct. 26
P-Z	Fri.	Oct. 23
Open	Tues.	Oct. 27 (Juniors only)

Tues. Nov. 10

L-Z	7:00 a.m. - 12:00 noon
A-K	12:00 noon - 5:00 p.m.
Open	5:00 p.m. - 10:00 p.m.

Wed. Nov. 11

A-K	7:00 a.m. - 12:00 noon
L-Z	12:00 noon - 5:00 p.m.
Open	5:00 p.m. - 10:00 p.m.

Sophomores

A-G	Thur.	Oct. 29
H-O	Fri.	Oct. 30
P-Z	Wed.	Oct. 28
Open	Sat.	Oct. 31 (Sophomores only)

Payment deadline for Spring 1993 Teleregistration is December 4, 1992.

SPRING 1993

Teleregistration

Plan Before You Call -- a Checklist to Help Organize Your Teleregistration

_____ 1. Check the date when you are scheduled to teleregister. (See chart, page 8) By this date you need to assemble all information described below so that you can call and register smoothly.

_____ 2. Check your department and college rules about course enrollments, prerequisites, restriction codes and any other requirements. If you don't meet the requirements for a course in which you enroll, you could be dropped from the course during teleregistration or later on without a fee refund.

_____ 3. Advising requirements for students in good standing vary from department to department. Check your department's catalog entry.

_____ 4. Students on academic probation MUST be advised and issued an advising clearance code before they will be allowed to register. Check with your department office if you are on probation. If you register early and are academically ineligible, you will be withdrawn from the university and notified by grade report. Acceptance of payment does not guarantee enrollment.

_____ 5. Do you know your official university classification? Check the front of your last grade report for your rank-- freshman, graduate, junior, senior or sophomore. You are classified by the number of hours completed and recorded as of that last grade report. Any transfer work accepted (evaluated and posted since the last grade reporting) will be included in classification hours. Transcripts submitted after February 15 may not be considered in determining your classification.

_____ 6. Plan your schedule using the appropriate catalog. Use the trial time schedule on page 15. Then fill out the teleregistration worksheet on page 14. PLAN ALTERNATE COURSES. Every section may not be open at the time of registration.

_____ 7. Planning to register for an overload (more than 19 hours for an undergraduate and 16 hours for a graduate in most cases--check your catalog for details)? You must contact the registrar's office at least 24 hours prior to registration. If you register for an overload and you are academically ineligible, you will be withdrawn from the number of hours constituting an overload.

_____ 8. Check the phone you plan to use to be sure it is a touchtone--not all phones with keypads are.
Many phones have a code on the bottom with a number ending in "T" or "R". The "T" phone is a touchtone, and can be used to teleregister. Numbers ending otherwise may not work; phones without number codes on the bottom are older and may or may not work. All phones on campus, including pay phones, are touchtone.

_____ 9. Always exit teleregistration by entering * *. If you just hang up, you may miss messages that are important to your registration.

_____10. Remember, to be eligible for schedule revision you must register and complete fee payment for at least one class.

On Your Teleregistration Date--A Step-by-Step Guide

1. The busiest times on teleregistration dates are between 7 a.m. and 9 a.m. Avoid these times if possible. If all lines are busy, you will receive a busy signal. If you hear more than four rings without a pickup, hang up and try a bit later.

2. Have your worksheet at hand before you dial. Punch in (817) 387-9646, and wait for instructions.
If you punch keys ahead of the prompts, you may miss important messages, or make a mistake in input. Don't key ahead. The system will hang up if you make two invalid entries during a transaction.
If you are disconnected, you will **not** lose your courses.

3. You will be asked to enter the numbers on your worksheet in the order they are listed there:

semester and year code   [OPER 0] [ABC 2] [WXY 9] [DEF 3]   Spring 1993

your Social Security number __ __ __ -- __ __ -- __ __ __ __.

your personal identification number (PIN) __ __ -- __ __ -- __ __.
    (birthdate)

if necessary, your advising clearance code __ __ __ __.

ALL SINGLE DIGIT NUMBERS SHOULD BE PRECEDED BY A 0.
You can carry out transactions--adding courses, dropping courses and adding or dropping fee options--in any order, though you should complete all transactions related to one course within one call (see notes on corequisites).

SPRING 1993

4. To schedule a course, enter the action request code as noted on your worksheet (11).

Wait for the prompt. Then enter the course ID number that includes subject, course and section. For example, for ENGL 1310 section 003, you would enter:

| 1 | 1 | OPER 0 | 1 | DEF 3 | OPER 0 | 1 | DEF 3 | 1 | OPER 0 | OPER 0 | OPER 0 | DEF 3 |

To enter a restricted or variable credit-hour course, follow the directions above, and wait for the prompt. Then enter the four-digit restriction code (which you have already gotten from your department) and the number of hours if the course has variable credit. Remember, ALL SINGLE DIGIT NUMBERS SHOULD BE PRECEDED BY A 0. That means when you have a 2-hour course, you will enter "02" after the variable credit prompt. For example, MUAS 1501.700 for 2 credit hours is a restricted course and would be entered:

| 1 | 1 | OPER 0 | TUV 8 | ABC 2 | JKL 5 | 1 | JKL 5 | OPER 0 | 1 | PRS 7 | OPER 0 | OPER 0 | (prompt) |

| 1 | ABC 2 | PRS 7 | TUV 8 | OPER 0 | ABC 2 |

If you schedule a course with corequisites--one or more additional sections in which you must enroll (labs, etc)--be sure that you teleregister for all the required sections before you disconnect from the teleregistration system. Otherwise, the system will drop you from the course. To change a section of a course that has corequisites, first request the new section then drop the old one.

If the section that you requested is closed, the system will register you for the next available section of that course that will fit in your schedule. The system will tell you for which section you have been registered and give you an opportunity to reject that section. If you hang up or key ahead at this point you will be registered for that section.

5. To drop a course from your schedule, wait for the action prompt, and press 12 and the course numbers and section codes as described in step 4.

| 1 | ABC 2 | OPER 0 | TUV 8 | ABC 2 | JKL 5 | 1 | JKL 5 | OPER 0 | 1 | PRS 7 | OPER 0 | OPER 0 |

6. After you have scheduled all your courses, press | 1 | DEF 3 | to hear a confirmation of your requests. (Confirming your schedule does not guarantee your registration if you have not included all corequisites.) The system will allow you to enter courses that are time conflicts. Listen for this message and clarify your choices.

7. After creating your schedule, you may want to purchase a yearbook or parking permit. To do so, refer to the fee option codes on the worksheet. Press | ABC 2 | 1 |, then the appropriate fee code. To drop a fee option press | ABC 2 | ABC 2 | and the appropriate fee code.

8. There are other help codes listed on your worksheet. To exit the system, press | * | * |

SPECIAL NOTICE TO GRADUATE STUDENTS

You may be provisionally admitted during the fall semester without taking the Graduate Record Examination or the Graduate Management Admissions Test. But you will not be allowed to register (by phone or otherwise) for the spring unless you have a satisfactory GRE score on file in the School of Graduate Studies. Only official score reports from the Educational Testing Service are acceptable.

SPRING 1993

PAYMENT OF TUITION

Student Billing and Payment Procedures for Teleregistration:

Your early registration tuition and fee bill, including a copy of your schedule of classes, will be mailed to your UNT box or local address on or about November 19, 1992.

If you do not receive your bill in the mail, contact the bursar's department BEFORE the payment deadline, December 4, 1992. All payments must be received by 5:00 p.m. on the payment deadline, with or without billing notice.

> **Address Changes** -- If your address has changed you must contact the registrar's office either by filling out the change of address form on page 5 and turning it in. Or you may call, give your student ID and your PIN, and make the change by phone. Be sure to delete any invalid P.O. Box # from your address. It is your responsibility to provide the university with a current valid address. Address changes must be received by November 11 to be reflected on your early registration schedule bill.

Instructions for regular payment and payment associated with grants, loans, scholarships, and third party billing are sent with your bill. Check the schedule, included with your bill, to be certain you received the courses you requested. Questions about course schedules should be directed to the registrar's office.

All payments, other than cash or credit card should be mailed to the LOCKBOX Collection System address on the reverse side of your payment coupon (bottom portion of your bill.) Cash and credit card payments must be made at the bursar's department cashier windows on the first floor of the Administration Building.

If you decide not to attend spring 1993, do not turn in your tuition and fee bill.

> Payment arrangements must be **received** by the bursar's department no later than 5 p.m. on the December 4, 1992 due date. Failure to complete this process by the deadline will result in cancellation of your course requests and will require that you register during Coliseum registration.

Tuition can be paid in three installments in the fall and spring semesters only.

If you cannot pay the total amount of your tuition and fees prior to the payment deadline, then pay the minimum amount due as shown on your teleregistration bill plus a $12.50 handling charge. By doing so you are accepting the terms of the contract, printed below.

INSTALLMENT PAYMENT OF TUITION - CONTRACTUAL PROVISIONS

INSTALLMENT DUE DATES FOR SPRING 1993
Payment must be received on or before the following dates, with or without billing notice:

Payment 1
  teleregistration   December 4, 1992
  Coliseum registration   the day of registration
Payment 2   February 19, 1993
Payment 3   April 2, 1993
Final Payment   April 30, 1993

SPRING 1993

(delinquent accts. only)

NON-REFUNDABLE FEES FOR PAYMENT OF TUITION BY INSTALLMENT:
Handling Fee $12.50
Delinquent Payment Fee $10.00

A student who fails to make full payment of tuition and fees, including any incidental fees, by the due date may be prohibited from registering for classes until full payment is made. A student who fails to make payment prior to the end of the semester may be denied credit for the work done that semester.

1) Payment must be received on or before each due date WITH OR WITHOUT billing notice. If mailing a payment, postmarks will not be a consideration. It is the student's responsibility to know when a payment is due, regardless of university billing procedure. The university attempts to notify students through monthly billings of the amount owed. Due to timing constraints, it is not always possible to give ten days advance notification. All billing questions should be addressed to the bursar's department, UNT Box 13736, Denton, TX. 76203-3736 or call (817) 565-3225.

2) A handling fee of $12.50 will be charged for installment payment of tuition. A $10.00 delinquent payment fee will be charged for any payment received after the due dates printed above. **This does not include the first payment, which must be received by December 4, 1992 if you teleregistered or by the end of the day you register at the Coliseum or your schedule will be cancelled.** These fees are NON-REFUNDABLE.

3) If full payment for the semester is not received by April 30, 1993, the student will be blocked from receiving transcripts and will not be able to complete registration for future classes until the entire past due balance is paid.

4) Installment payment of tuition is available for tuition, general use fees, student service fees, student union fee, computer fees, medical service fee, international education fee, I.D. card fee, and publication fee ONLY. Any other fees, including the installment handling fee, course-related fees, blocks, previous balances, etc must be paid with the first installment payment.

5) Any financial aid, scholarship, sponsorship, refund, or any other tuition and fee adjustment will be applied to the TOTAL balance due for the semester. A reimbursement will be issued only after all balances due the university for the current semester, or any previous semester, have been paid.

6) If a student voluntarily withdraws from the semester (drops ALL classes), the total balance of tuition and fees is due immediately. Withdrawal refunds are based on the amount owed the university for the semester, NOT the amount paid.

FINANCIAL AID INFORMATION FOR TELEREGISTERED STUDENTS

If you registered early and decide not to attend North Texas this spring you must reject your awards on your eligibility notice and return the reply copy to the financial aid office by January 5, 1993, for spring or notify the financial aid office by the above date to ensure the cancellation of spring 1993 financial aid. In either case, if you registered early, you must also contact the registrar's office to cancel your spring registration.

Note: You must complete this process by January 15, 1993 for spring or you will owe a repayment of financial aid funds. Also, if you fail to follow official withdrawal procedures prescribed by the registrar's office, you will be enrolled and will receive failing grades due to non-attendance.
    If you did not teleregister see "Coliseum Registration" on page 16.
    Follow these steps to receive your financial aid reimbursement.
    1. Sign the most recent reply copy of your financial aid eligibility notice.
    2. Bring your tuition and fee bill or printed course schedule at your assigned time to the Coliseum January 12-15 according to the registration schedule on page 18. (Printed course schedules may be picked up at the registrar's office in the Administration Building before you go to registration.) Eligibility must be verified at the financial aid area.

SPRING 1993

---

*Important GSL/SLS Disbursement Information
Due to a change in federal regulations, all first year students who are first time borrowers are not eligible to receive any GSL or SLS funds until 30 days into the loan period. For example: if you are a first year student who is awarded an SLS for spring and your loan period is January 19, 1993, through May 14, 1993, then the earliest you will receive your SLS funds is February 18, 1993.

---

3. Proceed to the special fees area where your tuition, fees and blocks will be deducted from your financial aid awards. Any housing payments due must be paid at the Housing Office in Crumley Hall. If financial aid does not cover your tuition and fee bill, you must pay the minimum due amount on your tuition and fee bill on or before 5 p.m. December 4 for spring 1993. If you are a first-year student with an SLS loan see the above note.

4. You may apply for a short term loan at the financial aid office for spring starting January 4, 1993, or inside door G at the Coliseum at your assigned time.

FINANCIAL AID HELPFUL HINTS

If you teleregistered and a financial aid message appears on your bill, your spring schedule will be saved until January 15, 1993 when you must make further payment. If a message does not appear on your bill, you may obtain a request for a hold on classes form from the financial aid office. If you elect to pay for your classes yourself, remember that payment must be received in the bursar's department by 5 p.m., December 4, 1992. Otherwise your check for payment may be returned to you.

Prior to January 12, regular office hours of 8 a.m.- 5 p.m. will be enforced. The Financial Aid Office will be open from 8 a.m. until 6 p.m. Tuesday through Friday, and from 9 a.m. until 6 p.m. on Saturday during registration.

If you decide to enroll for fewer hours than you indicated on your financial aid form for 1993, please contact our office for information about how this enrollment change may affect your financial aid eligibility.

STUDENT IDS and PARKING PERMIT DISTRIBUTION FOR TELEREGISTERED STUDENTS

Students who teleregistered and paid fees by December 4 may pick up their student IDs and parking permits any time during Coliseum registration. If you have a photo ID card from a previous semester, it is still valid and does NOT need to be encoded again.

Student ID cards are distributed and/or encoded upon presentation of a fee receipt or confirmation of payment arrangements for spring 1993 before registration at the ID Card Office in Stovall Hall, Room 111A.
During registration, IDs may be picked up at the Coliseum (Door C) January 12-16.

All students are required to carry a valid student ID and make it available upon request to academic and administrative officials. There is a $10 replacement fee for lost, stolen, or discarded IDs. ID cards are encoded one time only. ID card activation will be updated automatically based on enrollment.

Parking decals are distributed upon completion of a vehicle registration form and presentation of a fee receipt during registration at the Coliseum (Door C).

SPRING 1993

Exhibit G.1. Question and Answer Script, University of Southern California

Question 1:   I keep getting a busy signal when I access the system. What can I do?
Answer 1:   Keep trying. The system is not as busy between 8 a.m. to 10 a.m. and 4 p.m. to 7 p.m. The system is also available on Saturday between 10 a.m. and 4 p.m.

Question 2:   The system tells me I have a restriction and cannot register. Where do I go?
Answer 2:   First, call the office that has placed a restriction on your registration. You will receive instructions on how to clear the hold.

Question 3:   The office that has a restriction on my record will only stamp my permit and will not take the restriction off the computer. Can I register?
Answer 3:   Yes. Unfortunately, you cannot register on the voice response system, but as soon as you bring the permit to the Registration Office and obtain proper clearance, your classes will be processed immediately, provided your appointment time has passed.

Question 4:   My appointment time is not until the day after tomorrow. Must I wait until then to register on the voice response system?
Answer 4:   Yes, but remember that once you access the system, you may call anytime after that time and make as many changes as you need to.

Question 5:   One tagged class I really need is closed. What can I do?
Answer 5:   You can only add a tagged class in person in the Registration Office, but you must first obtain the departmental stamp on your permit or drop/add form.

Question 6:   The system will not accept my social security number and birth date. Why?
Answer 6:   Be sure you use the social security number and birth date on your Permit to Register.

Question 7:   The English Department assured me they have given me "D" clearance for a class but the system tells me I do not have it. What do I do?
Answer 7:   Call the English Department directly; their telephone number is 4566. They may have a backlog of "D" class processing and may not have processed yours yet.

Question 8:   The system will not allow me to register for ENGL 500. Why not?
Answer 8:   Your class standing needs verification since you may be an undergraduate and only graduate students may take that course.

Question 9:   The system tells me that I have a time conflict with two classes. What can I do?
Answer 9:   Finish your remaining registration choices, then come to the Registration Office for resolution to this problem.

Question 10:   I am being told that the system is unavailable. When is it normally available?
Answer 10:   Monday through Friday from 8 a.m. to 7 p.m., and Saturday from 10 a.m. to 4 p.m.

Question 11:   The system will not accept my registration in PSYC 590 for 8 credits. Isn't it variable credits?
Answer 11:   The Psychology Department has originally given you "D" class approval for 6 credits. They must first change the "D" class permission screen to 8 credits before you can change the credits to 8. Contact the Psychology Department for resolution.

Question 12:   May I cancel/drop all my classes on the system?
Answer 12:   Yes, you may drop all your classes through the third week of the semester.

Question 13:   I added a class by mistake. What do I do?
Answer 13:   Simply access the system again and drop the course section you do not want.

Question 14:   The system tells me that I have a missing lab (or discussion or lecture). Is this correct?
Answer 14:   Check the *Schedule of Classes* publication for special instructions on registering for that course, (e.g., "lecture requires lab") and access the system again. If you do not get resolution, additional evaluation is needed. Contact the Manager of Registration.

Question 15:   What is the appointment schedule based on?
Answer 15:   The appointment schedule is based on credits completed, including transfer credits. Graduate students receive the first appointment, seniors are next and entering freshmen are last.

Question 16:   My appointment time cannot be right. Who can I discuss it with?
Answer 16:   You must speak with either the Manager or Supervisor of Registration at 740-8500.

Question 17:   I want to take a class for audit and one for pass/no pass. How do I do it by touchtone?
Answer 17:   I am sorry, but enrollment options for audit and pass/no pass must always be processed in person in the Registration Office because a special application is required each time you select one of those options.

Question 18:   I tried to register for 26 units and the system will not accept all my courses. Why is this?
Answer 18:   The system is programmed to accept enrollment up to a maximum of 24 units. When you have consulted your advisor, come to the Registration Office and add more than 24 units.

Question 19:   I do not have a touchtone telephone at home. How do I register?
Answer 19:   You may use any touchtone telephone on campus, one of the phones in the Registration Office or any available touchtone telephone.

Question 20:   What can I use to find out what courses I already have?
Answer 20:   Just press the star key (*), the number 9 key and the pound sign (#) and the system will summarize all the classes you currently have.

Question 21:   If I make an entry and decide that I don't want the class, what can I do?
Answer 21:   Simply press the star key once, followed by the pound sign, to cancel your current entry.

Question 22:   How long can I drop and add by touchtone?
Answer 22:   You may add through the third week of classes and drop classes through the 12th week.

Question 23:   How many phone lines does your touchtone system have?
Answer 23:   32 lines.

Question 24:   If my class is canceled after week 3, can I drop it by touchtone in weeks 4 through 12?

Answer 24:   No. You must drop courses in person in the Registration Office because we must use a special code to insure that you receive a 100% refund when the course is dropped.

Question 25:   May I change course sections in the same course during weeks 4 through 12 by touchtone?

Answer 25:   No. Please make the change in person in the Registration Office because special codes must be used when inputting a section change.

Question 26:   I have been told to decelerate in a course by my department. May I do this by touchtone?

Answer 26:   No. Please make the change in person in the Registration Office because special codes must be used when inputting an acceleration or deceleration change of program.

Question 27:   I am a limited, nonadmitted student. May I use touchtone to register?

Answer 27:   No. Touchtone is only available to admitted USC students. Limited students may only register during the in-person period; staff and faculty, who are limited, may register early and also must enroll in person.

Question 28:   What voice response system are you using for touchtone?

Answer 28:   Perception Technology.

Question 29:   I am dialing outside the 213 area code. Do you have a toll free 800 number for touchtone?

Answer 29:   No. But the university is discussing the feasibility of arranging for one.

Question 30:   The system keeps telling me, "Please wait while I process your transaction." What should I do?

Answer 30:   Simply hang up and call again. Also remember to start your registration process from the beginning in case any data were lost when you received this message.

Question 31:   The touchtone system will not allow me to register. What is wrong?

Answer 31:   An operator will access the student's registration screen and   check the following items: no appointment assigned, invalid post, restriction/hold on registration, returning or newly admitted student, or a currently enrolled student who needs to be assigned to the touchtone screen.

Exhibit G.2. Script for U-Dial Video, Boston College

VIDEO	AUDIO
OUTDOOR SHOT, INTERVIEW WITH VARIOUS STUDENTS	ANNOUNCER: All we need is one word or one phrase to describe what you think of registration. FIRST STUDENT: Absolutely miserable. SECOND STUDENT: Not good. THIRD STUDENT: I think it's a waste of time. I mean, I think there are more productive ways to go about that. FOURTH STUDENT: Frustrating. FIFTH STUDENT: It took a lot of time and everyone's complaining that they couldn't get what they wanted anyway. SIXTH STUDENT: Well, I'm a freshman, and I haven't had to go through registration yet, but I hear it's hell. SEVENTH STUDENT: I would avoid it at all costs. Like, I'd stay in a class I hated just to avoid drop/add. EIGHTH STUDENT: I think that about captures it.
ANNOUNCER, OUTSIDE MAIN BUILDING	ANNOUNCER: We're outside Gasson Hall on the Boston College campus. It may look pretty quiet right now, but at registration time this peaceful Gothic building turns into a terror-filled maze of lines of students all trying to get their courses. But now, all of that's going to change.
GRAPHIC: UDIAL USING THE SYSTEM	
ADVISOR AND STUDENT	ADVISOR: Nice to see you, Tom. What can I do for you today? STUDENT: Well, as always, Prof. Corkum it's good to see you, too. I think the last time we saw each other was probably the last registration period. I'm afraid this time it's not as good.

ADVISOR: Why is that?

STUDENT: It's this new registration system.

PROFESSOR: The U-DIAL system?

STUDENT: Yeah, the U-DIAL. That's it.
I mean I was so confused before with
registration and now they bring in this new
system, and I don't know how to use it.

ADVISOR: Well, the new U-DIAL registration is
actually relatively simple to use. And all you
need for it is a touchtone telephone and your
normal registration materials. Did you bring
those with you today?

STUDENT: Yeah.

ADVISOR: Why don't you get them out? Did you
decide on which courses you want to take yet?
Or alternate courses you may want to take?

STUDENT: I sure did.

ADVISOR: Good. Why don't we get started. I'll
explain the U-DIAL system to you a little bit.
I think you'll find it easy to use.

STUDENT: Good luck.

ADVISOR: The first thing you need to do is dial
the telphone number, which is, 552-8800. This
connects you to the mainframe computer in the
O'Neill Library. From that point, there are
three numbers you have to enter into your
telephone. First, you have to enter your
student identification number, then your
personal identification number or PIN number,
and lastly your registration access code.

STUDENT: That's a lot of numbers.

ADVISOR: Well, it's not really. And it's
really simple once you get the hang of it. Why
don't we go ahead and try it. I'll dial the
number for you.

STUDENT: OK.

SHOT OF TELEPHONE   U-DIAL VOICE: You have reached the Boston
College registration system. Please enter your
nine-digit student ID number now.

STUDENT ENTERS NUMBER

> U-DIAL VOICE: Please wait.
> Please enter your five-digit PIN number now.

STUDENT ENTERS NUMBER

> U-DIAL VOICE: Please wait.
> To drop and add a course, press 1 now.
> To add a course, press 2 now.
> To drop a course, press 3 now.
> To list your courses, press 4 now.
> To check the status of a course, press 5 now.

> ADVISOR: Then all you have to do is follow the instructions you hear and enter the index numbers for the courses you want to take. Have you decided which course you want to register for right now?

> STUDENT: Yeah, I got one.

> ADVISOR: What is it?

STUDENT BITES ON HIS FINGERNAIL

> STUDENT: Introduction to Human Sexuality.

> ADVISOR: Could you speak up? What was that?

> STUDENT: Introduction to Human Sexuality.

> ADVISOR: Oh. OK. Well, why don't you enter the index number for that course into the telephone.

STUDENT ENTERS INDEX NO.

> U-DIAL VOICE: Please wait.
> The course you will add is index 5871, which is, HS016.

> ADVISOR: It's just as simple as that, Tom. The registration process works just like it did before, but the main advantage is you don't have to wait in those long lines anymore.

> STUDENT: Wow, that's great. So, actually I can even register from my own dorm room instead of waiting in those stupid lines. Even at a pay phone in Mary Ann's (local hangout). That's awesome.

> ADVISOR: Well, hopefully, you won't be registering from there.

> STUDENT: No, never.

ADVISOR: But that's right. Just remember, though, they won't let you register before your assigned time. So, don't try to do that.

STUDENT: Never, not me. You won't catch me doing that.

ADVISOR: That's good to hear. And once you register, if you want to change anything, you can always do that at a later time. You can add or drop a course.

STUDENT: Great. Allright. Thanks, professor.

GRAPHIC:
U-DIAL
BOSTON COLLEGE

ANNOUNCER: Keep in mind these five basic steps to the U-DIAL registration system.

GRAPHICS

ANNOUNCER SPEAKS THE GRAPHICS:

FIRST GRAPHIC: 1. Have index numbers of your courses and alternates ready before you call.

SECOND GRAPHIC: 2. Dial 552-8800, the university's registration line.

THIRD GRAPHIC: 3. Enter your ID number, your personal identification number, and your registration access code.

FOURTH GRAPHIC: 4. Follow the instructions you hear and enter the index number for the courses you want.

FIFTH GRAPHIC: 5. Call back anytime after registering to drop or add a course.

SHOT OF ANNOUNCER
OUTSIDE

ANNOUNCER: Just keep in mind those five simple steps to make your registration by U-DIAL go smoothly. And if you have any more questions, there's more information in your registration newspaper. And remember, if Tom can learn to register by U-DIAL anyone can.

GRAPHIC:
U-DIAL
USING THE SYSTEM

Source: Written, produced and directed by Jennifer Bubriski and Tom Hines, Boston College.

Exhibit G.3. BRUTUS Video Script, The Ohio State University

VIDEO (SHOOTING)	**AUDIO**
1. SCENE OPENS WITH BRUTUS WALKING OUT OF A DORM. HE IS BUNDLED UP WITH A SCARF AND MITTENS. HE BEGINS WALKING TOWARDS LINCOLN TOWER (SHOT OF HIM ON THE OVAL, WALKING BY LARKINS AND THEN WALKING INTO LINCOLN TOWER). AS HE COMES THROUGH DOORS TO THE THIRD FLOOR, HE SEES A LONG LINE WAITING FOR SERVICE. HE GETS INTO LINE AND WE SEE HIM STANDING AT THE END OF THE LINE, HALFWAY THROUGH THE LINE AND THEN AT THE COUNTER AS THE WOMEN BEHIND THE COUNTER PUTS UP A CLOSED SIGN. BRUTUS PUTS HIS HEAD ON THE COUNTER IN DESPAIR. CINDY STUDENT IS WALKING BY AND SEES BRUTUS AND MOTIONS FOR HIM TO FOLLOW HER AND LEADS HIM TO A PAY PHONE. CINDY DIALS THE PHONE AND BOTH PUT THEIR EAR TO THE RECEIVER.	1. During the entire scene the song "There's Gotta Be Something Better Than This" will be playing. Various sounds of blustering winds play during Brutus' walk across campus.
2. FADE TO SCHUSTER SITTING ON CORNER OF DESK (GRAPHIC TITLE GENE SCHUSTER, UNIVERSITY REGISTRAR FOR 10 SECONDS).	2. "Does the scene you just saw look familiar? Many of you have stood in lines like this but I'm sure you are all wondering what a phone is going to do for you in these instances. I'm Gene Schuster, Registrar of The Ohio State University and today I'd like to talk to you about Telephone Registration, a new system we are hoping will eliminate the hassles of registration. The concept was pioneered at Brigham Young and Georgia State Universities a few years ago and several other institutions in the United States have also made use of their students for classes."
3. CHANGE OF CAMERA ANGLE AND POSITION.	3. "Each student permitted to use the telephone registration process will receive a unique security code number with his registration instructions. This prevents anyone other than the students from using telephone registration. In addition, each student will be assigned an appointment time which will determine the earliest time to enter class requests. Student's scheduling priority is established by the time elapsing following his or her appointment time. So you'll want to complete your registration as soon after your appointment time as possible." "With this new registration system, you will notice modifications to both your Registration Form and your Approved Schedule/Fee Statement."
4. FADE TO MOCK UP OF REGISTRATION FORM, SCHUSTER SPEAKS HERE. VOICE OVER HERE, HIGHLIGHT SECTIONS AS MENTIONED.	4. "The new Registration Form will contain: Your personal security code number Your appointment time A listing of your current quarter schedule A worksheet for you to plan your course requirements before you call

BRUTUS VIDEO SCRIPT (continued)

A phone number to call if you need help"

5. FADE TO MOCK UP OF APPROVED SCHEDULE/FEE
    STATEMENT, SCHUSTER SPEAKS HERE.

    VOICE OVER SPEAKS HERE, HIGHLIGHT SECTIONS
    AS MENTIONED.

5. "The Approved Schedule will contain:

    A summary of personal data, degree pro-
    gram, and advisor for you to verify
    A listing of your approved schedule developed
    from the course requests you entered
    A re-listing of your current quarter schedule
    An application for Traffic and Parking sticker"

6. FADE TO STUDENT SITTING AT DESK WITH ADVISOR
    REVIEWING MASTER SCHEDULE AND COURSE DE-
    SCRIPTION BOOK, VOICE OVER SPEAKS HERE.

6. "Many of you will have to see your advisor in order
    to pick up your registration form. Some will pick
    them up at their department office while others will
    have the form mailed directly to them. The choice
    is at the college office discretion. In any case, prior
    to beginning telephone registration, it is important
    that each student consult with his or her advisor."

7. VOICE OVER SPEAKS HERE.

7. "When you are ready to register, make sure you
    have your telephone registration worksheet, Master
    Schedule of Classes Bulletin, and a touch tone
    telephone (rotary dial phones will not work with this
    system). In addition, please make sure that you
    have been in to see your advisor prior to beginning.

8. FADE TO STUDENT AND BRUTUS SITTING AT A DESK
    IN A DORM ROOM. STUDENT IS DIALING A PHONE
    WHILE BRUTUS LISTENS IN. SHOULD HAVE A
    MASTER SCHEDULE AND WORK SHEET ON THE DESK.

8. Dialing sounds as student dials and ringing sounds.
    As phone is answered, dialogue from tape starts.
    "Welcome to OSU's telephone registration."

9. GRAPHICS S P 8 7 FLASH ON LOWER PART OF
    SCREEN AS STUDENT DIALS.

9. "Please enter registration quarter and year."
    Dialing sound (4).

10. GRAPHICS 2 8 7 4 2 0 5 1 8 FLASH ON SCREEN AS
    STUDENT DIALS.

10. "Please enter your social security number."
    Dialing sound (9).

11. GRAPHICS 3 9 6 4 FLASH ON SCREEN AS STUDENT
    DIALS.

11. "Please enter your personal access code for
    Spring 1987." Dialing sounds (4). "You are re-
    gistering in Arts and Sciences."

12. VOICE OVER WILL SPEAK AT THIS POINT.

12. "Let's watch the student add a course."

13. GRAPHICS A 0 8 7 6 5 1 FLASH ON SCREEN AS
    STUDENT DIALS.

13. "Enter first request." Dialing sounds (7). "Adding
    087651, Math 415, Monday through Friday 8:00am."

14. VOICE OVER WILL SPEAK HERE.

14. "Now she will add a secondary course in case she is
    unable to get into Math 415."

15. GRAPHICS S 0 8 7 5 8 4 FLASH ON SCREEN AS
    STUDENT DIALS.

15. "Enter next request." Dialing sounds (7). "Adding
    secondary to Math 415, 087584, Math 366, Monday
    through Friday 11:00am."

BRUTUS VIDEO SCRIPT (continued)

16. GRAPHICS A 1 1 7 3 5 FLASH ON SCREEN AS STUDENT DIALS. GRAPHICS A 1 1 7 3 5 6 FLASH ON SCREEN AS STUDENT DIALS.

16. "Enter next request." Dialing sound (7). "Please re-enter, call number 11735 not valid." Dialing sounds (7). "Adding 117356, Physics 263, Monday through Friday 10:00am."

17. VOICE OVER WILL SPEAK HERE.

17. "The student will now attempt to add a course that requires permission of the instructor."

18. GRAPHICS A 0 7 0 7 1 5 FLASH ON SCREEN AS

18. "Enter next request." Dialing sounds (7). "Accepting subject to permission of instructor, 070715, German 262, Monday, Wednesday, Friday 1:00pm."

19. VOICE OVER WILL SPEAK HERE.

19. "She has completed entering all her course requests and will now request a listing of her fee options."

20. GRAPHICS * O FLASH ON SCREEN AS STUDENT DIALS.

20. "Enter next request." Dialing sound (2). "Currently you have student health insurance coverage for you and your spouse."

21. GRAPHIC Y FLASHES ON SCREEN AS STUDENT DIALS.

21. "Enter Y if OK or N to make changes." Dialing sound (1).

22. VOICE OVER SPEAKS HERE.

22. "Now she will request her schedule to be repeated to her."

23. GRAPHICS * L FLASH ON SCREEN AS STUDENT DIALS.

SCREEN COPY OF SCHEDULE WILL FLASH ON SCREEN AS SCHEDULE IS REPEATED.

23. "Enter next request." Dialing sound (2). "Math 415, Monday through Friday 8:00am, 087651; secondary of Math 415, Math 366, Monday through Friday 11:00am, 087584; Physics 263, Monday through Friday 10:00am, 117356; German 262, Monday, Wednesday and Friday 1:00pm, 070715."

24. VOICE OVER SPEAKS HERE.

24. "The student will now indicate that she has finished scheduling her courses."

25. GRAPHICS * # FLASH ON SCREEN AS STUDENT DIALS.

25. "Enter next request." Dialing sounds (2). "Please listen carefully to the address where your next fee statement will be mailed. 123 M-A-I-N Street, M-A-N-S-F-I-E-L-D, Ohio 44609.

Enter Y if OK or N to make changes."

26. GRAPHIC Y FLASHES ON SCREEN AS STUDENT DIALS.

26. Dialing sound (1). "Scheduled results will be mailed the fourth week of March. Thank you for calling." sound of phone hanging up.

27. FADE BACK TO SCHUSTER SITTING ON EDGE OF DESK IN OFFICE.

27. "You have seen and heard today only the highlights of OSU's Touch Tone Telephone Registration System, as system we have nicknamed BRUTUS, Better Registration Using Touch tone phones for University Students."

BRUTUS VIDEO SCRIPT (continued)

28. CHANGE OF CAMERA ANGLE AND POSITION.

28. "Details of this exciting new approach to course registration should be available in your College Office. You will be receiving information from your school or college indicating when you will begin using BRUTUS."

29. BRUTUS ENTERS OFFICE, CROSSES OVER TO GS AND SHAKES HIS HAND. BOTH LOOK INTO CAMERA.

29. "Remember BRUTUS; Better Registration Using Touch Tone Phones for University Students. Thank you for your time and attention."

30. FADE TO BRUTUS WALKING OUT OF LINCOLN TOWER (BACK VIEW). AS HE WALKS DOWN SIDEWALK, DOES

30. Music "There's Gotta Be Something Better Than This" will play until end of credits - music fades.

BELL KICK. FREEZE WITH BRUTUS IN AIR AND DO CREDITS.

CREDITS WILL ROLL UP IN THIS ORDER:

B.R.U.T.U.S.

Better
Registration
Using
Touch tone phones for
University
Students

A SPECIAL THANKS TO (BRUTUS) AND TO THE OHIO STATE UNIVERSITY ATHLETIC DEPARTMENT.

Exhibit G.4. Brent Registers via Telephone, A Skit, University of Washington

The following script by Melanie Moore Bell may be used without permission of the author. The skit was first performed during the 1988 implementation of TT/VR at the University of Washington by Melanie Moore Bell (Registrar and Associate Director of Admissions), Frank Byrdwell (Assistant Registrar for Registration), Bill Hevly (Director of Instructional Media Services), William (Bill) Shirey (Manager of Student Systems), and W. W. (Tim) Washburn (Executive Director of Admissions and Records).

SETTING. A typical student's room where a touchtone telephone sits on a desk along with other registration materials.

CHARACTERS. David and Brent, dressed like typical students, are sitting at their desks in their room. To add a touch of humor, the roles can be assumed by faculty or administrators instead of students. The computer [actor] is dressed in a computer-like box with leotards and a swim cap. The Voice Response System (VRS) [actor] has a very imaginative costume. The narrator is dressed in typical work clothes and is standing at the side of the stage in front of a microphone and podium.

The stage lights are raised and the action begins.

NARRATOR: The Touchtone Telephone Registration Players feature (Name of actor) and (Name of actor) as students, (Name of actor) as the Voice Response System (VRS) voice, and (Name of actor) as the computer.

Picture the following. It is 10:30 p.m., Monday, (date). Two college students, David and Brent, are sitting in their room in (Name) Hall. David, a senior, has registered and is helping Brent, a freshman, with the new touchtone telephone registration system. Brent has already met with his advisor and selected courses he plans to take. Now Brent is ready to register.

DAVID: Brent, telephone registration is easy as long as you follow the directions. Have you read the Announcement of Courses and filled out your worksheet?

BRENT: Most certainly!

DAVID: Well, Brent, you're ready for the latest t-e-c-h-n-o in registration. Go for it!

COMPUTER: (GESTURES THAT COMPUTER IS OPERATIONAL.)

BRENT: (PICKS UP TELEPHONE, PRESSES THE REGISTRATION ACCESS NUMBER AS HE SAYS ALOUD) 5-2-1 (HMMM), 5-4-5-5.

VRS VOICE: Welcome to the (college/university) Telephone Registration System. Enter the registration term code now.

BRENT: Okay, that's "4" for fall term.

VRS VOICE: The term code entered is invalid. Review the instructions on the worksheet and re-enter a term code now.

DAVID: See how important it is to fill out the worksheet correctly BEFORE you access the telephone registration system?

BRENT: Let me try code 2, just to see what happens.

VRS VOICE: The term code is invalid. For assistance, please call the registrar's office at 566-8900, that is 566-8900. Thank you for calling the (college/university).

BRENT: I've been d-i-s-c-o-n-n-e-c-t-e-d! I'm a freshman and that's not fair.

DAVID: That'll teach you not to fool around with the registration system! Now get on with it and do it right. Arsenio Hall comes on in an hour.

BRENT: (ENTERS THE REGISTRATION NUMBER AGAIN AND GOES THROUGH THE MOTIONS OF GETTING TO THE TERM CODE ENTRY.)

VRS VOICE: Welcome to the (college/university) Telephone Registration System. Enter the registration term code now.

BRENT: Okay, what does it say here for fall? So I press 1 for fall term. (PRESSES THE "1" KEY ON THE KEYPAD.)

VRS VOICE: Enter your social security number, now.

BRENT: All right! (RAISES HIGH 5 FINGERS AT DAVID.) We made it past that hurdle. So I press 478-89-3421.

VRS VOICE: Enter the month, day, and year of your birth as six digits, followed by the number sign key.

BRENT: Zero 8 zero 8 72, and the number sign key. I wonder why they call it the number sign key? Must be a fancy reference to the "pound key." Maybe some freshmen thought they pounded the keys to send the registration stuff to the big mainframe on campus.

VRS VOICE: Please wait while your transaction is processed.

COMPUTER: (Name of Voice Response System) is checking the eligibility of the student which includes checking for appropriate day to register, admission to (college/university), no holds on registration. After verifying that Brent is eligible to register, (VRS) prompts Brent on six decisions that he must indicate, e.g., insurance, addresses, the first time he accesses (VRS) each term.

VRS VOICE: Please enter the appropriate Student Health Insurance option code.

DAVID: Brent, don't you want annual insurance since you're so accident prone?

BRENT: Okay, I'll press 5 for annual student insurance.

VRS VOICE: You have selected annual student insurance.

COMPUTER: (GESTURES PROCESSING ACTIONS WHILE NARRATOR SPEAKS.)

NARRATOR: Brent continues through the worksheet making choices about associated student membership, contribution options to student lobbies, and address selections for mailing of registration confirmation/ID card, billing statements, and final grades. Brent only has to make these decisions once and that is the first time he calls (VRS) each term. When he makes subsequent calls, he will not be asked to make choices on these items. With these out of the way, Brent is now ready to begin entering transactions to register in his courses. Let's see how he goes about this with David's help.

VRS VOICE: Enter your transaction followed by the number sign key.

DAVID: Brent, now you're ready to follow your worksheet and enter the add transactions. Just always remember to end each transaction with the number sign key.

BRENT: David, isn't this exciting? No more standing in lines. Here I go to add my Accounting course. A for add. Schedule line number is 1234. I can skip the two optional boxes because this section is fixed credit and does not require an entry code. So I end with the number sign key.

VRS VOICE: Please wait while your transaction is processed.

COMPUTER: (GESTURES WITH SCHEDULE OF CLASSES PUBLICATION AND NODS HEAD ... NO!)

VRS VOICE: You are not presently eligible to register for that course. Refer to the Announcement of Courses for course restrictions.

DAVID: Brent, you didn't check the Announcement of Courses! Well, it says sophomore and junior priority and you are just a lowly freshman!

BRENT: Okay, now for my next class. This one requires permission, so I picked up my own entry code from the department yesterday. So, A for add code. Schedule line number is 7555. Star key. I don't want to forget the star key. Entry code is 89345. If only they would get rid of these entry codes; then the registration shuffle would be totally eliminated!

DAVID: Don't forget to end with the number sign key.

VRS VOICE: Please wait while your transaction is processed.

COMPUTER: (GESTURES THAT IT IS OKAY.)

VRS VOICE: You have selected SLN 7555, MUSIC 101, Section A, meeting on Tuesday and Thursday, from 3:30 to 5:45, in MNY 268. Your total credit is 1.

BRENT: David, how long did it take you to register on the telephone system?

DAVID: Less than five minutes because I was prepared in advance ... like the Army you know.

BRENT: Okay, now for my English 104 course. A for add code, SLN 35542, and the number sign key.

VRS VOICE: Please wait while your transaction is processed.

COMPUTER: (GESTURES "NO" AND THUMBS DOWN.)

VRS VOICE: The section you requested is closed. However, the following sections are open: SLN 5062, Section A meeting on Monday, Tuesday, Wednesday, and Thursday, from 8:30 to 9:20; SLN 5063, Section E meeting Monday, Tuesday, Wednesday, and Thursday, from 10:30 to 11:20. Enter your transaction, followed by the number sign key.

BRENT: Well, section E sounds good to me. A for add, SLN 5063, and the number sign key.

VRS VOICE: Please wait while your transaction is processed.

COMPUTER: (GESTURES "YES" AND THUMBS UP.)

VRS VOICE: You have selected SLN 5063, English 104, Section E, added for 5 credits, meeting Monday, Tuesday, Wednesday, Thursday from 10:30 to 11:20 in MEB 245. Your total credits are 6.

DAVID: Brent, I just remembered. You can't take your orchestra class in the afternoon. You're our star quarterback! You have practice when that class is scheduled.

BRENT: You're right! I'll drop that class so it's available for someone else. I'll call (VRS) tomorrow.

DAVID: No, don't wait. Someone else may need that class now.

BRENT: Press D for drop, then the SLN which is 7555, and press the number sign key.

VRS VOICE: Please wait while your transaction is processed.

COMPUTER: (GESTURES PROCESSING.)

VRS VOICE: SLN 7555, Music 104 Section A has been dropped from your schedule. Your total credits are 5.

BRENT: Let me see. To exit (VRS), I just press the T key for terminate, and the number sign key.

VRS VOICE: Your registration confirmation will be sent to your local address. Thank you for calling the (college or university).

COMPUTER: (WAVES GOODBYE.)

BRENT: David, we have plenty of time to order pizza, make popcorn, and call our girlfriends before the Arsenio Hall show. This telephone registration is fantastic ... not to mention a convenient way to register.

DAVID: And to think that I graduate next term after all those years of standing in line to register. Brent, you're a lucky guy!

(SCENE ENDS. CURTAIN.)

References

Bell, Melanie Moore. "The future of touch-tone telephone technology: Enhancing academic support services. Paper presented at conference sponsored by Brigham Young University, Provo, Utah, June, 1990.

Brigham Young University. "Design, Implementation, and Evaluation." Papers presented at conference on Touchtone Telephone Registration, Provo, Utah, June, 1990.

————. **1988.** "A conference on Registration and Other Future Systems." Papers presented at conference on Touchtone telephone, June.

————. **1991.** "Enhancing Academic Support Services." Papers presented at conference on The Future of Touch-Tone Telephone Technology, June.

Denny, Lou Ann and Genene Walker. "Students are getting InTouch ... Arizona State University touch-tone registration." *Computing News* (March 1991): 8-11.

EDUTECH International. "How To Choose An Administrative Information System." The EDUTECH Advisory Series. Report #1. Bloomfield, Connecticut. (September 1990).

Emerson, S. Thomas. "Voice response: Humanizing computer systems." *The Magazine of Bank Administration* (November 1981): 42-44.

Erikson, Charles. "Registration by telephone: Is it the answer?" *College & University* (Summer 1979): 347-48.

Evert, Herbert. "A day in the registrar's office circa 2003." *College & University* (Spring 1990) 65:171-75.

Fouche, James W. Jr. Keynote Address presented at a seminar on Telephone Bill Payment and Home Banking. Sponsored by the Bank Administration Institute, New Orleans, Louisiana, April, 1982.

Gawkoski, R. Steve, Laura Patterson, and Don Wermers. "From idea to implementation: Campus politics and communication." Paper presented at the Annual Meetings of the Wisconsin Association of Collegiate Registrars and Admissions Officers (WACRAO), 1989; and the American Association of Collegiate Registrars and Admissions Officers (AACRAO), 1990 at Honolulu, Hawaii. Published in *Proceedings of Selected Sessions of the 1990 AACRAO Annual Meeting.*

Harris, Joneel, Mike Allen and Martha Wheat. Presented at the Voice Response Pre-Conference Workshop, American Association of Collegiate Registrars and Admissions Officers, New Orleans, Louisiana, April, 1990.

Hunt, David. "'Person to person' phone-in registration." *College & University* (Spring 1987): 194-200.

Jass, Ruth. "The politics of implementing a touch-tone telephone registration." *College & University* (Winter 1988): 123-33.

Jones, Bonnie. "Imagine...for admissions officers and registrars." *College & University* (Spring 1990) 65:235-41.

Lonabocker, Louise. "Security in the age of distributed processing." *College & University* (Spring 1990) 65:203-12.

Koenig, William E. "The transition from telephone bill payment to home banking." Paper presented at a seminar on Telephone Bill Payment and Home Banking. Sponsored by the Bank Administration Institute, New Orleans, Louisiana, April, 1982.

Olwig, John W. "Let's talk registration: A process for developing a touchtone registration script." The Ohio State University. (October 1986).

Perception Technology Higher Education User Group. "Developing an application ... A how to guide." *Touchtones* (Winter 1992).

Perception Technology. "Guidelines for evaluating voice response solutions in higher education." Unpublished paper.

—————. Recording voice. Unpublished paper.

—————. Voice response vendor selection criteria. Unpublished paper.

Peterson, Erlend D. "The Brigham Young University touch-tone telephone data entry and computer voice response registration system: An analysis of student acceptability." Ed.D. diss., Department of Educational Administration, Brigham Young University, Provo, Utah, 1985.

Russell, John E. "Two approaches to implementing an on-line registration system." *College & University* (Summer 1981): 398-99.

Ryan, Robert E. Jr., and Henry Hobson. "Justifying telephone bill payment." Paper presented at a seminar on Telephone Bill Payment and Home Banking. Sponsored by the Bank Administration Institute, New Orleans, Louisiana, April, 1982.

Spangler, J. D. "To register, talk to this computer..." *American School and University* (Summer 1980): 337-38.

Spencer, Robert W. and Erlend D. Peterson. "Touchtone telephone registration." Paper given at the American Association of Collegiate Registrars and Admissions Officers Conference, Denver, Colorado, April, 1984.

Spencer, Robert W., Erlend D. Peterson, and Douglas J. Bell. "The Brigham Young University touchtone telephone registration system." *College & University* (Spring 1984): 218-26.

Teja, Edward. *Teaching Your Computer to Talk.* Blue Ridge Summit: Tab Books, Inc. 1981.

van der Velde, Marjolijn. State of the industry report presented at a seminar on Telephone Bill Payment and Home Banking. Sponsored by the Bank Administration Institute, New Orleans, Louisiana, April, 1982.

Wermers, Donald J. "Touchtone registration at the University of Wisconsin-Madison: A team approach." Paper presented at a conference on Enhancing the Advising and Registration Processes Through the Use of Technology, Provo, Utah, June, 1990.

—————. 1990. "Toward 2000: The excitement of opportunities unlimited." Keynote Address at the Annual Meeting of the Upper Midwest Association of Collegiate Registrars and Admissions Officers (UMACRAO), October, St. Cloud, Minnesota.

—————. 1991. "Touchtone telephone/voice response registration and other applications at University of Wisconsin-Madison." Paper presented at a conference on The Future of Touchtone Telephone Technology: Enhancing Academic Support Services, 20 June, Provo, Utah.

Wermers, Donald J., Laura McCain Patterson, and Thomas J. Scott. "SPEEDE simplified: The user perspective." Paper presented at the Annual Meetings of the Wisconsin Association of Collegiate Registrars and Admissions Officers (WACRAO), 1991; the American Association of Collegiate Registrars and Admissions Officers (AACRAO), 1992 in Dallas, Texas; and College and Machine Records Conference (CUMREC), 1992.

Wilkes, P. and D. Rosengren. "Phone registration: Design and implementation of an alternative process." *College & University* (Fall 1977): 124-28.

Other Resources

Greene, James A. and Mark Elliott. "Touchtone telephone/voice response registration: Issues and answers." CUMREC *1986 Conference Proceedings.* University of South Carolina, Columbia, 1986.

McGuire, Joseph P. and Edward J. Thompson. "Selecting and implementing a voice response system." CUMREC *1986 Conference Proceedings.* University of South Carolina, Columbia, 1986.

The following are available from CAUSE, the association for managing and using information technology in higher education. The ID number referenced is the CAUSE number.

Andersen, Peters. "New Applications for Touch-tone Systems." 1992. ID number: CMR9219.

Ball. "Voice Mail at the University of Maryland at Baltimore." 1986. ID number: CEM8666.

Baltzer. "Integration of Voice, Data, and Video Services Via a Wide Area Network: Technical and Organizational Issues." 1991. ID number: CEM9146.

Barrie. "Against All Odds: The University Wide Effects of a Touch-tone Registration System." 1989. ID number: CMR8928.

Bell, Nicholes, Peterson, Rasband. "BYU's Touch-tone Data Entry/Voice Response Registration System." 1984. ID number: CMR8416.

Bosse, Herman. "Affordable Touch-tone-Phone Student Registration and Self-Registration Without Mortgaging Your College." 1987. ID number: CNC8741.

Brown. "Touch-tone Telephone Registration and Common Sense Advice When You Take the Plunge." 1988. ID number: CMR8826.

Greene, Elliott. "Touch-tone Telephone/Voice Response Registration: Issues and Answers." 1986. ID number: CMR8614.

Hill. "Touch-tone Registration: Is It Worth It?." 1989. ID number: CEM8942.

James, Norwood. "Touch-tone Registration: Host Application Design Considerations." 1988. ID number: CMR8824.

McGuire, Thompson. "Selecting and Implementing a Voice Response System." 1986. ID number: CMR8619.

Metropolitan State College. "Touch-tone Registration." 1986. ID number: CSD0187.

Oakland Community College. "Touch-tone Telephone/Voice Response Registration System Survey." 1988. ID number: CSD0236.

Orwig. "Let's Talk Registration and Developing a Telephone Registration Script." 1987. ID number: CMR8720.

Rasband, Childs, Tomlinson. "BYU's Touch-tone Telephone Registration System." 1986. ID number: CEM8625.

Schafer. "Online Registration: Why Not?" 1986. ID number: CMR8626.

Szakal, Howard. "Let the Computer Collect: Using Credit Cards with Touch-tone Technology." 1991. ID number: CMR9120.

Telin, Keskinen. "Online Student User-Friendly Preregistration." 1991. ID number: CMR9128.

University of British Columbia. "Voice Response System." ID number: CSD0375.

University of Miami. "RFP: Pay Telephone System Agreement." 1987. ID number: CSD0216.

University of Wisconsin/Madison. "RFB: Computer-Based Voice Response System for Student Registration." 1987. ID number: CSD0253.

Index

fee payment option, 75

Ferris State College, 30

financial aid: benefits, 34, 44, 76, 112

Florida Community College at Jacksonville, 35, 56

Florida International University, 30

Florida State University, 30, 35

flow chart, 18, 28, 65, 66, 67, 194-195

funding options, 47, 48-49

Georgia State University, 26, 29, 30, 35

goals, determining, 38, 44, 45, 59, 64, 68

Gonzaga University, 35, 56, 122-123

grade options, 34, 35, 75, 110

hardware, 31, 46, 50, 52, 54, 79-80, 106

host environment, 79, 82

host transaction format: human interface/
conversational system, 65; screen-oriented/
transactional system, 18, 49-50, 65-66

implementing ideas, 34, 35, 37

information: campaign, 39, 99; sessions, 40, 98-99

interfaces: Binary Synchronous Communication, 82;
evaluation of on-line registration, 49-50, 52, 54;
telephone company, 52-53

International Standard Organization, 18

Iowa State University, 30

LAN, 18

Lane Community College, 30, 56

maintenance, 47, 79, 82

Maricopa Community Colleges, 30

messages, flow chart, 65

Metropolitan State College, 30

Miami-Dade Community College, 30, 35, 56

Michigan State University, 35

modem, 19

monitoring: computer, 81-82; project team, 54-55

needs analysis, 44-46

newsletter, 40

news releases, 40

North Carolina State University, 30, 56, 123-124

North Florida Junior College, 35

Northeast Louisiana University, 30

Ohio State University, The, 30, 35, 51, 56, 103,
124-125

on-line registration interface, 49-50

optical mark read, 19

outsourcing. *See* service bureau

PAC. *See* personal access code

pacing. *See* registration: early

passwords. *See* security

Pennsylvania State University, 30

Perception Technology Corporation, 27-28, 64, 79,
87, 137, 140-141

Periphonics Corporation, 29, 137, 142-143

personal access code, 22, 71-73

personal computer-based system, 50, 52, 81

personal identification number. *See* security

phonemes, 21

phrase, 53, 64

pilot program, 28, 29

PIN. *See* security

progression relationship, 54